# SHARED GROUND
# AMONG JEWS AND CHRISTIANS
## *A SERIES OF EXPLORATIONS*

### VOLUME IV

# Faith Without Prejudice

## Rebuilding Christian Attitudes Toward Judaism

*Revised and Expanded Edition*

**Eugene J. Fisher**

THE AMERICAN INTERFAITH INSTITUTE
CROSSROAD • NEW YORK

1993
The Crossroad Publishing Company
370 Lexington Avenue, New York, NY 10017

Printed in the United States of America

**Library of Congress Cataloging-in-Publication Data**

Fisher, Eugene J.
    Faith without prejudice : rebuilding Christian attitudes toward
Judaism / Eugene J. Fisher. — Rev. and expanded ed.
        p.  cm. — (Shared ground among Jews and Christians ; v. 4)
    ISBN 0-8245-1266-9(cloth)
    1. Judaism—Relations—Christianity. 2. Christianity and other
religions—Judaism.  I. Title.  II. Series.
BM535.F52  1993
261.2′6—dc20                                                    92-36342
                                                                      CIP

# Contents

# Foreword:
# Faith for the Future

## Irvin J. Borowsky

For 1900 years, the incredibly misguided concept of Jews killing Jesus has been so formulated that responsibility has rested not only on "Jews" living during the first century, but on all Jews of all ages, of all times, and in every geographical area. Catholics are now rejecting this blatantly incorrect deicide charge; for it is this unholy accusation that has led to the murder of two out of five Jews in this century alone.

Vatican II, in its Declaration on the Relationship of the Church to Non-Christian Religions, reaffirmed the best of Christian tradition concerning the Jews. The 1975 Vatican Guidelines spoke warmly of "the spiritual bonds and historical links binding the Church to Judaism." Subsequent statements emanating from the National Conference of Catholic Bishops in 1975 and 1988 and now the new universal catechism of 1992 are additional examples of the strong support Catholic leadership has taken to eliminate any form of anti-Jewish activity from local parishes.

Since the time of Hitler, there has existed a widespread reaction of shock and soul-searching concerning the Holocaust. Church leaders, divinity schools, and Catholic communities in abundance have expressed the inconsistencies of a Catholicism that incorporates anti-Semitism. True Catholics, those who embrace the doctrines and moral directives of the Church, fully renounce all forms of anti-Semitism.

At no time in the history of Christian and Jewish dialogue

has there ever been such a concentrated effort by both religions to build sincere bridges of communication. One of the supreme lessons of the Holocaust is that, when hate, intolerance, and prejudice are permitted to rule, even religious lines become frayed and death is visited upon all. It is a fact that while all Jews in Europe were designated for extermination, millions of Catholic civilians and clergy were also murdered.

Today, a growing number of priests and others within the Catholic teaching community are presenting Holocaust memorial programs that remind us to restate that any form of prejudice is anti-Catholic. Christians and Jews have long hoped that hatred of the Jewish people would fade away. That hope, sadly, in some quarters has dwindled into a fantasy. Despite the fact that there are less than fourteen million Jews left in the entire world, distrust and hatred of the Jewish people continue. Their vilification is neither emotional nor accidental. It appears in all editions of the New Testament. It is the inaccuracies about events of the first century that have fueled hatred of Jews, even in nations that have little or no Jews in their country.

In the last few decades the most brilliant minds in Christian theology have wrestled with this tragic factor. As a result of their impeccable research, scholarship, and now the remarkable technologies available for studying historical documents, an accurate portrait of the foundation of Christianity and the development of 1900 years of violence against the Jews is made clear. The *improperly translated Christian scriptures* taught each new generation of Christians that the Jewish people are to be blamed for the crucifixion of Jesus. These virulent translations have been so embedded in Christian thought that factual presentations of these events is startling new information to many.

Even now, ambitious bigots still use the derogatory biblical references to "the Jews" to market their hatred. These charlatans must be prevented from exploiting Christianity. And, it can be done via *accurate translations* that describe the true enemies of Jesus.

From the time Jesus was a child he was exposed to the barbaric treatment of his fellow Jews by the Roman invaders and their collaborators. Historians have estimated the number of Judean collaborators who assisted the Roman conquerors at a few thousand; these included Roman-appointed priests, tax collectors, money changers, and temple guards. These Jews were the authorities whom Jesus was against; he was spiritually close to the other 99 percent of his co-religionists.

Today, as we prepare to move into a bold new century, an additional threshold of enlightenment has been crossed as a result of solid research and promising accurate biblical translations. It is clear that Jesus addressed no hatred of his fellow Jews; that Jesus lived and died as an observant Jew; that it was Jewish followers of Jesus who wept as they watched his agony on the cross.

Theologians and scholars agree that if Mark, John, and Paul had the benefit of knowing that their writings helped define tragic realities for their own people, they would surely have modified the hate-filled references that are still published today as translations of the New Testament. There is no doubt that their intentions were to capture the spirit and leadership which Jesus exemplified, notably his courage, commitment, and, most of all, his love for all mankind. Jesus stood up to oppression. He spoke out against cruelty. He reflected a faith that inspired. He inspired the writers of the New Testament and, if permitted to be an example, will inspire the removal of the hate-filled and inaccurate references to Jews from the New Testament and from Christianity itself.

Let us join together to extend our outreach and resources to Bible publishers. There are millions of Christians who read the Bible as a daily newspaper. Let us help them understand that the use of the word "Jew" in the exclusive sense as the enemy of Jesus represents a misguided, incorrect, and ultimately harmful castigation of an entire people. Clearly, the success of this magnificent objective will be a major step in preventing bigots from, once again, arousing less-informed people to distrust and hate.

We invite the readers of Dr. Eugene Fisher's splendid book to absorb the remarkable insights he offers herein and to discover Jesus as a faithful Jew who brought the core of his heritage to Christianity.

IRVIN J. BOROWSKY,
*Founder and Chairman*
American Interfaith Institute
Philadelphia, Pennsylvania

# Foreword:
# Faith Grounded in History

## James H. Charlesworth

For almost two thousand years Jews have been castigated and murdered. Partly to blame, sometimes directly other times indirectly, are Christians who contend that Jews in their communities are responsible for Jesus' crucifixion. Not only were these actions a travesty of equating an ancient race with a modern group, but the historical setting of Jesus' time was distorted. Followers of Jesus Christ forgot the first-century setting of the Galilean Rabbi they called "Lord." It was virtually never contemplated that Jesus was a faithful Jew who obeyed the Torah, taught in the synagogues, and worshipped in the Temple.

Thanks to the vision of Irvin J. Borowsky and the generosity of the American Interfaith Institute, Eugene Fisher's magisterial *Faith Without Prejudice* is reissued now in a revised and expanded form. Dr. Fisher, widely lauded for his insightful perception of the way to build bridges of understanding among Jews and Christians today, clearly and forcibly demonstrates that the New Testament, when read carefully, discloses that "Jews" did not crucify Jesus, and they were not responsible for his death (pp. 72–81). Even if by twisting truth it might appear that "Jews" two thousand years ago in ancient Palestine made a mistake, why should Jews today be implicated for what happened long ago and far away?

Fisher examines the charge that the New Testament is anti-Semitic. On the one hand, he rightly rejects such a sweeping categorization and denunciation (pp. 56–71). On the other hand, he readily admits that there are some passages in the New Testament that are not only susceptible to anti-Semitic rhetoric, but do indeed, unfortunately, castigate "the Jews." Here we confront a major problem. What are we to do?

Should Christians abandon their sacred scriptures? Heavens no! Such drastic surgery would not only remove the heart from Christianity, it would cut the umbilical cord that binds Christians with Jews.

I am convinced that we dare not allow present concerns to dictate the means of translating or interpreting the New Testament. The last two centuries have demonstrated the fallacy of understanding the New Testament in terms of reigning philosophical systems, first Hegelianism and then Existentialism. We must not excise passages or words from the New Testament because they are offensively "anti-Jewish." That cannot be the rationale for our work; otherwise, we have no safeguard from doing what the Nazis did and what a future demagogue may demand. Or, even worse, in face of churches full of believers who want a Jesus "like me" we might unwittingly succumb to Marcion's attempt to depict a Jesus totally bereft of Judaism, and one removed far from history and time into a cosmic timeless realm (p. 40). The norm for translating and interpreting must *not* be present concerns or norms.

We need a scientific method. We need to be certain that we are much more sensitive to what was intended. Our question should be focused: What did the ancient author intend to say to whom, and how was he (or she) being understood? We need to "indwell" the social setting that gave rise to the words chosen, and then attend to the narrative and rhetorical thrust of the author and the type of literature he (or she) has produced. In light of the renewed appreciation of the varieties of Judaism in Jesus' time — thanks especially to the data preserved in the Pseudepigrapha and the Dead Sea Scrolls — and of the historical elements in the New Testament, we can more accurately reconstruct Jesus' time and large portions of his own life and teaching.

This method and perception is well received and widely followed, but we may run into another problem. We must not become so enamored with method that we become preoccupied with it. We should remember not only to improve our methodology but to apply it. We should also not expect the historical critical method to perform tasks for which it was not developed.

That means we Christians have a sacred text in which we come to know and indeed experience the word of God.[1] In hearing God's voice and comprehending his will we know assuredly that large sections of the New Testament have been misunderstood and even mistranslated. For example, a renewed sensitivity of Jesus' Jewishness, his death at the hands of Roman soldiers, and his pursuit and entrapment by *some* of the Sadducean aristocracy helps us better represent the meaning intended by the evangelists and other New Testament authors. This sensitivity is threefold: (1) to the historical and social setting of the writing and the episodes it refers back to, (2) to the narrative or rhetorical thrust of the passage (or document), and (3) to the renewed appreciation of Jesus' Jewishness and the attractive piety of the early religious Jews. Together these new perceptions help us see that the noun *Ioudaioi* does not always mean "Jews"; sometimes it means "Judeans," as in John 11:54:

> Jesus therefore no longer went about openly among the Judeans (*Ioudaiois*), but went from there (Judaea) to the country near the wilderness, to a town called Ephraim; and there he stayed with his disciples.

The "Judeans" stand for some of the Sadducean aristocracy who seek Jesus' death because he was a threat to their prosperity and power.[2]

Translating *Ioudaioi* as "Jews" unintentionally draws a direct line to those in our communities called "Jews."[3] To translate this noun in light of the meaning and narrative of the Gospel of John, and in harmony with what seems to be the most reliable reconstruction of what lead to the end of Jesus' life on earth — that is as "Judeans" — will open a future in which the New Testament can-

---

1. As Fisher states, "Theologically, it is important to recognize that God inspired not one but four Gospels" (p. 57).

2. See my article, "Caiaphas, Pilate, and Jesus Trial," in *Explorations,* forthcoming.

3. Father R. E. Brown, a gifted New Testament scholar, has influenced Fisher into thinking that in the Gospel of John "the Jews" represent "a generalized or symbolic meaning rather than a specific historical one.... 'The Jews' in John is a theological category, as symbol of anyone..." (p. 60). This exegesis is correct but it was made within a commentary. It is commentary on the text; it must not be confused with the text. The text itself must be more sensitively translated; it will simply no longer be acceptable to relegate critical comments on the meaning of terms to commentaries and scholarly works. Few people read our popular books; far less even consult a commentary. Our insights into the narrative and social setting of documents like the Gospel of John must be reflected in our translations of the New Testament.

not be used again to fan the flames of anti-Semitism, the hatred of Jews.

A Roman Catholic scholar, Fisher also illustrates why it is now undeniable that Jesus was a faithful Jew (pp. 39–55). This position is demonstrated by Jews, Protestants, and Roman Catholics in the American Interfaith Institute's second volume which is titled *Jesus Jewishness.*[4] Unfortunately, even today some Christians — like the woman who shouted in the face of Bishop Bernard Sheil (p. 39) — brand me as a "Jew" because I stress Jesus' Jewishness.[5]

As a Methodist minister and a scholar who has lived in Jerusalem and taught at the Hebrew University, I am honored to be invited to write this foreword. Along with everyone who has read this far and who will at least peruse this book, I admit that it is not easy for rivaling siblings — that is Jews and Christians today — to forget the egregious injustices and horrifying episodes of the past. It is tempting to forget. But, as historical creatures who know who we are and who others are because of our own past, especially when it crisscrosses with another's life, we know that the only way to insure a better future for our children and grandchildren is to remember and to live out — each moment of our lives — the commitment to live together as Jews and Christians dedicated to the survival, indeed joyous life, of the other. We need each other. We need to be united; but we also need to stand separately beside the other so that we can be there to receive help and to render assistance. That is, we need to celebrate with integrity and honesty our cherished similarities *and* differences.

In the endeavor to understand what "it is all about" we should not succumb to the temptation to explain away the incredible dimensions of life. As authors of some Dead Sea Scrolls, some Pseudepigrapha, and as Paul and the author of the Odes of Solomon stressed, in so many different ways, the human before the Almighty is left with an interrogative awe:

> Who can number,
> Who can calculate,
> Who can recount,

---

4. J. H. Charlesworth, ed., *Jesus' Jewishness: Exploring the Place of Jesus within Early Judaism* (Shared Ground Among Jews and Christians 2; New York: The American Interfaith Institute and Crossroad, 1991). The book contains chapters by Charlesworth, Harvey Cox, David Flusser, Daniel J. Harrington (S.J.), Hans Küng, John P. Meier, Alan F. Segal, Ellis Rivkin, and Geza Vermes.

5. See, for example, my *Jesus Within Judaism: New Light from Exciting Archaeological Discoveries* (Anchor Bible Reference Library 1; New York, London: Doubleday, 1988).

> The wonders
> And the mysteries of God?

Together — as Jews and Christians — wiping away each others' tears,[6] and joining together in adulation to God who has called us, we can affirm that God has not forsaken his promises to us.

JAMES H. CHARLESWORTH
*George L. Collord Professor of New Testament Language
    and Literature*
Princeton Theological Seminary

---

6. See the magisterial volume edited by Irvin J. Borowsky, titled *Artists Confronting the Inconceivable: Award Winning Glass Sculpture* (Philadelphia: American Interfaith Institute, 1992).

# Preface to the First Edition

My thanks go first of all to Rabbi Marc Tanenbaum and Ms. Judith Hershcopf Banki of the American Jewish Committee who gave me encouragement and allowed access to invaluable research data.

Second, I would like to thank those scholars, both Catholic and Jewish, who motivated and guided me into this field of study: Rev. John Castelot, S.S., of St. John's Seminary in Plymouth, Michigan, who first introduced me to the Hebrew Scriptures; Rev. Edward Loveley, S.J. and Professor Shlomo Marenof of the University of Detroit, who believed in me when I most needed it; Professors Cyrus Gordon, David Rudavsky and Nathan Winter, among others, of New York University, who led me to a deep appreciation for Judaism and the Jewish people.

Third, my thanks go to my predecessors in the field of intergroup analysis of Christian teaching materials, on whose work much of my own is based: the two great French scholars, one Jewish and one Catholic, Jules Isaac and Pere Paul Démann, who pioneered the field and whose work had an important impact on the Second Vatican Council; the late Bernhard E. Olson of Yale, whose work *Faith and Prejudice* established intergroup analysis in this country on solid methodological footing and to whose memory the present book is dedicated; the American Jewish Committee, which initiated and has supported self-studies of intergroup relations both in this country and in Europe from 1950s to the present; Sisters Rose Thering, Rita and Mary Gleason, whose dissertations for St. University in the early 1960s provided the first studies of Roman Catholic textbooks; Rev. John Pawlikowski and Claire Huchet Bishop, whose books made the American and European studies available to wide readership; and Gerald Strober, who undated the Olson study of Protestant texts.

Finally, my gratitude to my wife Catherine, whose love supports me and whose incisive critique improved the text.

# Preface to the Second Edition

For this second edition of *Faith Without Prejudice* (which is still a goal, though perhaps growing closer), in addition to the above I would like to acknowledge the assistance of the American Interfaith Institute and its Director, I. J. Borowsky, who inspired the idea of a second edition and brought it to fruition. Much has happened in Catholic-Jewish Relations in the fifteen years that have passed since this book was originally published. Indeed, a vast new literature of the dialogue has developed since then. This is reflected in the longer and completely new "Resource" bibliography developed for this edition and included here as Appendix D.

Indeed, the documentation appendices contain mostly new materials. Appendix B includes the major statements of the Holy See in 1974 ("Guidelines") and 1985 ("Notes" for Preachers and Catechists) along with the Second Vatican Council Declaration, Nostra Aetate no. 4. Complementing these documents are the key statements of Pope John Paul II in Mainz in November of 1980, and in the Great Synagogue in Rome in April of 1986.

Appendix C includes two significant statements emanating from the National Conference of Catholic Bishops (USA): the 1975 Statement on Catholic-Jewish Relations and the 1988 statement of the Bishops' Committee on the Liturgy, *God's Mercy Endures Forever: Guidelines on the Presentation of Jews and Judaism in Catholic Preaching,* and the Bishops' Committee for Ecumenical and Interreligious Relations 1988 *Criteria for the Evaluation of Dramatizations of the Passion.*

Chapter VII on Christian Teaching Today also includes a section updating my own study of Catholic teaching materials on which the chapter is based. This summarizes very briefly the results of Philip Cunningham's 1992 dissertation analyzing the Catholic textbooks of the 1990s in direct comparison with the results of my own study and employing exactly the same critical methodology. This illustrates that progress has indeed continued in the interim but also pinpoints where further progress is vitally needed.

Finally, I would like to dedicate this book to my wife, Catherine, who sustains me in love, and to my daughter, Sarah, who has given me a whole new understanding of love.

# INTRODUCTION

# John and Isaac

On June 13, 1960, Pope John XXIII received in audience a Jewish historian named Jules Isaac. The conversation lasted only twenty-five minutes, yet it began one of the most profound renewals of Church teaching and practice in a 2,000-year-long history.

Pope John was uniquely prepared for the meeting. When he was Apostolic Delegate in Istanbul during World War II, he had responded to the plight of the Jewish refugees and helped to save many lives. But he still remembered with frustration his inability to render more than individual aid. Despite his efforts, the Nazi death machine ground on, ruthlessly exterminating more than six million Jewish lives and decimating the Jewish population of Europe.

John also remembered the words of his predecessor, Pope Pius XI. Pius made his remarks in an earlier audience and in a most difficult time. It was September 6, 1938. The shadow of Hitler lay heavily over all of Europe. Pius was commenting on the text of the Canon of the Mass to a group of Belgian Catholics. He sensed the carnage that was even then beginning to happen. His voice choking with tears, the pope courageously spoke out on the most burning issue of the day: the so-called "Jewish problem:"

> The sacrifice of Abel, the sacrifice of Abraham, the sacrifice of Melchizedek, in three strokes, in three lines, in three steps show the whole religious history of humanity.... Abraham is called our patriarch, our ancestor. Anti-Semitism is not compatible with the thought and the sublime reality expressed in the Mass.... Through Christ and in Christ, we are the spiritual descendants of Abraham. Spiritually, we are Semites (*Documentation Catholique*, 39, 1938, col. 1460).

Clear as they were, these words did not halt the rising Holocaust. But John knew that they expressed the best in Catholic teaching and a consistent theme of the popes down through the centuries. He turned his attention back to the man before him.

Jules Isaac was presenting the pope with a carefully prepared dossier outlining a program designed to rectify the negative aspects of Christian teaching concerning the Jews that had grown up alongside of the more authentic Church doctrine. He had even brought with him extracts from the Catechism of the Council of Trent (sixteenth century). These statements showed that the charge that the Jews killed Jesus was contrary to the Church's tradition.

John knew that the Jewish scholar was right. And he knew that papal teaching had always forbidden violence by Christians against Jews, even though countless Christians through the years had violated the ban.

In the twelfth century, for example, Popes Alexander III and Innocent III set down a "Constitution for the Jews." Though approving of certain oppressive measures such as the establishment of ghettos, the popes declared that "since through the Jews our own (Christian) faith is truly proved, they must not be oppressed grievously by the faithful." The Papal Constitution explicitly forbade forced conversion of the Jews, the disruption of Jewish worship and feasts, desecration of Jewish cemeteries, and involuntary servitude. Importantly, it enforced the decree with the most stringent weapon available to the Church: excommunication!

Against those who would seek to destroy the Jews, Innocent III declared:

> Do not wipe out the Jews completely, lest perhaps Christians might be able to forget God's Law, which the Jews (although not fully understanding it) present in their books to those who do understand.

The statement is ambiguous because of its parenthetical note that the Jews don't fully understand their own Scriptures. But it is forthright in seeking to protect Jewish lives. By accepting this ancient constitution, pope after pope held to a significant point: the Jewish people continue to play an essential role in God's plan of salvation. Christian existence is dependent upon Jewish survival. As a result, the Papal States, which were under direct political control of the Roman pontiffs, were a place of refuge — if not prosperity — for Jews throughout the Middle Ages.

Jules Isaac had thus appealed in his short presentation to the best in the warm personality of Pope John and to the best traditions of the Church. At the end, he asked whether there was any hope of ridding Christian teaching of the many anti-Jewish myths that had become encrusted on it like barnacles on a ship. John replied with characteristic honesty: "You have every right to more than hope.... But this requires deliberation and study. What you see here is not an absolute monarchy."

In preparing for the Second Vatican Council, John kept his promise to start the wheels of reform in motion. He personally entrusted Cardinal Bea and the Secretariat for Promoting Christian Unity with the task of writing a special statement on the Jews. After much discussion, revision, and not a little bargaining, the Council finally promulgated the draft on the Jews as a part of its *Declaration on the Relationship of the Church to Non-Christian Religions.* A new age of dialogue between Jews and Catholics was born.

In the following pages, we shall discuss some of the major implications that this continuing dialogue has for us as Christians today. We shall look briefly at some of the highlights of Jewish-Christian relations, noting both the good and the bad. We shall take special care in treating the origins of the conflict between Church and Synagogue as reflected in the New Testament. The efforts of biblical scholars in recent generations have greatly increased our understanding of the historical context in which the New Testament was written. These studies have literally revolutionized our view of key New Testament passages, stripping away many of the prejudices and misjudgments with which we used to read the Scriptures.

Reading the New Testament in the light of modern scholarship and recent Church teaching not only will help us to be prepared for dialogue with Jews, but it can lead to new understandings of our own origins and of who we are as Christians. In 1975, the Vatican issued new Guidelines governing Jewish-Catholic relations. These tell us that it is when "pondering its own mystery" that the Church "encounters the mystery of Israel." Today we encounter the divinely inspired tradition of a living Judaism as a tradition, like our own, "rich in religious values." In learning to appreciate these values, we can greatly enrich our own spirituality and understanding of God.

This book, then, aims at providing the general reader, the catechist and homilist, with some of the wealth of new insights emerging from the dialogue begun by Vatican II. It will offer ways of overcoming past misconceptions and strategies for implementing in the classroom and at home the goal of a prejudice-free life of faith. Finally, it will present in summary fashion the results of the author's study of current American Catholic teaching materials. The study measured Christian teaching about the Jews according to the directives of the latest Vatican Guidelines and the results of biblical scholarship. In this way, it is hoped, the reader will find a practical and concrete guide to a renewed understanding of Judaism — and through it of Christianity itself.

# CHAPTER ONE

# A Bridge Across Time

Spring was blossoming in Paris. It was Easter in the year 1132, but despite the gentle beauty of the season, a dark shadow lay over the papacy. Pope Innocent II, elected only a few months before, had been forced to flee Rome. Cardinal Leonis, the leader of a rival faction, had held his own "election" and had himself proclaimed "Pope" Anacletus.

Innocent had taken refuge in the Abbey of St. Denis in Paris. That year the pope celebrated the Easter liturgy in exile, and not for the first time. During the liturgy, Innocent took part in a ceremony that was customary for papal coronations in the medieval period. The ritual, called the "Torah Roll Ceremony," was practiced by the popes well into the nineteenth century. In many ways it symbolized the relationship between Church and Synagogue. Adding to the poignancy of the ceremony this time was the fact that here an exiled pope was meeting with representatives of an exiled people: the Jews.

It was the custom for newly elected popes to receive delegations from the various groups within the Papal States and to accept some symbol of their fealty to him as a feudal prince. Since he could not be in Rome, Innocent did the next best thing and held the coronation ceremony in the Paris Abbey.

Among the official delegations was a group of French Jews. They presented the new pope with a magnificent, hand- lettered scroll containing the first five books of the Bible, the Torah. The pope received the sacred scroll from their hands with the greatest of reverence, for was it not the very word of God being offered by the descendents of the biblical authors themselves?

This official papal ceremony symbolized beautifully the fact that it is from the Jews that the Church has received essential elements of its knowledge of God's revelation. The Church thus celebrated ritually the continuity between Judaism and Christianity. The covenant made for Christians on Calvary finds its roots in God's covenant with the Jewish people on Sinai.

The required statement of acceptance spoken by Innocent on that Parisian Easter, of course, likewise emphasized the Church's own interpretation of the meaning of the Torah as fulfilled in Christ. But the act of giving and the response of accepting says more about what the relationship between our two covenant peoples should be than would a thousand volumes.

Gesture and response, gift and acknowledgement, shared meaning, common origins — such simple human actions are the basis for communication. Openness to and respect for the other, as other, form the basic supports for the bridge which can cross over the chasm of time that separates Jew and Christian. We share the same God, the same divinely inspired Torah.

But other actions were taking place during these years of Christendom's sway over Europe. These acts, committed by Christians against Jews in the name of Christ, also speak volumes. They were the Crusades.

## The Crusades

The Crusaders had been told by popes and preachers that to fight the infidel would insure for them a place of glory in heaven. The sermons, of course, had been aimed at inspiring the knights to go to the Holy Land and fight for the liberation of Jerusalem from Moslem control.

But it seems that the Crusaders took the advice rather literally. Why go all the way to Jerusalem, they reasoned, when there were infidels right at hand within Christendom? "Look," they cried, "we set out on a long road in order to reach the burial place (of Jesus) and to revenge ourselves on the Ishmaelites (Moslems) Behold! Here are Jews dwelling in our midst, whose fathers killed Jesus. . . . Let us take our revenge first on them and extirpate them from among the nations."

This Crusader battle cry is quoted from original sources by Father Edward A. Synan of the Pontifical Institute of Medieval Studies, Toronto (*The Popes and the Jews in the Middle Ages*, New York: Macmillan, 1965, p. 71). Fr. Synan proceeds to describe countless atrocities committed by the Crusaders on their way to free Jerusalem. As a mediaeval Christian writer, Ekkehard of

Aura, complains: "They (the Crusaders) ought to have traveled the road undertaken for Christ. (Instead) they turned to madness and shamefully and wantonly cut down with cruelty the Jewish people in the cities and towns through which they passed on their way" (*ibid.*, p. 70).

Fr. Synan also points out that some bishops attempted, with greater or lesser success, to give refuge to the Jews under their jurisdiction. But it was not enough to stem the tide of massacre.

More successful was St. Bernard of Clairvaux, the official preacher of the Second Crusade (1146), who stated in no uncertain terms: "Whoever touches a Jew so as to lay hands on his life does something as sinful as if he laid hands on Jesus himself!" But Bernard displayed a rather typical Christian ambivalence when he concluded that while "the Jews ought not to die because of their crimes," they ought "rather to suffer the diaspora (exile)."

It is against this history, good and bad, that Jews and Christians today are approaching a new stage in their centuries-long exchange.

### Disputation and Dialogue

As Christians, we must approach the present dialogue with honesty and openness. Seeing ourselves through the eyes of the other is a necessary part of coming to learn our own identity.

Dialogue is the opposite of debate. The point is not to convince the other side of the truthfulness of one's own position but to learn about the other position from the other person. Dialogue is a mutual search, not an attempt to convert. The "rightness" of positions is not what is at stake. What matters is opening oneself to the other as a person worthy of respect.

The skills of dialogue are not the skills necessary for debate, though the participants on each side should be firmly rounded in their own traditions. The key virtue of dialogue is humility. The chief vice that threatens dialogue is pride, the type of pride that says: "I alone have the whole truth. You must listen to me and be convinced by what I say."

Christians have not always approached the Jews in a sense of open dialogue as they do today. This needs to be faced. For to understand the Jewish side of the dialogue, Christians need to know their history well, since the wounds we seek to heal are historical realities. Unless these wounds are diagnosed, they cannot be treated.

In medieval times, then, formal "disputations" were at times forced upon the Jews. The rules of such debates were strict. At times they were slanted to favor the Christian side. Recalling the history of these "disputations" can help us today to see what *not* to do if we are to have a fruitful encounter that will bridge the historical gap separating us from the people from whom Jesus came.

When the great Spanish Jewish scholar Nahmanides was called by the King of Aragon in 1263 to participate in a formal disputation with Christians, he was allowed only to respond to the questions set for him by his opponent. It was understood that the truth of the Christian faith could not be impugned.

Despite the limitations Nahmanides did well. Referring to the biblical prophecies that the messianic age would be marked by universal peace and justice (Is. 2:4; Micah 4:3, etc.), he pointed out these promises had not yet been fulfilled. War and crime still prevailed throughout the world. Indeed, Christians themselves maintained armies and wrought destruction! How, he asked, could the Messiah have come if the messianic age had not?

Nahmanides perhaps argued too well. He was exiled from Spain and lived the remainder of his life in Palestine.

In another famous "dialogue" that lasted for three days, Rabbi Tehiel of Paris was asked to answer thirty-five charges directed against the Talmud. The major point of each was that the Talmud contained slanders against the person of Jesus and influenced Jews to act unfairly toward Christians. Tehiel painstakingly refuted each point. Afterward, 24 wagonloads of copies of the Talmud were thrown into the flames in a public square.

Those modern Jews, such as Eliezer Berkovits, who oppose the idea of dialogue with Christians thus have plausible reasons to do so. But to view history only negatively is as much of a trap as ignoring it altogether. To see the past only as a limit to what can be accomplished in the present is to be forced to repeat forever the errors and horrors of that past. Knowing the past is only useful to the extent that it enables us to work in the present to build for the future. In this book we will attempt to build for the future. By examining our common past, especially the biblical past, we will attempt to lay a few planks across the gap that separates us.

Today as in the time of Alexander III, the Church officially disavows any attempt to force the conversion of Jews. But other dangers threaten us. Anti-Jewish notions are embedded in our very thought patterns. They are part of the subconscious baggage that we bring with us to the dialogue. Who has not heard the phrase "to jew someone down"?

*Websters Dictionary* is illuminating on this point. The adjective "pharisaical," for instance, is defined as "resembling the Pharisees; outwardly but not inwardly religious; hypocritical, self-righteous." As we shall see, this stereotype of the Pharisees is as false as it is vicious. Yet it is part of our language.

The entry for the noun "Jewry" is even more frightening: "1. Judea; also, a district inhabited by Jews; a ghetto. 2. The Jewish people." Here the Jews are *defined* as victims!

The word "Shylock" is another anti-Jewish stereotype that is part of our daily language. According to Webster it is a noun that means: "1. A revengeful Jewish moneylender in Shakespeare's *The Merchant of Venice*. 2. An extortionate creditor."

Ignorance of and negative attitudes toward the Jews permeate each one of us. We need to rid ourselves of anti-Jewish bias by engaging in open dialogue. This "mini-history" will, hopefully, fill in some inadequacies in our knowledge of the Jewish people.

## Early Relations: Perspectives on the Conflict

The history of Jewish-Christian relations is a difficult one to write. It is especially difficult for the Christian since, for so much of the 2,000 years of shared history, the Christian side has enjoyed almost absolute dominance, politically, over the Jewish community. Admittedly, that power was all too often abused.

Yet one must go beyond guilt. The question today is not who is to blame but where we go from here. What caused the split in the first place? Christianity began as a Jewish sect. At what point did it break away? Why the bitterness of that early schism? To heal the wound we must first know its source.

### New Testament Background

In the beginning, as recorded in the New Testament, Christianity did not see itself as apart from but as a part of Judaism. The first apostles and disciples were all Jews. Even after Pentecost, they continued to worship in the temple, to attend the synagogue and to observe the Mosaic Law (Acts 2:42–47). It even took a special vision to convince St. Peter that non-Jewish converts to Christianity did not have to follow the Law (Acts 10).

Judaism in the first century was a vital, complex community. Jews lived not only in Palestine but also throughout the then known world. The first century was a period of tremendous religious creativity throughout that widespread community. This creativity took many forms, from the Hellenistic, philosophical religiosity of a Philo to the ascetic monasticism of the Dead Sea Scrollers. To the Jewish observer, Christianity would have been seen as one of numerous competing groups, each proclaiming its own Messiah.

The early unity of Christianity and Judaism is reflected in the fact that much of Christian liturgy and theology is based on Jewish precedents. The Mass, for example, combines the Synagogue practice of reading the Scriptures with an abbreviated form of the Passover meal. Christian feasts such as Easter and Pentecost were originally celebrated according to the Jewish calendar. Important beliefs, such as the resurrection of the dead, heaven and hell, angels, and the Last Judgment are direct borrowings from the doctrines of the Pharisees. Above all, there is a common Scripture, the Hebrew Bible, and the same faith in the one God who acts in history.

### A Family Quarrel

Perhaps it is because Christianity is so close to Judaism that the differences between the two came to be such a source of tension between us. We always quarrel most heatedly with those to whom we are closest. Even today the majority of violent crimes are committed not by those who are strangers to the victims but by those who are members of the victims' families or by close friends.

Add to this the fact that early Christianity was struggling for survival, a minority within a minority, and one can begin to see why the struggle became so bitter. Similar dynamics can occur within any family unit. When children reach adolescence, they strive earnestly to become adults overnight. They want to establish their own identity. This leads, often enough, to exaggerated self-assertiveness and even to a rejection of all that their parents are and stand for. Loud arguments, door slammings, stair poundings, and accusations later regretted become the order of the day.

Much the same sort of thing was happening between Christianity and its parent religion, Judaism, at the time when the New Testament was set down in writing. The Gospels were, we know, written long after the events they describe. The epistles were the earliest, but even they were not written until twenty or thirty years after Jesus' death. These letters show a community just beginning to see itself as separate from the parent Jewish community. Paul spends considerable time in his epistles striving to put into words the uniqueness of the Christian vision and how that relates to other forms of Judaism. The debate with Peter over requiring non-Jewish converts to follow the Mosaic Law is the reason Paul tends to stress only what is negative about the Jewish Law. He does not mean to reject Judaism absolutely but only as applied to Gentile "God-fearers" (Romans 9–11). Since he is arguing with fellow Christians as well as with Jews, he tends, in the style of the times, to argue passionately and at times may exaggerate his case for the sake of emphasis.

Next came Mark and Luke (A.D. 50–60). These Gospels reflect an escalating conflict between Jews and Christians. They are subtly harsher than Paul in their judgments on the Law and Judaism. Finally, Matthew and John were not written down until the last decades of the first century (80–90). They reflect a situation in which Christianity had totally severed itself from its parent and had gone on its own, resulting in a feeling of mutual bitterness.

## A Basic Disagreement

Though similar to Pharisaic Judaism in many ways, as we shall see, early Christians had a real need to define their specific identity. Jesus, they knew, was God. This belief set them apart from other Jews, and indeed from all other groups of the ancient world.

The early Christians saw in Jesus alone the fulfillment of all the biblical promises. Like another Jewish sect of the time, the Essenes who lived by the shores of the Dead Sea, they applied such passages as Jeremiah 31:31 to themselves: "The days are coming, says the Lord, when I will make a new covenant with the house of Israel." With the eyes of faith they saw that the end of days, the messianic age, was upon them. To them it was obvious. How could anyone disagree (cf. Acts 3:7)?

The problem was that not all Jews agreed on what signs would indicate the coming of the messianic age or what the biblical promises meant. Some saw it as political liberation from Roman oppression, a new Exodus. Others looked for a period of universal peace and social justice. The arguments presented by Peter (Acts 3) or Stephen (Acts 7) were thus unconvincing to those Jews who centered their messianic expectations on the qualities of the messianic age rather than on the person of the Messiah. War and injustice, after all, continued unabated.

The faith by which we know that Jesus is God is a gift. It is not, in the final analysis, the result of arguments, convincing or otherwise. God gives this gift freely to the chosen. If one follows the reasoning of Pope Innocent II (see Introduction), it is even possible to say that God's mysterious will never intended *all* Jews to be converted to Christ during the present dispensation. It is one of the Church's most ancient traditions that the Jews, as Jews, have a vital role to play in the economy of salvation — a role that will not end until the final end of time.

### Seeds of Mistrust

The early Christians were on fire with the love of Christ. They saw themselves as a besieged community. The Book of Acts records that there was suspicion on both sides. The high priest, a political appointee of Rome and thus more "Roman" than "Jewish" in his outlook, looked on Jesus as a threat to the Roman rule which sustained his own power. Jesus' followers likewise were viewed as political threats by the temple priesthood, which also mistrusted such groups as the Pharisees and the Essenes. Acts 5:17 and 7:1 show the lengths to which the high priesthood would go to protect its ties with Rome.

With rebellion brewing among the Jews of Palestine, the temple priests sought to have the early Christians silenced. The temple's loyalty was to Rome rather than its own people. This priestly party, the Sadducees, wanted no part of any movement, whether Christian or Pharisaic, that might disturb the status quo.

In such a volatile political situation, violence was bound to occur (cf. Acts. 7–8). The division between Christians and their fellow Jews, originally a dispute over the interpretation of Scripture, widened into a chasm.

### The Pharisees

The Book of Acts, like the passion narratives in the Gospels (as we shall see), clearly implicates only the priestly party of the Sadducees for the persecutions of Jesus and his followers. Indeed the Pharisee Gamaliel is said to have saved the lives of the apostles when they were arrested by the Sadducees. His reasoning is typical of the type of approach that the Pharisees, who were the great spiritual leaders of the common people, would have taken to Christianity had they had any effective political power at that period:

> If this movement (Christianity) is of human origin, it will break up of its own accord. But if it does in fact come from God, you will be unable to destroy them, but you might find yourselves fighting against God (Acts 5:38–39).

The Pharisees were men of profound religious vision. By emphasizing the spirit of the law over the letter, good deeds over temple sacrifice, they saved Judaism from disappearing when the temple was destroyed and its sacrifice no longer available to the people. As we shall see, Jesus' teaching is remarkably similar to that of the Pharisees in almost every particular. Why then do certain Gospels, especially that of Matthew, portray the Pharisees in such a bad light? For the answer we must look again at the dates of the composition of the books of the New Testament, and at the historical factors that changed what was a family quarrel into a fierce rivalry.

Matthew and John were not written down until about the year 80 or 90. Just prior to this a major crisis had occurred in the Jewish community. The temple at Jerusalem was destroyed by Roman troops in retaliation for an ill-fated rebellion against Roman rule. With the temple gone, the priesthood faded as an active force. The Zealots, the revolutionary leaders, were decimated. Only the Pharisees remained as viable Jewish leaders, and the people clustered around them for survival.

With the other leadership gone, the Pharisees alone remained as major competitors of the Christians as interpreters of the Hebrew Scriptures. After the year 70, then, the Christian apologetic was increasingly directed against the Pharisees. Because they were then the chief competitors of Christianity, the Pharisees figure prominently in Christian writings after the year 70. Because the rivalry was intense and the stakes were high (the conversion not only of Judaism but of the Roman Empire), the New Testament authors made use of the highly inflated language that was the style of the time.

## Competition for Converts

During this period, the Pharisees were highly successful missionaries. Throughout the Empire there were Jewish communities, each with numerous "God-fearers" or converts to Judaism. Paul, for example, made it a practice to go to the synagogue in every city he visited. Acts 13:43 shows how successful he was in convincing the Jewish converts that Christianity was the better path: "When the congregation finally broke up, many Jews and devout Jewish converts followed Paul."

Naturally the rabbis who led these congregations were concerned about the loss of converts. To them, Christianity might be tolerated, but not at the expense of the communities they led. Paul's actions, to them, would appear little else than "sheep-stealing," that is, proselytizing among the converts whom the rabbis had instructed in Judaism. Paul and the Christians were banned from many synagogues by rabbis who were trying to protect their congregations.

Tempers flared on both sides, and the gap widened into conflict. Some of this anger on the part of the Christians is reflected in the grim, austere presentation of the Pharisees in the later Gospels, such as those of Matthew and John.

The Gospel writers brought their human emotions with them in writing down the inspired Word of God. And we must remember that there are four Gospels, not one. In many cases one Gospel must be used to balance off another if one is to reconstruct an historical event or understand the context of a saying ascribed to Jesus. In the chapters that follow we will attempt to present a proper balance in relation to key events such as the trial and death of Jesus.

Other factors aggravated the split between the communities. As more and more non-Jews converted to Christ, and as the years passed, the Christian community had less and less direct knowledge of what Judaism really was. Statements such as those in Matthew, originally written in an emotionally- charged atmosphere, were taken as the full truth. While many of Matthew's original readers would have been familiar with the context of his approaches, later Christians were unacquainted with the other side of the picture. Stereotypes became established, and misinterpretation of the Gospels became widespread as Christianity became more and more divorced from Judaism. Without knowledge of Judaism, Paul's statements about the Law may be taken in a much more absolute sense than he would have originally intended. Misunderstandings solidified and developed into myths about the Jews.

Originally, the Gospel authors utilized strong contrasts in working out the differences between Judaism and Christianity. These words and images, taken out of context and read by persons with no knowledge of Judaism, sadly took on a force of their own. One final factor must be added here, a factor not under the control of either Jews or Christians: the phenomenon of pagan anti-Semitism.

## Pagan Anti-Semitism

The situation of the early Church, as described, was not one of anti-Semitism as we know it today. It was a case of a bitter rivalry between closely related communities that gradually got out of hand. Left on their own, it is possible that, in time, the Jewish and Christian communities might well have worked out some sort of amicable understanding. But anti-Jewish feeling in the Christian world does not stem from religious rivalry alone. Even before the birth of Christ, anti-Semitism was widespread in the ancient world of the Gentiles, and many Gentile converts to Christianity brought their negative views of the Jews with them when they entered the Church.

The reasons for this pagan anti-Semitism are not hard to discover. First, polytheism, the belief in many gods, was the normal practice among the Gentile peoples. By believing staunchly in only one God, the Jews became a suspect people. They were "different," so they were looked down on. Rumors and stories, once started, were taken as truth throughout the empires of the day.

Second, polytheism was bound up in the politics of the time. Conquered people had to show loyalty to their conquerors by worshiping the deities of the victorious nation. Good citizens worshiped the official gods of the city-state. Often, emperors and kings set themselves up as divine, and they demanded worship as a form of patriotism and political loyalty. To refuse to worship

the ruler was treason. The Jews, believing only in one God, refused. For their courageous faith they were persecuted and were
often martyred, as the Books of Maccabees illustrate. Citizens of
the Graeco-Roman world distrusted their loyalty and spread vicious anti-Semitic lies about them. Unfortunately, because of the
gap that had grown between Christianity and its parent religion,
Gentile Christians became easy prey for such falsehoods.

## Reconciliation: The Second Vatican Council

We have seen the beginnings of the tragic split between Christian and Jew. Let us turn to what is hopefully the beginning of
the end of the quarrel, though not necessarily of the unique role
of each of the two communities in God's plan.

Vatican II in its *Declaration on Non-Christian Religions*, n. 4, reaffirmed the best of ancient Christian tradition concerning the Jews.
More, it attacked the heart of the anti-Jewish myth by denying its
two central tenets: "What happened in his (Jesus') passion cannot
be charged against all the Jews, without distinction, then alive,
nor against the Jews of today.... The Jews should not be represented as rejected by God or accursed, as if this followed from
Holy Scripture" ((*Nostra Aetate*, Oct. 28, 1965).

In a single stroke, the bishops at Vatican II put aside all specu-
lation that the Jews could be considered guilty of deicide, which
means the killing of God. The corollary notion that Jewish suffering is the result of God's punishment for that so-called crime was
likewise explicitly rejected.

Going further, the Council points out the basis for a fully positive theology of Judaism. The Jews continue, it proclaims, to be a
people specially chosen by God to play a role in salvation. What
was implied by Innocent III in the twelfth century is here made
plain: "Now as before, God holds the Jews most dear for the sake
of their fathers. He does not repent of the gifts he makes or the
calls he issues." In other words, God has not revoked the call to
the Jewish people.

In the *Constitution on the Church*, the most solemn statement of
the Council, the Jewish people of today are spoken of as *populus
secundum electionem*, "a people according to election" (n. 16). These
statements open the way to a whole new approach to Judaism, for
they mean that the Sinai covenant with the Jews is still in force
today. Our view of the relationship between Judaism and Chris-

tianity becomes from this perspective a much deeper mystery. A major task of the dialogue today lies in exploring the relationship between two peoples, both of whom are in valid covenant with the same God. The implications, to say the least, are immensely exciting.

## The 1975 Vatican Guidelines

In the wake of the Council, great strides were made in Jewish-Christian relations. On January 2, 1975, the Vatican issued new "Guidelines" for implementing the decree. This document marked the progress made in the intervening period.

The document specified much that had been implicit in the conciliar statement of a decade earlier. It spoke warmly of "the spiritual bonds and historical links binding the Church to Judaism." Reaffirming Vatican II's condemnation of anti-Semitism, it called for a positive reformulation of the Christian understanding of Judaism based on the "essential traits the Jews define themselves in the light of their own religious history." This last is a crucial point given the ignorance and misunderstanding that have prevailed for so long between the communities.

The Vatican document also notes the many "common elements of the liturgical life" which we share with the Jews. The fact that much of our ritual is based on Jewish liturgy is thus admitted. The Guidelines go on to note that, in essential ways, "the Old Testament retains its own perpetual value." It calls on all catechists and homilists to explain thoroughly "those phrases and passages which Christians, if not well informed, might misunderstand because of prejudice." The present book is in large part written to give practical background material for implementing this mandate.

In its section on "Teaching and Education," the document lists and corrects a number of common misunderstandings, for example:

> The Old Testament and the Jewish tradition rounded on it must not be set against the New Testament in such a way that the former seems to constitute a religion of only justice, fear and legalism, with no appeal to the love of God and neighbor. The history of Judaism did not end with the destruction of Jerusalem. Rather it went on to develop a religious tradition . . . rich in religious values. (See Appendix B.)

Finally, the Guidelines call for joint social action and common prayer that remain sensitive to the uniqueness of each tradition. But the document does not advocate joint liturgical worship, which would be unwelcome to Jews as well as Christians, since the communities must retain their distinctiveness.

## The American Bishops

In 1967 the American bishops issued "Guidelines for Catholic-Jewish Relations in the United States." These were remarkable for their candor and represented a significant step in the dialogue in this country. They acknowledged "the manifold sufferings and injustices inflicted upon the Jewish people by Christians in our own times as well as in the past." They mandated the analysis of Catholic textbooks for their treatment of Jews and Judaism, the establishment of courses and programs in Judaism and anti-Semitism in Catholic schools and seminaries, and the revision of the presentation of the crucifixion story "in such a way as not to implicate all Jews of Jesus' time or today in a collective guilt." The 1967 statement explicitly rejected "the historically inaccurate notion that Judaism of that (Jesus') time, especially that of Pharisaism, was a decadent formalism and hypocrisy." And in a very clear way it took the implications of Vatican II to their logical conclusion by acknowledging "the permanent election of Israel (Rom. 9:29)." This notion, the bishops declared, should be incorporated into all Catholic teaching, a directive whose implications will be felt for decades yet to come.

On November 20, 1975, the National Conference of Catholic Bishops of the United States issued another major "Statement on Catholic Jewish Relations." (See Appendix C.) Like the 1967 statement, this one was widely praised throughout Jewish and Catholic circles. Briefly summarizing the history of Catholic-Jewish relations since the Council, the bishops made some key contributions to the dialogue and charted a course for future work. For example:

> Most essential concepts in the Christian creed grew at first in Jewish soil. Uprooted from that soil, these basic concepts cannot be perfectly understood.... By the third century, however, a de-Judaizing process had set in which tended to undervalue the Jewish origins of the Church.

Such an admission that the Church can understand its own nature *only* in dialogue with a living Judaism is literally breathtaking to one who knows the history of the dark days of suspicion and polemic. Even more importantly, the American bishops open up a new area of dialogue for the future based on a reinterpretation of Romans 9–11. Some exciting implications of these insights will be discussed in a later chapter.

Today a new spirit of openness is in the air. By going back to the sources and searching the Scriptures in the light of this new spirit, we can hopefully discover a new way to view the Jews and — incidentally — ourselves as well. The child Christianity is learning to accept its parentage.

Another important aspect of the American bishops' statement has been more recently highlighted by the furor caused by the various votes in the United Nations seeking to defame Zionism as racism. Zionism is simply a modern expression of an ancient longing, one to be respected and one that is as inherently valid as any of the other "liberation" movements of the twentieth century. The bishops state:

> In dialogue with Christians, Jews have explained that they do not consider themselves as a church, a sect, or a denomination, as is the case among Christian communities, but rather as a peoplehood that is not solely racial, ethnic or religious, but in a sense a composite of all of these. It is for such reasons that an overwhelming majority of Jews see themselves bound in one way or another to the land of Israel. Most Jews see this tie to the land as essential to their Jewishness. Whatever difficulties Christians may experience in sharing this view, they should strive to understand this link between land and people which Jews have expressed in their writings and worship throughout two millennia as a longing for the homeland, holy Zion.

Such a statement, coming during a period of increasing controversy around this sensitive issue, must be seen as both courageous and significant. There are many complexities, both political and theological, surrounding Zionism and the state of Israel. The bishops themselves go on to caution that "appreciation of this link is not to give assent to any particular religious interpretation of this bond" nor "to deny the legitimate rights of other parties in the region." In the mind of the American bishops, the political existence of the state of Israel does not depend upon an interpretation of the Hebrew Scriptures. Rather, like other new nations it is rounded on the legal decision of the United Nations following universally held principles of international law at a point in time when the United Nations had proper and recognized jurisdiction of the dispute. The bishops are therefore careful not to adopt any political stance in the controversies over the Middle East, beyond clearly affirming Israel's right to exist in peace.

Such cautiousness is vitally necessary today. But one must also respect the forthrightness of what the statement does say. Here there is no room for such inflammatory charges as "Zionism is racism." For the stance is one of openness and dialogue rather than emotional rhetoric. Such openness is our best hope for the future.

# CHAPTER TWO

# Understanding Jesus,
# The Faithful Jew

## Introduction

Bishop Bernard Sheil, an auxiliary bishop of Chicago, who in 1931 rounded the Catholic Youth Organization which has become internationally famous, was delivering a lecture in the school which he had founded. His subject was a very unpopular one with many people — the relationship which should exist between Christians and Jews. "Was not Jesus Christ a Jew?" he asked. "Was not Mary?"

Boos and hisses mingled with the applause. A wild-eyed woman pushed herself straight into the bishop's path and began to scream: "You're not a Catholic. You're not a bishop. You're a rabbi!"

When the bishop broke the silence that followed, his words were calm: "I thank you, Madam, for the compliment. Rabbi? That's what they called our Lord."

This story, a true one, which is taken from a current junior high school Church history text, *The Pearl and the Seed* (Allyn and Bacon), illustrates a need and a promise. The need is to correct our traditional teaching that sought to approach Jesus in isolation from his people. The promise is that by recapturing his Jewishness we can come to a new appreciation of his person and his teaching. For the denial of Jesus' Jewishness is, in fact, a denial of his humanity. To miss the distinctively Jewish context of Jesus' teaching is, often enough, to miss the point entirely.

At the beginning of the second century, a son was born to the Catholic bishop of Sinope (celibacy not becoming a common practice among the clergy until centuries later). The child was named Marcion, and he grew to become a powerful preacher. Marcion wanted to make Jesus relevant to his own time. He wanted to present Jesus in a way that would appeal to the sophisticated, philosophically-oriented Greeks and Romans of his time. In his view the Jesus of history, the itinerant Jewish teacher, was not sufficiently universal. The Jewish Jesus needed to be replaced with a metaphysical concept corresponding to the best traditions of Greek philosophy. So Marcion preached a "cosmic Christ," above all history and national particularism. The Jewish origins of Christianity, and the Jewish particularity of Jesus, Marcion felt, were an embarrassment.

Marcion wanted to preach a "pure" Christianity, stripped of all Judaic vestiges. The Hebrew Scriptures were "crude" in comparison to the abstract categories of Greek philosophy. They should be discarded for the sake of the converts to be won. The God of the Hebrew Scriptures was harsh and vindictive, a cruel God fundamentally opposed to the pure God of love preached by Christ. The New Testament not only fulfilled but completely replaced the revelation of the Hebrew Scriptures. It alone contained everything necessary for salvation, and even it should be de-Judaized.

In the year 144, the Church excommunicated Marcion for heresy. His theory of a total opposition between the Sinai and Christian covenants was rejected in order to affirm the essential continuity between the Testaments. It is, the Church declared, the same God who speaks through both Scriptures.

Though defeated, Marcionism did not entirely disappear. Throughout history the temptation has arisen to present a de-Judaized version of Christianity, to see in the Hebrew Scriptures a God of fear and in the New Testament a God of love. Perhaps some of us can even remember similar views from our own religion classes as children.

Marcionism represents an extreme view, a notion which in its blatant form has been consistently rejected by the Church. It represents a view in which Judaism and Christianity are seen as opposites, as "Law" versus "Gospel" or "justice" versus "love." The 1975 Statement of the American bishops notes:

> Christians have not fully appreciated their Jewish roots. . . . The Jewishness of Jesus, of his mother, of his disciples, of the primitive Church, was lost from view. That Jesus was called rabbi, that

he was born, lived and died under the Law, that he and Peter and Paul worshiped in the temple — these facts are blurred.

Marcion's attempt to make Jesus relevant to the culture of his own times is understandable. Each generation must relate to Jesus as the Christ in its own way. It is always necessary to make our catechesis come alive for our students. But we should always remember the lesson of Marcion. The real Jesus of history will never wholly fit into the neat categories of philosophical trends. His message is ever challenging and, to be understood, must be seen as rooted in the history and religious convictions of his people, the Jews.

Jesus is no more a modern existentialist than he was a Greek philosopher. He considered himself to be a faithful Jew. He was brought up to observe the Jewish Law, the Torah. Like other pious Jews of his day, he cherished that teaching as the inspired word of God. When he spoke, he spoke to his fellow Jews and presumed their knowledge of and love for the Hebrew Scriptures. Stripped of its base in the Hebrew Scriptures, the New Testament can make little real sense. Jesus' teaching depends for its understanding on an appreciation of the Jewish context in which he spoke. This chapter will present a few of the insights to be gained by reading the New Testament in the light of Jesus' personal commitment to Judaism.

## The Law of Love

When the scribe asks Jesus "Which is the first of all the commandments?" (Mk. 12; Mt. 28; Lk. 10), Jesus does not answer by formulating a "new" law of love. Instead, he quotes two key passages from the Hebrew Scriptures. "Love God with your whole heart, your whole soul and your whole mind" is taken from Deuteronomy 6:5. It is part of a larger passage called the *Shema* ("Hear, O Israel, the Lord is your God, the Lord is one"). This is one of the central prayers of Judaism. Like Jesus, every pious Jew prays this prayer three times every day. It is important to know the context of this prayer in the Scriptures, since the Jews who listened to Jesus would have had the entire section memorized and would have been reminded of the whole by the small part quoted by our Lord.

The fifth chapter of Deuteronomy, which immediately precedes the *Shema,* records the giving of the Ten Commandments, which biblically stand as a symbol for the whole of the Law. Chapter 6, of which the *Shema* forms a part, is meant by the Deuteronomist as an explanation of the meaning of the essence of the entire Sinai covenant with all its numerous commands. The Hebrew author is thus giving what he or she considers to be the "first" of all the commandments: wholehearted love of God. Deuteronomy 6:6, which immediately follows the passage quoted by Jesus, gives the primary characteristic of this law of love: "Let these words I urge on you today be written on your heart." The Sinai Law *is* the law of love. It is not mere externals but a law meant to be written on the heart. In giving the law of love, Jesus stands within the mainstream of Judaism. This is why Marcion had to be condemned. Jesus' law is not a "new" law in the sense that it is opposed to an "old" law of fear. Christianity and Judaism are in complete agreement on this point. The Law, the "Torah" (which means the "teaching" and not "law" in our sense at all), is the one Law of the one God: the law of love.

The second part of Jesus' answer to the scribe's friendly question is also a quotation from the Hebrew Scriptures. "Love your neighbor as yourself" is found in Leviticus 19:18. Again, Jesus teaches a central tenet of contemporary Judaism. The Pharisees, like the prophets before them (Jer. 7:22–23; Is. 1:11–18), stressed that the covenant Law was best fulfilled not by ritual sacrifice, but by "good deeds" (*mitzvoth*), i.e., by acting in love and justice toward one's neighbor. Jesus shows his appreciation for the Jewish Law, and the Pharisaic understanding of the Law, by focusing on this teaching.

In his answer to the scribe, Jesus would have appeared to his audience to be a typical Pharisee of his time. Among the Pharisees, it was a major concern to show the inner spirit or intention (*kavanah*) of the law of the heart. The following passage, perhaps dating to a short time after the death of Jesus, is but one of many examples:

> Ben Azzai quoted the verse, "This is the book of the generations of Adam" (Gen. 5:1) and said: This is the greatest principle of the Law. Rabbi Akiba said: "Thou shalt love thy neighbor as thyself" is the greatest principle in the Law (*Genesis Rabbah, Bereshit* 24:7. The translation is based on Montefiore and Loewe, *A Rabbinic Anthology,* New York: Schocken, 1974. Subsequent quotes from the

Talmud are either from here or from N. Glatzer, *Hammer on the Rock: A Midrash Reader,* New York: Schocken, 1974).

## Jesus and the Talmud

Christ, in many instances, took his stand on the teaching of the Old Testament.... Jesus also used teaching methods similar to those employed by the rabbis of his time (1975 Vatican Guidelines).

Modern scholarship has reclaimed the image of the Pharisees and shown us who they really were. In New Testament times, the Pharisees formed a complex, vitally creative movement. They represented the common classes as against the aristocratic Sadducees who represented the moneyed class. They preached that God could be approached directly by the people through prayer and study of Torah without the necessity of the mediation of temple sacrifice. Lively debates, such as the one recorded above, were commonplace. Their masterwork, the Talmud, composed over a period of approximately eight centuries and spanning the time of Christ, records those debates and the conclusions of various "schools" or followers of particular rabbis. Like Jesus, each of the great rabbis had disciples dedicated to working out the implications of his particular style of interpreting the Law.

One aspect of the genius of the Talmud is that it records not only the final resolution of a discussion, but the minority opinions as well. The Talmud is thus a particularly rich and flexible body of religious insight. Often it can provide us with the background for Jesus' sayings. From the New Testament we can see that Jesus often took part in the spirited debates taking place between groups of Pharisees. Sometimes he sided with one group, sometimes with another. If we read the New Testament in the light of the Talmud, we can see that Jesus would never have attacked the Pharisees as a whole. Rather, he acted and taught as a participant in their movement. The following example, possibly dating to the century before Jesus, illustrates this:

A heathen came to Rabbi Shammai and said: "I will become a convert (to Judaism) on condition that you teach me the whole Law while standing on one foot." Shammai drove him away with the measuring rod he held in his hand. Then the man went to Rabbi Hillel with the same challenge. Hillel said: "What is hateful to you do not do to your fellow. That is the whole Law. All the rest is commentary. Go and learn" (*Shabbath* 31a).

Hillel, like Jesus after him, is here echoing a biblical proverb which is the real source of the Golden Rule: "Do to no one what you would not want done to you" (Tob. 4:15).

Knowledge of the Talmud is often crucial to our understanding of the New Testament. Jesus is called "rabbi" in the New Testament for good reason. The people of his time viewed him as such, which is to say as a Pharisee. This fact can help clear up many misunderstandings.

Reading the Gospel of Matthew, for example, we often gain the impression that Jesus is condemning all Pharisees as hypocrites. It is a surprise to learn, then, that the Talmud, the book written by the Pharisees, condemns hypocrisy no less harshly than does Jesus.

> Who is the crafty scoundrel? Rabbi Huna says: "He is the man who, lenient to himself, teaches others the hardest rules" (Sotah 3:4).

In condemning hypocrisy, Jesus is preaching in a way typical of the Pharisees.

Self-criticism was common among the Pharisees. Their integrity demanded it. They fought hard against hypocrisy of all sorts. They also had a healthy sense of humor. The following passage from the Talmud illustrates these Pharisaic virtues, which Jesus shared. It provides a background for Jesus' "sevenfold indictment" of the Pharisees found in Matthew and shows that Jesus' original sayings were not directed against the Pharisees as a whole. Indeed, Jesus is most a Pharisee when he is attacking hypocrisy.

As we have seen, Matthew felt a need in the last decades of the first century to debate against the Pharisees. When he wrote down his Gospel, the Church was in bitter competition with the Pharisees for the conversion of both Jews and the Roman world. Matthew preserved the authentic sayings of Jesus but placed them in a new context. In this way a teaching of Jesus that was most Pharisee-like could be subtly changed into an attack on the Pharisees themselves (see Chapter 3).

The Talmud presents seven "classes" of Pharisees. These were not actual groups or real-life divisions. These categories were a literary device to set up the scene and were basically a satire on false notions of Pharisaism. The seven classes parallel Jesus' sayings fairly closely. In Matthew, however, the humor of the scene is lost. What was originally a lesson in which the Pharisees reminded themselves of the nature of true humility and love — their goal in life — thus became, by altering the context in which Jesus spoke, an apparent attack on the movement as such. This usage was probably far different from what Jesus originally intended.

The seven classes of Pharisees as listed in the Talmud are:

1. The "Shoulder" Pharisee, who ostentatiously carries his or her good deeds on the shoulder to be seen by all.

2. The "Wait-A-While" Pharisee, who when someone needs him or her says, "Wait until I have done this good deed."

3. The "Reckoning" or "Book-keeping" Pharisee, who calculates virtue against vice. This Pharisee may sin deliberately and then attempt to cross off the fault by adding a good deed to his or her list.

4. The "Bruised" Pharisee, who breaks his head against a wall to avoid looking at a woman or is so ostentatious in his "humility" that he keeps shuffling his feet together and wounding them.

5. The "Pestle" Pharisee, whose head is bent in sham humility like a pestle in a mortar.

6. The "God-fearing Pharisee," who is like Job.

7. The "Pharisee of Love," who is like Abraham (Ber. 9:7; Sot. 5:7).

The seventh class, of course, is the ideal the Pharisees set for themselves. It is the law of love which Jesus also preached. It is interesting that St. Paul follows the Pharisees in holding up Abraham as a model of faith (Rom. 4).

In preaching a halachah ("way") of love, in opposition to the hypocrisy of legalism, Jesus is at one with the major leaders of the Pharisees. He is joining in their attempt to center observance of the Law on its inner spirit while still preserving the notion that the *mitzvoth* ("good deeds") are necessary to the full life of faith.

### Hillel and Shammai

Many New Testament passages become clearer when one sees Jesus as a part of rather than opposed to the Pharisaic movement. In the century before Jesus, great debates took place between the followers of two major schools: those of Rabbis Shammai and Hillel. While Shammai favored a strict interpretation of the Law, Hillel tended to a more lenient view, interpreting the Law to fit the needs and realities of daily life. Majority opinion in the Talmud usually follows Hillel's less strict approach, as does Jesus.

The guiding spirit of the Pharisaic approach to the Law can be fairly summed up in the Talmudic saying: "The Sabbath is committed to you; you are not committed to the Sabbath" (*Mekilta* 31:13).

Jesus' saying preserved in Mark 2:27 thus shows how close he was to the followers of Rabbi Hillel: "The Sabbath was made for man, not man for the Sabbath." Its context in Mark is also revealing. Here Jesus' disciples are being censured by some of "the Pharisees" (probably Shammaites) for plucking ears of corn to eat on the Sabbath (compare Mt. 12). The Talmud (*Shabbath* 128a) shows that opinion was divided among the Pharisees on this question. Jesus sides with the Hillelites against the Shammaites. Interestingly, the more lenient rule of Hillel is also favored by the *Mishnah*, which prohibits "winnowing" and "grinding" with tools as labor which violates the Sabbath law, but allows individual plucking by hand.

For the Talmud, any law of the Sabbath could be ignored if a life was at stake. Jesus' cure on the Sabbath of the man with a withered hand would thus have been praised and not condemned by many Pharisees of his time, especially the followers of Rabbi Hillel.

## How Much More?

The Pharisees of Jesus' time saw the need of adapting the biblical Law to meet the changing circumstances of their times. The Pharisees thus had to develop principles of interpretation which would allow for updating the Law yet remaining within the spirit of the Law. In this process, the Pharisees had biblical precedent to follow.

If one compares the laws found in the book of Exodus, for example, with the same laws as written in Deuteronomy, one finds that the latter often revised the earlier legislation to keep pace with changing times. The ritual for the feast of Passover, for example, evolved significantly between the period reflected in Exodus 12 and the later period in which Deuteronomy 16 was set down. Again, the law on the seduction or rape of an unmarried virgin (Ex. 22:15–16) is expanded by Deuteronomy 22:28–29 to give added protection to the victim. Likewise, close comparison of the two versions of the Ten Commandments (Ex. 20 and Deut. 5) reveals development of moral insight.

By the time of Hillel and Shammai in the century before Jesus' birth, the Pharisees had worked out various logical principles for interpreting and adapting the Law. For them, the letter of the Law at times needed to be reinterpreted in order to remain true to its spirit or original intent. Rabbi Hillel gathered together seven of these *middoth* or rules of interpretation.

Jesus and the New Testament authors often made use of the rabbinic *middoth* in interpreting the Scriptures. The first of the seven will serve as an example. This is the rule of "Light and Heavy." Under it, a principle that applies in a lesser case can be applied as well to a weightier or more important matter. Often, the phrase "how much more?" in the form of a rhetorical question indicates that a rabbi is making use of the principle of "Light and Heavy." Jesus also uses this Pharisaic approach:

> If you, with all your sins, know how to give your children what is good, how much more will your heavenly Father give good things to anyone who asks him? (Mt. 7:11).

> If God clothes in such splendor the grass of the field, which grows today and is thrown on the fire tomorrow, how much more will he provide for you? (Lk. 12:28).

These sayings of Jesus are typically Pharisaic and have parallels in the Talmud. One parallel is striking for its virtual identity.

*Matthew 6:26:* Look at the birds of the heaven they neither sow nor reap . . . yet your heavenly Father feeds them.

*Kiddushin 4:14:* Did you ever see an animal or a bird that had a trade? Yet they support themselves without trouble. Does it not follow that I shall be supported without trouble?

## The Sermon on the Mount

The Sermon on the Mount (Mt. 5–7; Lk. 6) represents a collection of some of Jesus' most famous sayings as preserved by the early Church. It is rightly considered to contain the core of Christian moral teaching.

The Sermon, properly understood, reveals the close similarities between rabbinic Judaism and Christianity in the moral sphere. For both the Sermon and the Talmud begin with the Hebrew Torah as their starting point. And both apply the principles of the *middoth* for interpreting the spirit of the Law.

The Beatitudes, for example, find their source in the Hebrew Scriptures and have parallels in the Talmud. The second, "Happy are the lowly (humble, meek); they shall inherit the land," is found in Psalm 37 as "The humble shall have the land for their own, to enjoy untroubled peace" (v. 11). The following saying from the Talmud captures much the same spirit as the Sermon on the Mount:

> Isaiah said, "Sovereign of the Universe, what must a man do to be saved?" God said to him, "Let him give charity, dividing his bread to the poor, and giving his money to those who study Torah; let him not behave haughtily.... If he humbles himself before all creatures, then will I dwell with him (Is. 57:15). I testify that he who has these qualities will inherit the world to come: whoever has Torah, good deeds, humility and fear of heaven" (*Pesikta Rabbati*, 198a).

Note that here it is not an earthly kingdom but the spiritual Kingdom of God that is promised to the humble of heart.

For "Blessed are the peacemakers" the Talmud has this, among others:

> Elijah said to Rabbi Baruka, "These two will share in the world to come." R. Baruka then asked them, "What is your occupation?" They said, "We are merry-makers. When we see a man who is downcast, we cheer him up. When we see two people quarreling with one another, we try to make peace between them" (*Ta'an* 22a).

In the Sermon, then, Jesus does not oppose rabbinic Judaism. He does not seek to create his own Torah ("teaching") but to interpret, as do the Pharisees, the spirit of the one Law of God. We should take him seriously when he points out within the Sermon itself: "Do not imagine that I have come to abolish the Law or the Prophets.... Not one *yod* (the smallest letter of the Hebrew alphabet), not one tittle (a small curl on the end of certain letters)" (Mt. 5:17–18).

The Sermon, like much of Jesus' teaching, appears in the light of the Talmud to be an application of the Pharisaic concept of the "oral Torah." The rabbis felt that this oral law contained the means by which the written Law could be reinterpreted from age to age. The concept is to some extent similar to the Catholic Church's notion of the "tradition of the Church" by which the written word of God is to be authentically interpreted. The major difference is that the measure of authenticity of the oral Torah is not so much that the interpreter stands in a line of succession with the original biblical authors but that the interpreter follows precisely the rules of interpretation (*middoth*).

The concept of an oral Torah emphasizes the importance of the spirit of the Law, of proper intention (*kavanah*) over mere externalism. The oral Torah tradition was bitterly opposed by the Sadducees of the temple party, who felt that one must follow the written Law only. The Pharisees argued this way:

> It matters not whether you do much or little, as long as your heart is directed to heaven (Ber. 17a).

> The Torah that is practiced and studied for its own sake is a law of love. The Law (followed) not for its own sake is a Law without love (Suk. 49b).

Much of what Jesus says in the Sermon can best be understood within the context of internal Pharisaic discussion over the meaning of the oral Torah through which the written Torah was to be interpreted. The reasoning behind Jesus' ruling on divorce (Mt. 5:32), for example, is found in Matthew 19. Here, Jesus is applying the *peshat* or "literal" form of interpretation that was favored by the school of Rabbi Shammai. Marriage, for him, means that "the two are one body" and that only God can end the relationship. Jesus gives as evidence for his position the passage in Genesis 2:24: "For this reason a man shall leave his father and mother and cling to his wife." The record of the Pharisaic discussion as preserved in *Mishnah Gittin* 9:10 shows that Jesus is quite close to the *peshat* interpretation of the Shammaites. He is not opposing rabbinic Judaism as such, but taking a stand within its broad context.

Jesus' teaching on adultery (Mt. 5:27) also has a close Talmudic parallel:

> It is written, "The eye of the adulterer" (Jb. 24:15). Resh Lakish said: "The eye: lest you should think only he who sins with his body is an adulterer. He who sins with his eye is also an adulterer" (*Lev. R., Ahare Mot* 23:12).

Likewise, the saying "If anyone orders you to go one mile, go two miles with him" (Mt. 5:41) finds its rabbinic parallel. Hillel was once approached by a poor man to whom he gave a horse. Unable to find a servant for the fellow, who was "of good family," Hillel himself "ran before him for three miles," in order to restore his sense of self-worth.

Jesus bases his teaching on love of enemies (Mt. 5:43–44) on passages from the Hebrew Scriptures: "If your enemy be hungry, give him bread to eat, and if he be thirsty, give him water to drink" (Prv. 25:21; see Lev. 19: 17). The Talmud also appeals to passages from Proverbs in order to preach the idea of returning good for evil and love for hatred:

> Rabbi Hama ben Hanina said: "Even though your enemy has risen up early to kill you, and he comes hungry and thirsty to your house, give him food and drink. God will make him at peace with you." Rabbi Simeon ben Abba said: "The verse (Proverbs 17:13) means that if a man returns evil for evil, evils shall not depart from his house."

## Parables and Parallels

Jesus' stories are justly famous for their simplicity and depth. Scholars tell us that most parables have three levels of meaning: (1) how Jesus originally told them; (2) how the early Church used them in preserving them in oral form in its early liturgies; (3) how the Gospel writers used them in putting them into written form.

A parable is a story with a point, and Jesus often used stories to describe our relationship with God and the meaning of the Kingdom whose coming he had been sent to proclaim. The early Church and the Gospel writers then used Jesus' stories to make their *own* points for their own situation and times.

By the time the Gospels were written down, the Church was in competition with rabbinic Judaism for the conversion of the pagan world. Both held the same Hebrew Bible to be the word of God, but the two groups often interpreted that word in a different manner. The Gospel writers used biblical quotes as proofs that Jesus was the Messiah. In the same way, they took the sayings of Jesus and put them into a new context. In this way they used his words as a part of the Church's debate with the Judaism of their time. Parables that Jesus had originally told *within* and as a part of the Jewish tradition came to be understood by the Church as being against the Jewish tradition.

Thus a new meaning was often added to the original intent of Jesus' parables after his death. Today we are most interested in the original, authentic message of Jesus. By taking into account this later meaning, we can hear the parables as Jesus himself spoke them.

Here are just a few examples.

### Parable of the Talents (Mt. 25; Lk. 19)

In this story a property owner taking a journey gives money to three servants, demanding an accounting on his return. The first two invest wisely and are rewarded. The third simply buries the money for safekeeping and so is punished.

As used in the Gospels, this parable has to do with the Last Judgment and the accounting the individual will have to make to God. But what may have been the original intention of Jesus in telling it is suggested by the following parallel taken from the Talmud. Here the point of the story is once again the controversy between the Sadducees, who held to the written Bible alone, and the Pharisees, who accepted the principle of the oral Torah. Jesus may have told the story originally in order to side with the Pharisees against the strictness and literalism of the Sadducees. In this parable the wise servant can be understood as a symbol of the Pharisees and the foolish servant as a symbol of the Sadducees.

Once when I was on a journey, I came upon a man who went at me after the manner of the heretics. Now, he accepted the written but not the oral law. He said to me: "The written law was given us from Mount Sinai; the oral law was not given us from Mount Sinai." I said to him: "But were not both the Written and the Oral Law spoken by the Omnipresent? Then what difference is there between the written and the oral law?"

To what can this (case) be compared? To a king of flesh and blood who had two servants, and loved them both with a perfect love. One day he gave them each a measure of wheat, and each a bundle of flax.

The wise servant, what did he do? He took the flax and spun a cloth. Then he took the wheat and made flour. He cleansed the flour, ground, kneaded and baked it, and set it on a table. Then he spread the cloth over it and so left it until the king should return.

But the foolish servant? He did nothing at all. After some days the king returned from his journey and came into his house and said to his servants: "My sons, bring me what I gave you."

The first servant showed the wheat bread on the table with the cloth spread over it. The other servant showed the wheat still in the box, with a bundle of flax upon it. Alas for his shame! Alas for his disgrace!

Now when the Holy One, blessed be He, gave the Torah to Israel, He gave it only in the form of wheat, for us to extract flour from it, and flax to extract a garment. (*Seder Eliyahu Zutta II*)

Another Talmudic parable shows the approach of the Pharisees to the question of material possessions and the Kingdom of God (the life of Torah). This parallels Matthew 13 and similar parables of the Kingdom:

Rabbi Yohanan was walking from Tiberias to Sepphoris,
and Rabbi Hiyya bar Abba was supporting him.
They came to a certain field, and Rabbi Yohanan said:
This field was mine and I sold it in order to gain the Torah.
They came to a certain vineyard, and he said:
This vineyard was mine and I sold it to gain the Torah.
They came to a certain olive grove, and he said:
This olive grove was mine and I sold it to gain the Torah.
Rabbi Hiyya began to cry.
Rabbi Yohanan said: Why are you crying?
He said to him: Because you left nothing for your old age.
He said to him: Is what I have done a small thing in your eyes?
For I have sold a thing which was created in the course of six days,
and I have gained a thing which was given in the course of forty
    days;
as it is said: "And he was there with the Lord forty days and forty
    nights" (Ex. 34:28).
When Rabbi Yohanan died, his generation read the Scripture over
    him:
"*If a man would give all the substance of his house for love*" —
like the love which Rabbi Yohanan had of the Torah —
"*would he be condemned?* (Cant. 8:7) (*Leviticus Rabbah* 30:1; see Mt.
    13).

## Sayings

Almost all of Jesus' sayings have parallels in the Talmud or the Hebrew Scriptures. The following should be immediately recognizable:

Rabbi Yose says: Woe to the creatures that see and know not what they see, stand and know not upon what they stand. Upon what does the earth stand?...Upon one pillar. Its name is "The Righteous" (Hagigah 2b).

Everyone that humbles himself the Holy One, blessed be He, lifts up. Everyone that lifts himself up the Holy One, blessed be He, humbles (Erubin 13b).

Rabbi Yohanan said: Not like the Jerusalem of this world is the Jerusalem of the world to come. The Jerusalem of this world: All who wish to ascend to it may ascend. That of the world to come: They only will enter through who are called. (Baba Batra 75b)

Remember that Yahweh your God led you for forty years in the wilderness, to humble you, to test you and know your inmost heart... to make you understand that man does not live by bread alone but on everything that comes from the mouth of Yahweh (Deut. 8).

Even St. Paul's most famous description of the Kingdom has a rabbinic equivalent:

Do I at all favor an Israelite or a Gentile? A man or a woman? A man-servant or a maid-servant? But whoever keeps a commandment, the reward is at its heels (*Seder Eliyahu Rabba,* 14) (Gal. 3:28).

The entire Our Father can be paralleled in Jewish literature. It is a very Jewish prayer. For example:

*Mt. 6:9:* "Hallowed be thy name."

*The Kaddish:* "Let the great name be magnified and hallowed."

*Mt. 6:10:* "Thy will be done on earth as it is in heaven."

*Berakoth T 3.7:* "Do thy will in the heavens above and give tranquility of spirit to those who fear thee on earth."

*The Alenu:* "Lead us not into temptation, but keep us far from all evil." (Ber. 16b)

Other famous sayings of Jesus have close rabbinic parallels. The following are taken from the book, *Tannaitic Parallels to the Gospels* by Morton Smith (*Society of Biblical Literature,* 195 1):

*Mt. 6:30:* "Do not think, "What shall we eat?...."Take no thought for the morrow. It will take thought for itself. Sufficient to the day is the evil thereof."

*Mekilto 16:4:* "He who says 'What shall I eat tomorrow?' lacks faith, for it is said, 'The day's lot in its day!' "

*Mt. 7:7:* "Seek and you shall find."

*Sifre on Dt. 12:5:* "Seek and find the place the Lord your God will choose."

*Lk. 6:38:* "Give and it shall be given to you."

*Midrash Tannaim 15:8* "As you open your hand to the poor, so others shall open to you."

## Conclusion

This chapter has emphasized the similarities between Jesus' teaching and that of the Pharisees. There are, of course, significant differences between Judaism and Christianity today, and these should not be overlooked. But the differences by and large stem from the faith of the Church in Jesus as the Messiah. More, they stem from our belief in Jesus as divine. For there is no precedent in Judaism for the idea of a divine Messiah. The Messiah would be one sent by God. But for Judaism there is only one God. The Messiah is sent by God, but the Messiah is not God.

Such differences however would not have been apparent to Jesus' hearers. The Gospels clearly show that much of Jesus' teaching was private instruction given only to his immediate disciples and apostles. The apostles themselves did not fully realize that Jesus was divine until after the resurrection, at Pentecost.

Jesus thus would have been understood by his disciples and his Jewish audiences as a great rabbi. The differences between Judaism and Christianity only became apparent after his death. They can be appreciated honestly once we accept the similarities between Jesus and other great teachers of his people.

Many basic aspects of traditional Christian theology go back to the Judaism of the Pharisees. Our liturgy is based on the synagogue service. The order of the Mass follows the order of the Passover Seder, the Jewish feast celebrating the Exodus from Egypt. Pentecost, which comes fifty days after Passover in Judaism and fifty days after Easter in Christianity, celebrates the rounding of the people of God. For Christians this means the descent of the Spirit on the apostles. For Jews it means the giving of the Torah on Mount Sinai.

Major beliefs are also part of our heritage from Pharisaic Judaism. Heaven and hell, the Last Judgment, the spiritualization of the temple sacrifice, angels and devils, the resurrection of the body, the direct worship of God as Father — all of these were distinctively Pharisaic beliefs. They were rejected by the Sadducees because of the latter's strict interpretation of the Bible. Jesus and the Pharisees both preserved them as part of the oral Torah.

Christianity is thus essentially Jewish in origin, and it owes much of its faith to one special branch of Judaism: the Pharisees. To understand the teaching of Jesus one must be open to the teaching of the Pharisees, for in many ways Jesus shows himself to be one of them.

# CHAPTER THREE

# Are the Gospels Anti-Semitic?

The answer to this question, asked in this way, is of course "no." Nor is it true to say that the Gospels are the source of anti-Semitism in the Western world. As we know, anti-Semitism predates the Christian period by some time. The Books of the Maccabees in the Bible testify to the anti-Semitic persecutions committed by the Greeks even before the New Testament period, and an Egyptian inscription dating over a thousand years earlier records the boast of the Pharaoh Merneptah: "Israel is laid waste. His seed is not." Merneptah, of course, was somewhat premature in his judgment.

The Gospels do not preach race hatred. On the contrary, Jesus strongly condemns all forms of prejudice. Yet it must be admitted that many New Testament passages, if not properly understood within the context of their times, show Judaism in a bad light. And it is a sad fact that modern anti-Semites, like the Nazis, have been able to exploit misunderstandings of such passages to foster their own contempt for the Jews.

In the 1975 Vatican Guidelines such misuses of the New Testament are clearly condemned. They stress that an informed awareness of the history of the period is necessary to preacher and teacher alike if serious misunderstandings are to be avoided. The Gospels are the inspired word of God in human words, and, like any written literature, they are historically conditioned. That is to say, the passions and crises of the times in which they were written are reflected in the way their human authors retold the story of Jesus. We have seen the conflicts that were happening between Judaism and Christianity in the latter decades of the first century when the Gospels were written down. These conflicts are reflected in the Gospel accounts. The evangelists, leaders of communities in the midst of struggling for the conversion of the Roman Empire, told the story of Jesus in a way that would most effectively promote this evangelization.

Gregory Baum, the author of *Is the New Testament Anti-Semitic?* (Paulist, 1965), recently noted that the New Testament authors tend to describe the religion and institutions of Judaism with "a polemical edge." This represents a change from the position he took in 1965, as a result of further advances in biblical scholarship since that time. In his 1975 essay on the subject, Baum gives us a model of faith to follow:

> The Gospel needs no false protection: if the Christian message were in need of being shielded from a critique of its destructive implications, it would not be God's "word of salvation."

Had the Jewish and Christian communities remained in close contact through the centuries, there would have been no need for the present book. To an audience deeply familiar with Judaism, as were the first readers of the Gospels, there would be no need for lengthy background explanations of the ways in which the New Testament speaks of Jews and Judaism. But as the American bishops remind us, the "de-Judaizing process" which took place in Christianity after the close of the New Testament period led to a tendency "to undervalue the Jewish origins of Christianity."

## Human Emotion and Divine Inspiration

Matthew and John wrote their versions of the Jesus story quite late, almost a half century after his death and resurrection. This fact is important because Matthew and John, affected by their times, seem to have a harsh view of Judaism. Mark and Luke, on the other hand, are earlier. While they reflect tension with the Synagogue, it is clear that there has been no complete break as yet. But Matthew and John wrote after the fail of the temple and after the split with Judaism had become for the time being irreparable.

Theologically. it is important to recognize that God inspired not one but four Gospels. This plurality of approaches gives us, as a whole, the secure footing necessary to reconstruct the meaning of the life and words of our Lord. But at times it is necessary to compare one version with the others in order to separate what Jesus said and did from editorial comments that reflect the later period in which the Gospels were actually set in writing.

The epistles, too, must be taken into account, as we shall see. Many of them were actually written earlier than *any* of the four Gospels, so they can give us yet another valuable perspective.

The point here is that the believing Christian need not be shaken by discovering the all too human motivations of individual Gospel writers. It is the New Testament *as a whole* that is inspired and is a source of divine truth for us. We cannot take one passage or one book in isolation from the whole and hope to interpret it correctly. We must take each section in relation to other sections in order to reconstruct the essential message of Jesus.

We are used to this process in approaches to other areas of biblical study. For example, when we read in the Hebrew Scriptures "an eye for an eye and a tooth for a tooth," we do not immediately assume that the Bible encourages vengeance. For we know that the Bible also tells us: "Vengeance is mine, says the Lord."

Furthermore, we also take care to see such statements in their original context, and thus we see that Hebrew law applied the "eye for an eye" precept only in very limited cases. In Exodus 21, for example, the case cited is that of a fight between two men in which a pregnant women is injured in the process. If she miscarries, then she can receive money in compensation for damages. But if she dies, then "a life for a life" is applied.

The second case in which the precept is applied is found in Deuteronomy 19. Here, if a witness in a criminal trial gives false testimony, there is to be "no pity." The punishment for giving false witness is harsh because the crime is considered particularly heinous by the people of the time: "As he would have dealt with his brother...a life for a life." In other words, whatever would have happened to the defendant, if the false testimony had influenced the case, should be done to the perjurer.

Finally, the "law of the talon" is recited in Leviticus 24 to support the ritual prohibition of blasphemy and the death penalty for anyone "who curses his God," another particularly heinous crime. In lesser cases monetary restitution is allowed.

But aside from these particular (and rare) cases, the law of love and forgiveness prevails in the Hebrew Scriptures. Knowing this, we do not jump to conclusions when we read Exodus 21 and Deuteronomy 19. We see the human situation of the biblical authors and discover the biblical message from an understanding of the whole revelation.

This is true of the New Testament as well. If we, for example, take out of context Paul's statement that "his faith is considered as justifying him," we might conclude that good deeds were unnecessary for salvation. This would be teaching hypocrisy. But in the proper context one can see that Paul often insists that people should live out in practice what they believe. To understand Paul's teaching in Romans 4 concerning faith, one must understand the context in which it was written and take into account the limitations of human language.

## John and "the Jews"

The anti-Jewish implications of many passages in Matthew and John must be understood within the context of the times in which these Gospels were written down. For these later Gospel writers are relying on long oral traditions for their reconstruction of the story of Jesus, and neither is writing "history" in our modern sense of newspaper reporting. Rather, they are seeking to make the meaning of the Christ-event come alive for the readers of their own time (see Chapter 4).

Jesus' sayings are at times placed into contexts different from those in which they were originally spoken. Sometimes the material is arranged in such a way as to illustrate a theological interpretation applying a statement to a current debate at the time of writing. At other times, key words are added or omitted so that the original saying can be seen as relevant to an issue current in the late first century.

The unwary reader, failing to take into account the historical circumstances of the last decades of the first century, can thus be led to believe that Jesus attacked or even condemned his own people. A major instance of this danger can be found in St. John's use of the term "the Jews" in his Gospel.

John uses the term "the Jews" some seventy times as compared with five or six occurrences each in Mark, Luke and Matthew. Father Raymond Brown, S.S., points out in his "Introduction" to *The Anchor Bible* (p. lxxi) that in only a small number of these seventy cases is the term used in what we today would consider to be its normal meaning, that is, as a designation of a real, historical people or group. In a few passages that speak of Jewish feasts and customs, for example, "the Jews" is merely a religious, nationalistic designation and carries no negative connotations (e.g., Jn. 4:22; 18:33; 2:6; 7:2). And in Chapters 11 and 12, John uses the term simply to refer to Judeans, regardless of whether they happen to accept or oppose Jesus.

But such neutral and properly historical uses of the term "the Jews" are an exception among its seventy occurrences. For the most part, "the Jews" is in reality a technical title symbolizing all those who are hostile to the message of Jesus as Lord. And because of the context of the times in which the Gospel was written, this hostility primarily refers to those who are opposed to Christianity in the late first century. Fr. Brown comments:

> It is quite clear that in many instances the term "the Jews" has nothing to do with ethnic, geographical, or religious differentiation. People who are ethnically, religiously and even geographically Jews...are distinguished from the Jews. For instance, in (John) 9:22 the parents of the blind man, obviously Jews themselves, are said to fear the Jews (*The Anchor Bible*, "Introduction," p. lxxi).

Fr. Brown also points out passages in which the terms "chief priests" and "Pharisees" are used interchangeably with "the Jews" (Jn. 18:3 and 12; 8:13 and 18). And whereas in Mark 15:1 it is the Sanhedrin that brings Jesus before Pilate, in John 18:28–31 it is "the Jews." Evidently by John's time the term had come to take on a generalized or symbolic meaning rather than a specific historical one.

From such facts, among others, Fr. Brown is able to conclude that "this peculiar use of the term...is obviously anachronistic in the ministry of Jesus." That is, John is thinking of his own time and from a theological rather than historical point of view when he uses such terms. They do not refer to real groups of people, such as the Jews who lived in Palestine at the time of Jesus. "The Jews" in John is a theological category, a symbol of anyone, Christian or non-Christian, Jewish or pagan, who would knowingly reject the person of the risen Christ or the preaching of the Good News.

Many different classes and divisions among the Jewish people of Jesus' time are reflected in the earlier Gospels: Sadducees, Herodians, Zealots, scribes, tax collectors, rich, poor etc. But by John's time (that is, after the destruction of the temple in 70) most of these distinctions and groupings no longer existed. Hence only two general groupings remain in John's Gospel: the chief priests because they played so major a role in Jesus' trial, and the Pharisees because they alone survived the destruction of the temple as a viable form of Jewish leadership.

Again it must be noted that it was precisely in this period following the destruction of the temple that ill-feeling between Church and Synagogue reached its height. Is it not understandable that John would use a term like "the Jews" to denote opposition to Christianity in his own time? The consequences of misunderstanding John's usage have, of course, been tragic. But in this light we can accept Fr. Brown's assessment: "John is not anti-Semitic; the evangelist is condemning not race or people but opposition to Jesus" (p. Lxxii).

Yet it is equally important to realize how easily misunderstood are such passages, and how carefully one must approach them. This is especially true in the context of the liturgy, where there is often little time for the full explanation warranted by the situation. For this reason the 1975 Vatican Guidelines caution:

> Obviously, one cannot alter the text of the Bible. The point is that with a version destined for liturgical use, there should be an overriding preoccupation to bring out explicitly the meaning of a text while taking scriptural studies into account. . . . Thus the formula "the Jews" in St. John sometimes, according to the contexts, means "leaders of the Jews" or "adversaries of Jesus," terms which better express the thought of the Evangelist and avoid appearing to arraign the Jewish people as such. Another example is the use of the words "Pharisee" and "Pharisaism" which have taken on a largely pejorative meaning.

Another helpful suggestion has been made by Professor Lee Belford of New York University. Belford notes that the term "the Judeans" can be used in many places, since it is the actual transliteration of the Greek and can help to avoid the tendency to overgeneralize.

St. John's point is to challenge the people of his own time to the acceptance in their lives of the Gospel of love. In the same spirit of theological relevancy, phrases like "the overly scrupulous" or "legalists" might be employed as substitutes for "the Pharisees" from the pulpit or in the classroom. At some point, however, a full explanation of the entire problem needs to be presented to all Christians, especially in view of the increasing use of Sacred Scripture since the Second Vatican Council.

## Matthew's Apologetics

*Webster's Dictionary* defines "apologetics" as "systematic argumentative discourse in defense, especially of the divine origin and authority of Christianity." Apologetics has been an important aspect of Christian theology from its very beginnings. St. Peter, in the first sermon preached after the Spirit's descent on Pentecost, is shown using it when he argues that Jesus has fulfilled in his person certain of the prophecies of the Hebrew Scriptures (Acts 2).

Indeed, much of the material in the New Testament reveals this "prophecy fulfillment" style of apologetics. We have seen that Matthew's Gospel represents one of the latest books of the New Testament. By the time it was written the Christian community had become largely dominated by its Gentile converts. It had begun to lose its original, close identification with Judaism.

The growing separation and tension between the communities explains to a great extent the almost bitter tone of Matthew's Gospel in its treatment of Jews and Judaism. Especially in Chapters 11–13, Matthew appears to picture Jesus as rejecting Judaism and replacing it with the "true Israel" of the Church.

This notion of a rejection of Judaism, of course, does not reflect the mind of Jesus but the controversies and apologetical styles prevailing between Church and Synagogue at the end of the first century. This fact is of great importance in understanding the message of Matthew. Matthew is using a style familiar to his readers in this period.

A similar style, and a similar "replacement motif," can be found, for example, in the writings of another Jewish movement of the period which, like the late first-century Church, identified itself as "the true Israel." This was the sectarian movement whose remains were uncovered by the spectacular finds at Khirbet Qumran on the shores of the Dead Seas in the 1940s and 1950s.

In his book, *Biblical Exegesis in the Apostolic Period* (Eerdmans, 1975), Richard Longenecker analyzes parallels between the Dead Sea Scrolls and the New Testament. He points out numerous examples in Matthew which make use of a Qumran-like style of interpretation. At Qumran, as for Matthew, "the (Hebrew) biblical texts were looked upon from the perspective of imminent apocalyptic fulfillment" (p. 39). The point here is not to assess the validity of this procedure, but merely to note it as an example of the Gospel's use of a style of argumentation (apologetics) typical of its time.

It is important to note, however, that not all of the books of the New Testament contain a portrait of Israel as rejected. The earlier Gospels, Mark and Luke, do not hold such a "replacement theory." And John, though late, has no such picture of a rejection of Jews in order to make room for the Gentiles in the Kingdom of God (Joseph Grassi in *Root and Branch*, New York: Roth, 1973, p. 83). For John, "salvation is from the Jews" (Jn. 4:22). Finally, St. Paul, as we shall see, has a much different theology of the relationship between Judaism and Christianity in God's plan.

The notion of a rejected Judaism, therefore, comes not from Jesus nor, really, from Matthew himself. It was inherent in the apologetical style which he had to adopt, given the needs of the community for which he wrote. Though his Gospel contains certain elements negative in their treatment of Jews in general and of the Pharisees in particular, these elements must be interpreted in the light of the overall message of the New Testament. When one judges objectively the thrust of the New Testament message, one must conclude that the "replacement theory" has no place in the Good News.

Matthew, more than any other Gospel writer, aims his apologetic against the Pharisees. It is not Judaism in general, but the Pharisaic interpretation of it that Matthew pictures Jesus rejecting. And it is not the Pharisees of Jesus' time, but those of Matthew's own that the Gospel author is arguing against.

To accomplish this task, Matthew often inserts the Pharisees into scenes in which the other evangelists do not place them, and he constructs some chapters, like the Sermon on the Mount, in such a way as to give the impression that Jesus is arguing with his fellow Pharisees (see Grassi, pp. 79–82). Father Peter Ellis, C.SS.R., of Fordham University, comments: "The evangelists took great liberties with the chronological and topological order of events in our Lord's life and even greater liberties with our Lord's words" (*Matthew: His Mind and His Message.* Liturgical Press, 1974).

The Second Vatican Council in its *Dogmatic Constitution on Divine Revelation* (n. 19) and the Pontifical Biblical Commission in its statement of April 21, 1964, "Instruction Concerning the Historical Truth of the Gospels," both accept the fact that the Gospel writers took such liberties. The documents instruct those working with the Scriptures to take the author's intent into account when interpreting the New Testament message.

An example, often missed, of Matthew's apologetical style can be found in his use of the word "hypocrite." This word is almost never used in Mark's Gospel, which scholars agree was a basic source for Matthew's later version. Matthew adds "hypocrite" to Mark's text some fourteen times, especially in Chapter 23, where it appears that Jesus is directing it against the Pharisees (Grassi, p. 80).

The use of highly charged language to make a point was a well-known literary device in the ancient world. The Hebrew prophets themselves employed strong language — e.g., Jeremiah 9, Isaiah 3, etc. — and their tone was in turn mild in comparison with that of the ancient Assyrians or the Egyptian execration texts (Pritchard, *Ancient Near Eastern Texts*, pp. 328–329). As with the prophets, Matthew's literary style must be taken into account. One cannot conclude to an absolute indictment of Israel in Matthew any more than in Isaiah or Jeremiah. Matthew is writing a narrative, not a textbook on doctrine. To confuse emotional language stemming from conflicts in which Matthew was a participant with the absolutism of dogma is to confuse imagery with theology. The fact that such an historically-conditioned literary style, appropriate for its own age and narrow intent, has been mistaken for more than it intended has been one of the real tragedies of Jewish/Christian history. Ironically, it has led to a closed-mindedness on the part of some Christians remarkably similar in effect to that which Matthew imputes to the Pharisees of his time.

### The Antitheses in Matthew's Sermon on the Mount

Matthew's version of Jesus' great discourse is, scholars agree, a carefully worked-out section. In it Matthew at once records Jesus' words and sets them in a context suitable to the situation of tension with the Jewish community of Matthew's own time.

The section of the Sermon commonly called "the Antitheses" (Mt. 5:17–48), can serve as an example of Matthew's literary style, for it has long been understood by Christians as a prime instance of the presumed differences between Jesus' moral teachings and those of his fellow Pharisees.

In the Antitheses the refrain "You have heard it said . . . but I

say" appears to those unfamiliar with Judaism to be an abroga-
tion of the Mosaic Law by Jesus. But as Daube points out in *The
New Testament and Rabbinic Judaism* (p. 58), this formula is actually
a Pharisaic device for introducing an interpretation of Scripture.
That is, it was commonly used among the Pharisees not as an attack on the Scripture, but as a means of understanding it. Jesus
is thus not arguing with the Law but with certain interpretations
of it. His own interpretations, as usual, closely follow those of the
Pharisees. Ellis comments:

> For his audience in the eighties, Matthew is preparing an indict-
> ment of the Pharisees. Part of the bill of particulars is the charge
> that the Pharisees and Jews in general have heard the messianic
> Torah of Jesus, the Sermon on the Mount, and have rejected it.
> (*Matthew: His Mind and His Message*, p. 35)

We have seen already in Chapter 2 that a Jewish audience of
Jesus' time, and especially the Pharisees, would have been in full
agreement with the Sermon on the Mount, for it expresses a typical Pharisaic spirit. While Matthew sets up the scene in such a
way that there appears to be a conflict between Jesus and the
Pharisees, the reality is that the conflict was between Church and
Synagogue in Matthew's own time. Given the times in which
Matthew lived, the device must be presumed to be valid and
necessary. Christianity was on the cutting edge of survival and
in need of such an apologetic. But today we must interpret that
apologetic in the light of the same times which gave it its original
authenticity.

Matthew also preserves in the introduction to the Antitheses
words of Jesus that must be kept in mind: "Do not suppose that
I came to destroy the Law" (Mt. 5:17–20). Albright and Mann
comment about these words:

> [They] express the convictions of orthodox Judaism, both Pales-
> tinian and Alexandrian, in the time of Jesus. It should be em-
> phasized that those to whom Jesus speaks at this juncture in the
> ministry were Jews. There is no shred of evidence that Jesus at any
> point repudiated his obligation to the Law to which both his birth
> and his circumcision committed him *The Anchor Bible*, p. 57).

Jesus' interpretations are the ones to be expected from a Pharisee of his time. In the first two (Mt. 5:2129), Jesus cites two of the
Ten Commandments (against killing and adultery). He expands
the literal precepts into demanding spiritual maxims, reflecting

an approach based on the oral Torah. The extension of the prohibition of adultery to include lust, for example, is found in the
Talmud as: "If one gazes at the little finger of a woman, it is as if
he gazed at her pudenda" (Talmud Babli, *Berakhoth* 24a).

Even Jesus' harsh dictum that mutilation of the body is prefer-
able to sin ("If your right hand causes you to sin, cut it off...")
finds Talmudic parallels in *Shabbath* 88b and in the Midrash *Nid-
dah* 2:1. In the Talmud there are no instances of the advice
being taken literally. As in Christianity, such statements reinforce the idea that intention as well as act comes under the
judgment of God, and that one should avoid even the occasion
of sin.

The remaining four Antitheses differ from the first two. While
those dealt with the Decalogue, the rest involve more general
laws. They are:

1. *On Divorce (Mt. 5:31–32):* "But I say, whoever divorces his
wife, except in the case of lewd conduct *(porneia)*, forces her to
commit adultery." This ruling is in fact a strict interpretation of
Deuteronomy 24:1: "When a man, after marrying a woman and
having relations with her, is later displeased because he finds in
her something indecent, let him write a bill of divorce."

Jesus, in fact, even allows the same exception as Hebrew law.
The Talmud shows that the issue of what constituted "indecency"
in the exception was debated among the Pharisees. The school of
Shammai, like Jesus, held to a strict view: "No one shall divorce
his wife unless there is found unchastity in her" (Mishnah *Gittin*
90:1), while others allowed for various other reasons.

2. *On Oaths (Mt. 5:33–37):* "Do not swear falsely, but pay your
vows to the Lord." This saying appears to bring together two
quite different passages from the Hebrew Scriptures. Exodus 20:7
is one of the Ten Commandments, prohibiting false testimony in
court. Numbers 30:3 is a law promoting specific performance of
vows made to offer sacrifice in the temple.

Swearing "by heaven" and "by earth" was originally an attempt to avoid saying the holy name "Yahweh." By Jesus' time
such a pious practice may have led some to take their oaths lightly
since they were not bound in God's name. Jesus, like the Pharisees, here reminds people that all promises are solemn even if
God's name is not specifically invoked. The Talmud states for example that "yes" and "no" are oaths if repeated twice *(Sanhedrin*
36a). And *Baba Mezia* 49a, much in the manner of Jesus, advises:

"Let your 'yes' be righteous and let your 'no' be righteous." Jesus is thus contradicting neither the Mosaic law nor the Pharisaic interpretation of it, as was once thought. His view is at one with that of the Pharisees.

3. *"An Eye for an Eye" (Mt. 5:38–42):* This has traditionally been one of the most damaging of the Antitheses, for it seems to bolster a view that the Hebrew Scriptures emphasize only fear while the New Testament preaches a law of love. However, it has been shown by modern scholarship that the "law of the talon" was in fact not in practice in the Judaism of Jesus' time.

The law of the talon is referred to only three times in the Hebrew Bible. In each instance (Ex. 21; Deut. 19; Lev. 24), it is attached to a spectacular and rare case, as we saw above. And even there it does not guide the rulings but follows them. It is called on as one would call on an ancient proverb to support more current legislation.

Originally, the law of the talon was looked on as a check against the practice of the blood feud. Its intent was *"only* an eye for an eye, *only* a tooth for a tooth, etc."* That is, it intended to halt the dangerous escalation of blood vengeance between clans or tribes. By Jesus' time it had been replaced altogether by monetary substitution (damages and fines) in most cases. And after the Babylonian Exile, when the Covenant Code (Ex. 20–23) was replaced by the Holiness Code (Lev. 17–26), it would seem that the death penalty was entirely replaced in Judaism by the system of ritual excommunication (the *herem)* in normal practice (see Lev. 20). Here, a person was ostracized from the community rather than actually killed. The fact that Jesus must have known that the law of the talon was no longer in force would indicate that his point is moral rather than the rejection of Judaism we have often been led to presume.

The last section of this passage, "Give to the man who begs from you," again contains no contradiction to biblical law. It merely summarizes Deuteronomy 7:8: "You shall open your hand to him and freely lend him enough to meet his need."

4. *Love of Enemies (Mt. 5:43–48):* "You have heard it said, You shall love your neighbor and hate your enemy." This passage has long troubled scholars because there is no command anywhere in biblical or rabbinic literature to hate one's enemy. As we have seen (Chapter 2), both require returning good for evil, as does Jesus. The full passage from Leviticus is instructive:

You shall not hate your brother in your heart. Though you may have to reprove your fellow man, do not incur sin because of him. Take no revenge and cherish no grudge against the children of your people. You shall love your neighbor as yourself. I am the Lord (Lev. 19:17–18).

Because of recent discoveries, there is now one reference to a command to hate that can be pointed to in Jewish literature, but is not from any of the "mainstream" movements of Jewish history. Rather it is from the works of the Dead Sea sectarians, who separated themselves off from the Jewish community at an early date. The passage is in the *Manual of Discipline* in a section describing the ritual of initiation into the Qumran community:

Everyone who wishes to join the community must pledge himself to respect God and man; to live according to the communal rule . . . to love all that God has chosen and hate all that he has rejected; to keep far from all evil and cling to all good works . . . and to hate all the children of darkness, each according to the measure of his guilt, which God will ultimately requite.

It may be against this group that Jesus' original saying was pronounced, but it was certainly not against Judaism as such nor against any of the Pharisees.

The commonly held notion that Jesus broke with Judaism in the Sermon on the Mount, then, stems from a misreading of Matthew's Gospel. Some of the sayings that Matthew has gathered together here for convenience were originally directed against the Sadducees. Some take a side within the scope of a Pharisaic debate while remaining true to the spirit of Pharisaism. One even appears to condemn the practice of a group forgotten to history until the 1940's. But in each, Jesus stood well within the boundaries of the standard Jewish teaching of his day. There was a real conflict between some Pharisees and some of the followers of Jesus. But this conflict as it is reflected in Matthew occurred in Matthew's time, not Jesus'.

## Matthew's Additions to the Sources

A comparison of the three Synoptic versions of Jesus' summation of the Law as love of God and neighbor is illuminating for understanding the mentality of Matthew. Remember that Jesus responds to the question in a typically Pharisaic way. Mark and

Luke describe the event as a person sincerely asking a question of Jesus out of admiration for his knowledge of the Law. The Pharisees are not involved according to these early versions. The additions that Matthew makes to Mark's account are in italics:

Mark 12:28:  One of the scribes came up, and when he heard them (i.e., Jesus and the Sadducees) arguing, he realized how skillfully Jesus answered them. He decided to ask him, "Which is the greatest of the commandments?"

Luke 10:25:  On one occasion, a lawyer stood up to pose him this problem....

Matthew 22:34–36:  When *the Pharisees* heard *that he had silenced* the Sadducees, *they assembled in a body;* and one of them, a lawyer, *in an attempt to trip him up* asked him, "Teacher, which commandment of the law is the greatest?"

Matthew's additions to the Parable of the Tenants shows just how far the break between Judaism and Christianity had gone by his time. As told in Mark 12 and Luke 20, the vineyard is Israel and the wicked workers are the Sadducean aristocrats. In a manner reminiscent of the Pharisees themselves, Jesus charges the Sadducees and temple priests with perverting the true nature of Judaism. Matthew records the same parable in Chapter 21 of his Gospel, but instead of an attack on the Sadducees, it becomes an attack on the Pharisees and their view of Judaism. Matthew adds to the earlier accounts the words: "Therefore I tell you the Kingdom of God will be taken from you and given to a nation that yields proper fruit." These words are found in neither Mark nor Luke.

In the Parable of the Marriage Feast (Mt. 22; Lk. 14) we see an escalation of the emotional intensity of the language. In Luke the invited guests merely stay home. In Matthew they brutally seize and kill the servants of the king. In Luke the king simply invites other guests. In Matthew the king sends out his troops to kill "those murderers" and to burn their city. This last, of course, would seem to be a reflection of the destruction of Jerusalem by the Romans which took place in the year 70, at least a decade before Matthew wrote his Gospel.

In the Parable of the Seven Woes (Mt. 23) Matthew gathers together sayings that, in the words of Professor Joseph Grassi *(Root and Branch.* 1973), "Jesus could never have uttered at one time." We have seen how this passage is remarkably similar to one in the Talmud which denounces false forms of Pharisaism. It should also be noted that in the earlier versions of Matthew 23:1–6, preserved in Luke 20:45–47 and Mark 12:38–40, the sayings are directed against the scribes, not the Pharisees. Matthew alone includes the Pharisees at this point. Likewise a comparison with Luke 11:37–54 shows that Matthew escalates the language of Luke, adding phrases like "you snakes, you vipers" not found in Luke. The person is changed from the third ("they") to the second ("you"). And the distinction Luke carefully draws between "Pharisees" (vv. 37–44) and "lawyers" (vv. 45–54) is dropped in Matthew so that *all* the charges implicate the Pharisees. General phrases like "who perished" become accusations like "whom you murdered."

In Luke 13:31–33, we see that it was the Pharisees who tried to save Jesus' life by warning him that Herod Antipas wanted to kill him. In Luke, this is the introduction to Jesus' lament over Jerusalem. Matthew, however, omits the Pharisees' warning and includes Jesus' lament over Jerusalem as the climax of his attack on the Pharisees.

The story of the centurion (Mt. 7; Lk. 7) is another example of the difference in relations between the Church and Synagogue from Luke's earlier version to Matthew's later one. Once again we can see that positions had hardened. In Luke, Jesus replies to the faith of the centurion by saying: "Even in Israel I have not found such faith." In Matthew, the statement reads:

"Among nobody in Israel have I found such faith." This changes positive praise for the centurion into a negative judgment on Judaism. In Luke, the saying functions to show Jesus' desire to include Gentiles into his Kingdom. In Matthew, a negative verdict is added: "The children of the Kingdom will be thrown out into the dark."

## Conclusion

Today we are fortunate to have the results of modern biblical scholarship at our fingertips in the form of tools such as Gospel parallels, commentaries, and dictionaries of the Bible. These tools need to be used by anyone seriously approaching the New Testament, and most especially by anyone charged with the mission of teaching the Gospel message to others. History has shown us how easy it is to fall into misunderstanding if we attempt to read the New Testament out of the context of the time in which it was actually set down. Some of these misunderstandings can be most harmful, especially if the young are exposed to them without adequate preparation. Finally, a solid pedagogical principle should always be adhered to: If there is no time for preparation, or if the children are too young to understand the *full* background necessary for understanding a biblical passage, don't use the passage. Try another passage instead.

# CHAPTER FOUR

# Who Killed Jesus?

In this guilt are involved all those who fall frequently into sin; for, as our sins consigned Christ the Lord to the death of the cross, most certainly those who wallow in sin and iniquity *crucify to themselves again the Son of God, as far as in them lies, and make a mockery of him.* This guilt seems more enormous in us than in the Jews, since according to the testimony of the same apostle: *If they had known it, they would never have crucified the Lord of glory;* while we, on the contrary, professing to know him, yet denying him by our actions, seem in some sort to lay violent hands on him (Heb. 6:6; 1 Cor. 2:8).

The above quotation is from the Catechism of the Council of Trent, Article IV, as promulgated in the sixteenth century. It shows clearly what has always been essential Christian teaching on responsibility for the death of Christ. Theologically, all humanity bears the blame. It is not one particular group, but the sins of us all that are responsible for his death. That same Council also declared that the crucifixion was Christ's free decision: "It was the peculiar privilege of Christ the Lord to have died when He Himself decreed to die, and to have died not so much by external violence as by internal assent...."

Sin is universal. The meaning of Christ's death and resurrection is that through Christ's self-sacrifice, our sins have been forgiven. In order for humanity to be saved through Christ's redeeming passion, all humanity must be seen as sharing in the guilt for the deed.

## Sacred History

The New Testament does not present history in our sense of the term. It reveals the *meaning* of history. As revelation, it is not intended to give us merely a listing of facts and events. Rather, it aims to teach us the salvific will of God that underlies all human events. Only in this way is it "relevant" to us: that it reveals to us our *own* sins and our *own* salvation. To the question "Who Killed Jesus?" the Christian replies: "I did." "He (Jesus) himself bore our sins in his body on the tree, that we might die to sin and live to righteousness" (1 Pet. 2:24).

As Christians, we are saved only to the extent that we identify ourselves as the crucifiers of Jesus. The mystery of salvation is that in this same guilt lies our main hope. Jesus forgave his crucifiers: "Father, forgive them, for they know not what they do" (Lk. 23:34). We, the crucifiers, are forgiven. Being forgiven for the sins which brought about Jesus' death, we are saved.

This sacred history is the object of biblical inspiration. God inspired the evangelists to tell us the meaning of the life, death and resurrection of the Savior. This is the content of the divine revelation which we hold to be true as Christians. Theologically, it is clear. We as sinful humanity, not "the Jews," must bear the blame, for if we do not accept the guilt for his death, we cannot hope to share in the glory of his resurrection.

## Reconstructing the Event

According to the *Declaration on the Relationship of the Church to Non-Christian Religions:* "What happened in Jesus' passion cannot be charged against all the Jews then living, without distinction, nor upon the Jews of today" (n. 4).

Christianity's essential teaching is one of sacred history. Yet because that teaching is an interpretation of the meaning of real historical events, we are also interested in reconstructing, as accurately as possible, the actual event itself. Who did what, when, and why are always pertinent questions. As has been noted, the question of theological "blame" is settled. All of us, as sinful humans, must bear it together.

The Second Vatican Council reminds us that even historically the picture of what happened at Jesus' passion and death is by no means a simple one. While individual Jews may have played a part, it is far from clear whether they played that role because they were Jewish or because they were under the control of the Roman governor. If the latter was indeed the case, we may have to revise considerably the way in which we have traditionally told the story. What, then, were the motivations of the people who brought Jesus before Pilate? What was, according to the evidence, the most likely motivation of Pilate in sentencing Jesus to die?

We must remember that it was Pilate and Pilate alone who had the power to condemn Jesus to death (Jn. 19:10). Despite the washing of the hands, despite the charade with Barabbas (Mk. 15:11), it was Pilate alone who made the decision. This is clear in all the Gospel accounts (Lk. 23:24; Mt. 27:26–27; Mk. 15:15; 19:16).

Likewise it needs to be remembered that Jesus enjoyed tremendous popular support. Mark, for example, reports that it was this acceptance by the people that made certain of the rulers of the day uneasy: "The chief priests and the scribes heard of this and began to look for a way to destroy him. They were at the same time afraid of him because the whole crowd was under the spell of his teaching" (Mk. 11:18).

## The Chief Priests and the Sadducean Aristocracy

Who, then, were these "chief priests and scribes" and why did they have reason to fear Jesus' popularity with the people? History shows us that the temple priesthood and the Sadducean party which supported the priesthood were at that time closely allied with the interests of the Roman rulers of Palestine. Indeed, their wealth and position were dependent upon the power of Rome and even sustained by it. The priesthood and the Sadducees formed the aristocracy of the land at that time. They maintained that position only to the extent that it served the Roman interest to allow them to maintain it. In short, the temple priests and the Sadducees were what we would today call collaborators.

Arrayed against the Sadducees and the temple priesthood were the religious movements of the day. The Pharisees, as the lay leaders of a popular movement seeking to go back to the observance of the covenant in the spirit of the prophets, bitterly opposed the Sadducees and disagreed with them on almost every significant point of doctrine, from the manner of interpretation of the Bible to the belief in the resurrection of the body after death. In spirit and belief, as we have seen, the teaching of Jesus and the early Church was remarkably similar to that of the Pharisees.

Also opposed to the temple priesthood were the Essenes, the ascetic separatist group which had established a monastic-like community on the shores of the Dead Sea and from there issued ringing denunciations of the temple as vile and corrupt.

The temple priesthood and the Sadducees supported Rome not for religious but for political and economic reasons. In this sense, they could not be called "Jewish leaders" at all. Cut off from the people and living by collaboration with Rome, the temple priesthood must have developed a quite natural "siege mentality." Eager to please their Roman superiors, they would zealously seek to bring to the attention of Pilate even the slightest hint of rebellion.

Palestine in the time of Christ was, we know, seething with revolutionary movements. Indeed, a few decades after his death these erupted into full-scale rebellion against Rome, a rebellion only quashed by the destruction of the temple itself. Thus the temple priests had every reason to be afraid of Jesus. For them the only safety rested in preserving the status quo. Anything new, anything that would arouse the people, would threaten their precarious position.

Jesus may have exacerbated his situation with the temple priests by his attempts to reform the temple worship. Like the Pharisees, he was critical of the high priesthood. The scene in which he overturns the tables of the temple money-changers (Mark 11) is a good example of his opposition to the temple authorities.

Historically, then, we know that the only group of Jews who had any reason to fear Jesus or wish him harm were the Sadducees, the temple party. The reaction of the Pharisees would have been acceptance of him as a peer or, as in the case of Rabbi Gamaliel, a "wait and see" attitude. At any rate the Pharisees and the Essenes, unlike the Sadducees, had no political power. They had no temple guards to enforce their will as did the chief priest. They were as powerless before the Roman conqueror as were Jesus and his small group of followers.

The testimony of the Gospels is remarkably clear on this issue. In all of the Synoptic accounts (Mt. 26:3; Mk. 14:1; Lk. 22:2) it is the chief priests of the temple and not the Pharisees who have Jesus arrested to deliver him to Pilate as an insurrectionary. And Jesus does not name the Pharisees when he predicts his Passion-only the chief priests and the scribes, the elders, and the Gentiles (Mk. 10:32–34; Mt. 20:17–19; Lk. 9:22).

The chief priest was appointed by Rome and held office only

at the will of Rome. The Roman procurator even kept the chief priest's vestments. If the Roman authorities became displeased with a high priest, he was deposed and a new one, more suitable to Rome, was appointed in his place. In this sense the chief priest cannot fairly be called a "Jewish" leader at all. Though always a Jew by birth, he gave loyalty only to Rome and did the will of Rome.

When we teach or preach on the passion, then, we should be careful in how we phrase things. We should not say "the Jewish leaders" but "some" Jewish leaders, and we should be clear as to *which* Jewish leaders we are referring. They were not the truly religious leaders of the day, the Pharisees. Rather the individuals involved were only "the chief priests and the scribes," the Sadducean party of the aristocracy, who had sold out to Rome in the view of the people and represented no more than their own selfish interests.

## The Role of Rome

Crucifixion is a Roman form of capital punishment. In Jewish law, the punishment for blasphemy is death by stoning. The people must participate in the execution since blasphemy involves a violation of a covenant commandment (Lev. 24:10–16). If Jesus were convicted of blasphemy under biblical law, crucifixion would not have satisfied the law. If some Jews were concerned about possible blasphemy, they would not have been satisfied with Jesus' death by crucifixion. The sentence was the wrong one and carried out by the wrong people. The covenant violation of blasphemy would not have been appeased. Thus it is unlikely that Jesus was charged or convicted by Jews of blasphemy.

Jesus was condemned for political — not religious-reasons (Lk. 23:2–5). The charge was insurrection, as the inscription on the cross shows: "King of the Jews" (Jn. 19:19). By threatening the temple establishment, Jesus threatened Roman rule. The Sadducees, the temple priesthood and Pilate all shared a common reason for wishing to dispose of Jesus: they saw his popularity as a threat to Roman power.

Pilate is often viewed as a sympathetic figure. The Gospel of Matthew is taken to be a source for this portrait of a kindly ruler who believes in Jesus' innocence but is pushed by Jews into killing Jesus. Since the Gospels were written at a time when the survival of the Church depended on Roman tolerance, it is understandable that the role of Pilate would be toned down by the evangelists. The Gospel writers must have felt that it was not expedient to condemn Rome just when Christianity was becoming successful in converting Romans.

Contemporary accounts of Pilate, however, show another picture of him. Pilate was so brutal that even Rome could not take him for long, and he was eventually called back by Rome because of excessive cruelty. He was known to line the roads of Judea with crucified victims, sentenced to death on the barest hint of "revolutionary" actions or attitudes. Jesus was probably one of these.

A letter of the period reveals Pilate's true character. It charges him with "corruptibility, violence, robberies, ill-treatment of the people, grievances, continuous executions without trial, endless and intolerable cruelties."

Father Gerard Sloyan asserts in his study, *Jesus on Trial* (Fortress, 1973):

> Jesus' historical opponents, therefore, were certain of the chief priests and their associates. It is probable that they became the whole Sanhedrin in a (later) dramatization of the story in Christian circles (p. 131).

The Gospels as a whole present us with sufficient evidence, when viewed objectively, to reconstruct a true picture of Jesus' death. That picture does not include "the Jews" or even "the Jewish leaders." It is an event in which the Roman governor is the primary actor, along with certain key figures of the temple party which he controlled.

## St. Matthew's Passion Account

The additions introduced by Matthew into the material from Mark's Gospel on which he based his account reveal how the idea of Jewish guilt may have gotten its start. That start, as we have indicated before, does not lie in the historical events of Jesus' life. It comes from the later conflicts between the early Church and the Synagogue which took place some forty to fifty years after the events being described. These later events, such as the persecution of the early Christians by the temple authorities, are "read back" into the telling of the story of Jesus, as St. Stephen does in his famous sermon before his death (Acts 7). Even these events, of course, must be attributed not to the Pharisees but to the Sadducees. Acts 5:17 makes this clear: "But the high priest rose up, and all those who were with him, that is, the party of the Sadducees, and being filled with jealousy seized the apostles and put them in the public prison."

However, competition and tensions were rising between the churches and "some from the synagogue" (Acts 6:9), and so what was originally done by the chief priest and his party alone gradually came in Christian circles to be applied to all the Jewish leaders without distinction. Today we must be very careful to make the distinctions as they are presented in the New Testament, though blurred by a casual reading.

Matthew's additions, dictated by the pressure of his times, to the passion account are often small but provocative. As we have seen, he expands a questioning of Jesus by the temple authorities into a formal trial before the Sanhedrin. This trial, many scholars agree today, could not have taken place that night in the way Matthew describes it.

Matthew adds only a single phrase to Mark 15:15, but it changes the whole picture:

Mark 15:15: "So Pilate, wishing to satisfy the crowd, released to them Barabbas; but Jesus he scourged and delivered to be crucified.

Matthew 27:26: Then he (Pilate) released to them Barabbas; but Jesus he scourged and delivered *to them* to be crucified.

Matthew himself, of course, knows that Jesus was executed not by the crowd but by Roman soldiers, for he states in the very next verse: "Then the soldiers *of the procurator* took Jesus into the praetorium" (Mt. 27:27).

Matthew's additions tend to improve the image of Pilate. Mark, in an attempt to appease Roman sensitivity, had described Pilate as somewhat hesitant about whether to kill Jesus or not. What is hesitancy in Mark becomes conviction in Matthew. Matthew's Pilate is wholly convinced of Jesus' innocence. He washes his hands to illustrate it, a scene preserved in no other Gospel. In Matthew alone do we find the words ascribed to Pilate: "I am innocent of the blood of this just man. See to it yourselves" (Mt. 27:24). Since Roman law prohibited Jews from exercising capital punishment in such cases, it is doubtful whether this statement could be historical. Romans alone could carry out a death sentence at the time (Jn. 18:31). Likewise, the ritual washing of the hands was a Jewish religious custom. It is not likely that a Roman governor would follow it.

The scene in which the chief priests use the thirty pieces of silver to buy a potter's field for a cemetery is also found only in Matthew (27:3–10). Matthew refers to the words of a Hebrew prophet (Zech. 11:12–13) to show how Jesus fulfilled a biblical prophecy: "And they took the thirty pieces, the sum at which the precious one was priced by the children of Israel." Matthew then adds to Mark's text another verse: "And *all the people* shouted back, 'His blood be upon us and our children'" (Mt. 27:24–25). This passage has caused serious tensions over the centuries. It is noteworthy that it is found only in Matthew and that the other Synoptics make a sharp distinction between the small mob before Pilate and "the people" who sympathized with Jesus. Today, scholars' research has shown that this phrase — if used — was a specific legal term, but with a slightly different twist. The original would have been: "His blood be on him and on his children." (Michael Wyschogrod)

In Luke, the Jewish people as a whole are described as struck with sorrow over what the Roman governor and the temple priests have done: "Now there was following him (Jesus) a great crowd of the people, and of women, who were bewailing and lamenting him" (Lk. 23:27).

The scene in which the priests and the Pharisees assemble to convince Pilate to post guards before the tomb (27:62–66) is another one that is found only in Matthew. So too is the story of the dream of Pilate's wife (27:19), which serves to bolster the idea that Pilate thought Jesus to be innocent. Finally, Matthew adds the story that the chief priests bribed the tomb guards into spreading a rumor that Jesus' body had been stolen by his followers (Mt. 28:11–15). Fortunately, we have the other Gospels to help us balance the picture and reconstruct the history of the event.

The Gospels as a whole do give us a true picture of Jesus' life and the events of his passion and death. They are historical and also serve to teach us sacred history. But no one said it had to come easy. At times we must study carefully in order to put things into perspective. The Gospels were written in particular times and particular places. Each author reflects the trials and conflicts of his time. We must view the Gospels as a whole in order to comprehend the inspired and saving word which they contain.

## Practical Applications: Preparing for Holy Week

In certain periods, Holy Week has been a time of particular tension for Jewish communities living in Christian societies. Pope John XXIII, during the Vatican Council, began a process designed to ease those tensions when he ordered the phrase "perfidious Jews" to be taken out of the Holy Week liturgy. Originally, the term "perfidious" in the Latin simply meant someone who did not share the Christian faith. It did not carry the pejorative connotations which later ages added to it. But John knew history. He knew, for example, that in Tsarist Russia Holy Week was the time when pogroms, or riots against the Jews, were most likely to occur. And so he began a commitment on the part of the Church that is still going on today.

The passion accounts should never be read from the pulpit or in the classroom without an adequate catechesis and preparation. Classes in the period before Holy Week should include sound historical and theological background for both teacher and student. This chapter, for example, might be useful as required background reading for teachers or as an addition to the teachers' manuals of existing textbooks. Some of this background should also be present in homilies given during Holy Week.

Children and adults alike should approach the passion accounts only with a good awareness of the complex political events surrounding the events and with an understanding of the historical context of the Gospel authors. The Roman role should not be whitewashed, and Pilate should be seen in his true guise as a brutal tyrant. Phrases such as "the Jewish leaders" should be avoided and care taken to point out that the Pharisees had nothing to do with the event.

Holy Week represents the high point of the liturgical year. It is a time when the highest motivations of Christian love and reconciliation are appealed to and fostered. During this period we celebrate the central mysteries of our faith, the institution of the Eucharist, and the death and resurrection of Christ. Holy Week should today be a special time of healing between Christian and Jew, since so much of its theology is based on the theology of the Jewish Passover. We should exploit this opportunity for understanding our heritage with care and loving openness.

A group of prominent Catholic and Protestant scholars, called "The Israel Study Group," has recently published a version of the passion narrative based on the results of modern biblical scholar-ship (J. T. Townsend, *A Liturgical Interpretation of Our Lord's Passion in Narrative Form*, New York: NCCJ, 1977). This version can be highly recommended at least for para-liturgical and catechetical use, since it avoids or corrects many of the previous distortions in our understanding (write: 43 W. 57th St., New York, NY 10019).

# CHAPTER FIVE

# Dialogue for the Future

## New Understandings of the Relationship Between the Covenants

Reconciliation between two communities is a task that cannot be successfully accomplished by one side acting alone. Each must seek to get behind the misunderstandings of the other's beliefs and practices that have developed during the period of separation. To understand the other, and to understand oneself anew in the light of the other, can only come about when there is open and honest dialogue.

In such a dialogue, both sides must admit their need for the other. For in dialogue we see that it is to our interest to foster the prosperity and health of the other as other, just as in a good marriage the happiness of each spouse is seen to be dependent on the other. We cherish the sameness that we share. And we delight in the differences that make us worth being known by the other.

In a good marriage the dignity and uniqueness of each partner is carefully respected. So in the dialogue is the "otherness" of the other a carefully guarded treasure. In the ideal marriage the two personalities do not blend into one and lose themselves. Rather, the relationship fosters the self-actualization of each and seeks the realization of his or her best potentials. Dialogue, properly understood, should seek to help Jews to become better Jews and Christians to become better Christians.

It is such an understanding of pluralism as mutual respect that infuses the 1975 Vatican Guidelines and gives them their distinctive character:

Dialogue presupposes that each side wishes to know the other, and wishes to increase and deepen its knowledge of the other. It constitutes a particularly suitable means of favoring a better mutual knowledge and, especially in the case of dialogue between Jews and Christians, of probing the riches of one's own tradition. Dialogue demands respect for the other as he is; above all, respect for his faith and his religious convictions.

Official Vatican statements seldom reach this level of near poetry. Yet this statement sets the tone for today's attempt to bridge the ancient gap between the Jewish and Christian communities. Discussions between scholars of the two faith communities are on-going and enriching further and further the fruits of that official dialogue.

But it is up to us, in our individual parishes and synagogues, to make the dialogue come to life. Unless the new insights gained by our respective leaders are given flesh concretely in the classroom, from the pulpit, and in our daily lives, the great hopes raised by Vatican II and subsequent theological encounters will remain unfulfilled, mere academic "dry bones."

In the following section I will present what I believe to be some basic Church teachings as rounded on Scripture and tradition. These I will suggest as one way in which we, as Christians, can affirm the role of Judaism in God's plan without diluting our own faith.

## God Is Faithful

The first teaching to be realized if we are to understand Judaism's role in the divine plan is that the Sinai covenant between God and the Jews remains in force today. The Jewish people, elected by God to play a unique role in the divine plan, continues to be the chosen people, for God is faithful to his promises.

To hold that the Jews are today, as in biblical times, a chosen people is thus to uphold God's faithfulness to the biblical promises. It is significant that the Second Vatican Council proclaimed this truth in its *Dogmatic Constitution on the Church*. A dogmatic constitution, as opposed to a decree or a declaration, carries the highest authority and solemnity of any conciliar statement. The statement on the Jews is placed in the Council's basic statement on the nature of the Church itself: "On account of their fathers (i.e., their election) this people remains most dear to God, for God does not repent of the gifts he makes nor of the calls he issues (cf. Rom. 11:28–29)" (n. 16).

Here the Council refers us to St. Paul, as it does quite often in its *Declaration on the Relationship of the Church to Non-Christian Religions.* The American bishops have recently expanded on this theme: "In effect, we find in the Epistle to the Romans, Chapters 9–11, long-neglected passages which help us to construct a new and positive attitude toward the Jewish people" (*On Catholic Jewish Relations,* NCCB, November 20, 1975). (See Appendix C.)

## Romans 9–11

The Pauline epistles contain some statements that are negative toward the Jews and Judaism. Indeed, many Jewish scholars feel that it was Paul alone who changed early Christianity from a Jewish sect into a competitor with Judaism.

It is ironic therefore that a basic plank in our bridge toward dialogue should be laid on Paul's foundations. Yet it is in Romans 9–11 that we can see most clearly that it is not possible for Christians to teach that Judaism was deprived of its own special election because of Christ's coming.

Paul faces the question squarely: "I ask, then: Has God rejected his people?" (11:1). And he answers the question with equal candor: "Of course not! I myself am an Israelite, descended from Abraham, of the tribe of Benjamin. No, God has not rejected his people whom he chose so long ago" (11:2).

Paul wrote this around the year 57. Thus it predates the later Gospels of Matthew and John by some decades. Interestingly, his aim is to establish the validity of admitting Gentiles into the Church without making them submit to the precepts of the Mosaic Law. To do this he opposes, for the sake of argument, the concepts of Law and Gospel. Yet Paul's main point is not to demean Judaism but to challenge Christians. To do this, he uses the image of the olive tree.

## Root and Branch

Paul's image of the relationship between Judaism and Christianity is significant. Judaism is the continuing source, the life-giving root of which Christianity is but a branch. Without the living root, the branch will wither. To survive, Christianity must remain in close relationship with the Jewish people. He states: "If the root is consecrated, so too are the branches." If some of the branches were cut off and you (Gentiles), a branch of the wild olive tree, have been grafted in among the others, and have come to share in the rich root of the olive, do not boast against the branches. If you do boast, remember that you do not support the root: the root supports you" (Rom. 11:16–18).

Paul's statements provide a firm biblical base for us today. For 2,000 years, as the American bishops remind us, the negative side of Paul's doctrine has been stressed. Clearly, it is time we listened to the positive side as well (see also Eph. 2–3).

The Jewish role in the divine plan did not end with Jesus. Judaism is to be seen today as living in valid covenant with the one God.

The Christian role in the divine plan does not cancel out a continuing role for the Jewish people. Our Christian covenant, as Paul says, is grafted onto the Jewish covenant. This may be difficult to accept, and even more difficult to work into our present theological structure. But it is a divine mystery that we are bound to accept if we would enter into fruitful dialogue with our parent faith community. In concluding his treatment, Paul stresses this aspect of mystery. "How deep are the riches and the wisdom and the knowledge of God! How inscrutable his judgments, how unsearchable his ways" (Rom. 11:33).

Surely God's riches are deep enough to look with favor on both Jews and Christians. Surely his wisdom is deep enough to devise a plan that would include both faith communities. If we have difficulty searching out this plan, the limitation is ours, not God's. We must not reject what God accepts.

We are saved in Christ by being grafted unto the on-going covenant between God and the Jewish people. Mysteriously, our covenant with God in Christ is mediated to us through the Jews.

It is perhaps in this sense that the Christian dispensation fulfills the biblical prophecies. It does not replace the Sinai covenant, nor does it exhaust its meaning. As God promised Abraham in making the covenant with him: "In your descendants all the nations of the earth shall find blessing" (Gen. 22:18). In today's Jews, as well as in the Jew, Jesus, we Christians can find that blessing.

Christianity continues to take spiritual nourishment from and to receive God's revelation through the Jewish people today. "God does not forsake those whom he chooses." Somehow, in the mystery of God's will, we know that both Jews and Christians hold a special place in God's divine plan. We are only prepared for dialogue with Jews to the extent that we are prepared to accept them as our spiritual partners in fostering in the world the belief in the one God, the loving parent of us all.

The destinies of Church and Synagogue are divinely linked. This we know. The question that remains is how to work out our common destiny and mission in a way that will preserve the uniqueness of each.

## One Covenant or Two

How are we to see each other, we two peoples in covenant with the same God and yet so different? This is a question that Christians cannot answer alone. A solution will be found only through the process of dialogue.

Jewish thinkers as well as Christians have been grappling with the problem. Granted, we are both in full and valid covenant with God. How do we see our relationship with each other? Is there one covenant or two?

The great Jewish philosopher, Franz Rosenzweig, and more recently such Jewish thinkers as Will Herberg and Rabbi Hershel Matt, have offered one solution. They would see not two covenants, but one covenant with two forms.

The Jewish covenant is the means by which Jews are saved. And through the Jews the world is given such essential revelation as the one God, the idea of social justice, and the concept of individual and communal morality.

In the risen Jesus as the Christ, on the other hand, God's covenant with Israel is made available to the rest of humanity. The Church as the "new" Israel does not replace the role of Judaism in God's plan. It merely extends the one invitation to others. Christianity is an alternate form of the one Sinai covenant, which remains in force.

This theory has both advantages and disadvantages. The advantage is that it establishes close ties between Judaism and Christianity today. We are seen as having different roles, different emphases within the one divine dispensation. The disadvantage is that neither side wishes to be, nor should be, wholly identified with the other. We are unique, each an integral community in itself, and dialogue insists that we preserve our uniqueness.

Some scholars, such as Father Edward Flannery, would thus prefer a "two-covenant" theory, a sort of divine "separate but equal" scheme. This theory would point to biblical precedents. God first makes a covenant, through Noah, with all humanity (Gen. 9). The second covenant, through Abraham and Moses, perfects the first for one special people, the Jews. This covenant does not abrogate or threaten in any way the validity of the first covenant between God and humanity. Rather, it deepens it, and through the Jewish covenant all nations are blessed (Gen. 12; 17; 22).

Just as the covenant with Abraham did not cancel but rather enhanced the covenant with Noah, so the covenant with Christ does not cancel the lasting validity of Sinai. Jesus as the Christ extends the revelation of the Sinai covenant to the Gentiles, to us as Christians. The two covenants complement rather than compete with one another. The Christian covenant thus perfects and fulfills, not Sinai, but the covenant with Noah.

These two theories, in point of fact, have much in common. Both adequately encompass the basic facts we know to be true: (1) The Jewish covenant remains valid after Christ. It is sufficient for salvation on its own terms. It does not need to be "perfected" by Christianity. (2) The Christian covenant is rooted in the on-going reality of the Sinai covenant as its living source. (3) Stripped of its relationship with a living Judaism, Christianity would soon cease to exist. Without on-going contact with its living source, Christianity would soon lose touch with its own identity.

### Waiting for the Messiah

One final truth is needed to complete this list of facts we can hold, no matter which theory we might choose as best articulating these facts. This one may again be startling to some Christians, but again it holds great hope.

Though we believe in faith that the Messiah has come, we admit that the messianic age which we await has not yet dawned. While we have confidence that it will come because of our faith in Jesus as the Messiah, we admit that the biblical prophecies have not all been fulfilled (1 Th. 5; 2 Pet. 3).

Nahmanides' argument of long ago rings true today. We can read the prophecies ourselves — Isaiah 2:4, Micah 4:3, and the rest. These promises were not mere allegories; they meant what they said with their promise of universal peace and justice. Paul understands this when he speaks of "neither Jew nor Gentile, slave nor freeman, male nor female" (Gal. 3:28).

But this messianic sign, signaling the end of oppression of people by people, has not yet come to be. No less than the Jews, we Christians are faithfully awaiting the final coming of the Kingdom of God on earth. In Christianity, this event is known as the "second coming." Whatever one calls it, it has not happened yet.

So we wait. However, we do not wait alone. Judaism stands by our side, also firm in the faith. Together, then, despite our differences of belief, we can work toward a common goal. Together we can work to build the Kingdom of God on earth. Together we can await the final coming of the Messiah. And while we wait, we can pray together to our one Father, who is in heaven: "Hallowed be thy name."

# CHAPTER SIX

# Celebrations and Activities

## How Attitudes Are Formed

A teacher in a suburban Catholic high school tells this story of what happened when he tried to find out what his students thought of Jews. The responses he got intrigued him: "very strict," "mean," "bossy." These did not fit the normal stereotypes, but were quite negative. It was also interesting that almost all the kids seemed to say pretty much the same thing.

The teacher tried to find out what experiences the kids had had that would lead them to such opinions. "Where did you get such ideas?" he asked. "How many Jews do you know?"

After much prodding, it turned out that the youngsters had personally known only one Jew in their lives: their sixth grade teacher! The negative reactions were not typical of a sixth grader's reaction to Jews as Jews but a reaction to teachers as adult authority figures.

The teacher probably never realized that she was representing an entire community of people. This sort of generalizing from a single instance is one of the basic dynamics of prejudice (literally, "pre-judgment"). It shows the danger to Catholic education in separating ourselves too completely from the larger society in which we live.

But more is needed than mere contact between groups. A recent study of teenagers in three communities, conducted by the University of California under a grant from the Anti-Defamation League of B'nai B'rith, for example, came up with some startling conclusions (see Glock et al., *Adolescent Prejudice*, New York: Harper & Row, 1975). Contrary to what one might expect, the report shows that there has been little or no lessening of anti-Jewish feelings in recent years. The traditional anti-Semitic "stereotypes win allegiance from a majority of respondents." Finally, the youngsters in the community without Jews proved to be *less* anti-Semitic than those who had had more contact with Jews during their school years.

Obviously, mere contact between Jews and non-Jews is not enough to break down the set of stereotypes and pre-judgments that has been carefully worked into our culture for thousands of years. Prejudice must be actively combated. Merely making blatantly anti-Semitic remarks unpopular will not do the job. The underlying, deeply rooted attitudes that remain need to be challenged as well.

These culturally ingrained, deeply held negative beliefs about the Jews, if allowed to remain unchallenged, will alter our perceptions of the Jews we meet in life. This is why the California teenagers, even though many of their school friends were Jewish, were able to hold onto a set of negative stereotypes about Jews virtually identical with stereotypes from the Middle Ages. Programmed to see only the negative, they used any single negative experience to "verify" their pre-formed stereotypes. Good qualities in individuals were ignored. "To the extent that he or she is generous and warm," one thinks, "my friend is not like other Jews."

One can find the same dynamic in other forms of prejudice, such as racism and sexism. Thus, activities and, among Christians, liturgies and para-liturgical celebrations need to be developed that are aimed at replacing negative views and feelings with positive ones. This chapter will give a few examples of the types of things that can be done in the home, in the classroom, and at dialogue-meetings between Christians and Jews. It is not a complete list of what can be done. You may have some ideas of your own. Hopefully, it will also illustrate the positive benefits to Christians that can come from sharing Jewish prayer and liturgical practice.

## 1. Prayer

It is interesting that while Christians have no theological difficulties in using any Jewish prayer, Jews have great troubles with many Christian prayers. This imbalance is a mark of the differences between the two groups. It should be kept in mind, especially by Christians involved in dialogue with Jews. While we pray to a common Father, the central point of distinction between us is the Christian belief in Jesus as the Messiah and as divine. While Christians can wholeheartedly accept almost everything that Judaism teaches, the reverse is not true.

The Our Father is one of the few great Christian prayers that is acceptable to both sides of the dialogue. Indeed, as we saw in Chapter 2, every element of it finds a parallel in Jewish literature. The great prayer that Jesus taught us is first and foremost an intensely Jewish expression of worship.

Through the centuries, Judaism has developed forms of prayer from which we Christians can. learn much. Christianity, for example, has had the tendency at times to overemphasize the transcendence of God. We often approach God with fear and trembling, as one "up there," as all-powerful rather than all-loving. The trend today toward more intimate and spontaneous forms of prayer is thus a mark of what Robert Gordis has called the "re-Judaizing" of Christianity. We are getting away from the abstract "first principle" deity of Greek philosophy and back to the Yahweh-as-lover concept of Hosea and Jesus.

In Judaism, God is seen as living within the covenant community, immediately accessible to all. This immediacy and closeness with God often lends Jewish prayer a sense of familiarity with the divinity that can be quite startling to the Christian. Consider, for example, this late eighteenth-century Hasidic prayer:

> Good morning, Almighty God, Master of the world!
> I, Levi Yitzhak, son of Sarah, of Berditchev,
> Come before you to plead the cause of the people Israel.
> What do you want of your people?
> Why do you afflict Israel?
> You are always saying: "Speak to the children of Israel."
> At every occasion you turn toward us.
> Our Father, there are so many peoples on the earth:
> Persians, Babylonians, Edomites.
> Russians — what do they say?
> That their emperor is the real emperor.
> Germans — what do they say?
> That their empire is the real empire.
> And the English? That theirs is the real empire!
> But I, Levi Yitzhak, son of Sarah, of Berditchev,
> I say: May the glorious Name be exalted and sanctified!

In Jewish prayer, one can challenge God's judgment and even quarrel with him. Many rabbinic prayers, for example, confront God with the suffering of the people. There are precedents in the Hebrew Scriptures for this, of course. One thinks immediately of Abraham bartering with God over the fate of Sodom (Gen. 18): "Will you sweep away the innocent with the guilty? Suppose there were fifty innocent people in the city?" When God allows that if Abraham can find fifty good people, the city will be spared, Abraham bargains for forty-five, then forty, thirty, twenty and finally ten. The irony, of course, is that Abraham cannot even find the ten!

Moses also carries the day in an argument with God. After the incident of the golden calf (Ex. 32), God threatens to destroy the people. Moses counters that this would make God look foolish in the eyes of the Egyptians: "Why should the Egyptians say, "With evil intent he brought them out, that he might kill them in the mountains?"

The rabbis picture God as being delighted by such audacity in prayer. The Talmud relates the following:

> On that day Rabbi Eliezer brought all the proofs in the world, and the masters would not accept them.
> He said to them: If the law is according to me, let this locust tree prove it.
> The locust tree moved a hundred cubits.
> They said to him: The locust tree cannot prove anything.
> Then he said to them: If the law is according to me, let this stream of water prove it.
> The stream of water turned and flowed backward.
> They said to him: The stream cannot prove anything.
> Then he said to them: If the law is according to me, let the wails of the House of Study prove it.
> The walls of the House of Study began to topple.
> Rabbi Joshua said to them: If the law is according to me, let the heavens prove it.
> A voice came forth from heaven and said:
> Why do you dispute with Rabbi Eliezer?
> The law is according to him in every case.
> Rabbi Joshua rose to his feet and said:
> "It is not in heaven" (Deut. 30: 12).
> What is the meaning of: "It is not in heaven?"
> Rabbi Jeremiah said:

The Torah has already been given once and for all from Mount Sinai.

We do not listen to voices from heaven.

For you have already written in the Torah on Mount Sinai:

"After the majority must one incline" (Ex. 23:2).

Rabbi Nathan came upon Elijah.

He said to him: What was the Holy One, blessed be he, doing at that moment?

Elijah said to him: He was smiling and saying: My children have defeated me, my children have defeated me! (Baba Metzieh 598)

## 2. Celebrating Jewish Feasts

It is well known that the Mass as we celebrate it is a development of the Jewish synagogue service and the Passover seder. Jesus on Holy Thursday instituted the Eucharist during a Passover seder. More and more Christians are coming to celebrate the seder as a part of Holy Week. This is a healthy sign. Such seder celebrations can be done at home or in the parish hall.

Sofia Cavaletti writing in *SIDIC* magazine (Winter 1973), schematizes these startling parallels between synagogue and early Christian services:

| *Synagogue Service* | *Liturgy of the Word* |
| --- | --- |
| Profession of Faith (the *Shema*) | Prayer of Praise and Thanksgiving (The Gloria) |
| The "18 Blessings:" Praise, Petition, Thanksgiving | Readings (Law, Prophets, Gospel) |
| Psalms | Psalms |
| Readings (Law and Prophets) | Sermon |
| Sermon | Profession of Faith (The Creed) |
| Priestly Blessing | Prayers of the Faithful (Petition) |
| Collection for the Poor | Collection for the Community |
| | Priestly Blessing following Eucharist |

The recent reform of the Roman rite of the Eucharist reintroduced a structure which was used in Rome during the early Christian period. Its structure, and even some of the wording of the prayers, show its Jewish origin. Cavaletti has:

| *Jewish Passover* | *Christian Eucharist* |
|---|---|
| 1. Praise to God for creation of the people of Israel through Abraham | 1. Praise to God for the creation of the world |
| 2. Praise to God for the redemption of Israel through Moses | 2. Praise to God for the redemption of humanity through Christ |
| 3. Re-enactment of the salvation of Israel in the person of every Jew who shares in the meal | 3. Re-enactment of salvation — the Eucharistic meal |
| 4. Expectation of the coming of the Messiah | 4. Expectation of the return of the Messiah |
| 5. Psalms of Praise | 5. Doxology of Praise |

Copies of the Passover seder can be easily obtained from local Jewish bookstores or community councils. While we must not forget the meaning that the Mass has for us as Christians, it is important to celebrate the seder as a Jewish feast if one is to experience it rightly. Passover commemorates the Exodus from Egypt. It is a feast of freedom from slavery. Attendance at a Jewish seder or sabbath service is an excellent experience for child and adult alike.

Other Jewish feasts are less popular among Christian groups. But these, too, can provide both spiritual enrichment and greater understanding. What motivates us here, of course is love for all people, but especially the Jewish people who have remained "most dear to God" (*Nostra Aetate*) despite the tragedies of history.

*Hanukkah*, for example, comes shortly before Christmas. A feast of lights in the dark time of winter, it celebrates the victory of the Maccabean revolt against Greek tyranny. On each day of the eight days of the feast, a candle is lit to commemorate the miracle of the temple lamp, which had oil for only one day but burned for eight until fresh oil could be prepared.

*Hanukkah*, like many Jewish feasts, is celebrated essentially in the home and directed toward the children. In these days when Christians are struggling to set up viable programs of family religious education, we can learn much from Jewish practices of family-centered liturgy.

*Purim* takes place in February or March. It tells the story of the biblical book of Esther, where an attempt at genocide against the Jews was foiled. Purim is a time for carnivals and entertainment, a time to give to charity. Again, Purim is a particularly happy time for the family. Children are encouraged to boo and use noise-makers whenever Haman (the bad guy) is mentioned in the reading.

Such participatory home Bible services may lack the "dignity" we normally associate with reading from the Bible, but they encourage identification with it. Children who go through such experiences, of course, should know that they are taking part in a ceremony in the same way as their Jewish neighbors.

*Sukkoth* ("Tents" or "Booths"), a fall harvest festival much like the American Thanksgiving, commemorates the period when Israel wandered in the desert after the Exodus and had only tents in which to live. Like Hanukkah and Purim, Sukkoth is particularly suitable for Christian groups. It is in fact a very creative "simulation game." Booths are made in the home or the backyard and decorated with fall fruits and vegetation. Meals are eaten in the booths and thanksgiving for God's bounty is offered. If possible, the family even sleeps in the tent as a reminder of how the Hebrews lived while in the desert.

*Simhat Torah* means "rejoicing in the law." It falls on the last of the eight days of Sukkoth. The Torah is read through in its entirety every year in the synagogue, but on this day the last chapter is read. The Bible scrolls are carried in procession, while the children join in with banners and song. Hasidic Jews even dance with the scrolls to show this joy. Catholics, who tend to see the Bible as an external authority giving rules of conduct, would do well to celebrate this feast of joyful thanksgiving for the freeing gift of God's revelation.

*Shavuoth,* or Pentecost, really means the feast of "sevens." It comes seven weeks after Passover and celebrates the giving of the Ten Commandments on Mount Sinai. The account of Pentecost in the New Testament is carefully constructed to play on this theme. Just as God descended in fire and glory on Sinai to reveal himself to the people, so the Spirit descends in tongues of fire on the apostles to reveal to them the meaning of Christ.

Openness to Judaism not only means that we, as Christians, are enabled once again to know the origins of our liturgical and prayer life. It also means that we are open to the rich spirituality that has evolved within Judaism since the time of Christ.

*Yom Hashoah,* which occurs shortly after Passover in the spring, is a recent Jewish feast that is particularly appropriate for Christians. Also known as "The Day of the Holocaust," it commemorates the victims of Nazi genocide in World War II.

The following prayer, recommended for use in the Archdiocese of Detroit, can be a model for a Prayer of the Faithful in parishes on the Sunday closest to the Jewish celebration of the feast.

*Leader:*   Almighty God, whose loving care extends to all humanity, we confess our failure to respond in love, prayer and action to the tragic fate of millions of Jews whose lives were destroyed by the Nazi Holocaust.

We pray that you will guide us in developing such attitudes of charity that in our thoughts, words and deeds we may show forth your love for all humankind so that such an atrocity may never occur again. This we ask through Jesus Christ our Lord. Amen.

Let us pray.

For the growing dialogue between Catholics and Jews, that we may achieve the mutual understanding and respect to which the Church has called us.

*All:*   Let us pray to the Lord.

For all Christians, that we may live out in practice the words of Jesus that we preach: "Let us love one another."

*All:*   Let us pray to the Lord.

For all Jews, especially the survivors of the Nazi death camps of World War II who live among us, that they may live in peace and harmony and ever "walk with the Lord."

*All:*   Let us pray to the Lord.

For all persons, that we may be reconciled in faith in the one God, Father of us all.

*All:*   Let us pray to the Lord.

What motivates Christians in sharing such Jewish feasts or in recreating them in their own homes or classrooms is love of

God and neighbor. Since Jewish feasts such as those above re-create biblical events, which we accept as our history too, they can help us in our own catechesis. Two things should be noted in celebrations such as putting on a seder service.

First, we are not trying to teach that Judaism and Christianity are the same. We are two different communities, but there is a natural closeness between us based on shared respect for the same revelation of the Hebrew Scriptures and the fact that Christianity is an offshoot of Judaism. The purpose of having Christians experience Jewish feasts in the same way that Jews do is to teach respect and a special love for this people that of all non-Christian groups is closest to us. It is to build bridges in the most graphic way possible — by actual experience.

Second, we must take care not to try to "Christianize" the Jewish religious practices. In the seder, for example, it is important to point out to the children that a seder was the occasion for Jesus' institution of the Eucharist, but the seder itself should not *become* a Eucharist. This would be to confuse the two religious traditions. The ultimate goal of all catechesis is to communicate love of God and neighbor — in this instance love of a particular neighbor who through the tragedies of history has become alienated from us — but it is not to become that neighbor, or, worse, to try to make that neighbor into an image of ourselves.

## 3. Holy Week and the Passion

In Chapters 3 and 4 we have seen some of the historical and theological background that Catholics need to know if they are to approach the mystery of Jesus' passion with a mature understanding. Such explanations should be worked into homilies at the liturgy, especially during Holy Week. This material also needs to be made a part of the formation process of every catechist, since it is not currently included in most Catholic textbooks or teachers' manuals (see Chapter 7).

In the period prior to Holy Week and during the Week itself, catechetical classes center on preparing children and adults for the celebration of this most sacred time in the Church year. Full background material for each of the Gospel accounts, stressing the historical Roman role and the theological responsibility of every Christian, should highlight religious instruction during this period.

Because of the almost overwhelming difficulties of Matthew's passion narrative, it might be wise to discontinue its reading in the liturgy for Holy Week, at least for the children. Pastoral reasons alone indicate that a thorough catechesis needs to be developed before this text can be used without precipitating misunderstandings.

Currently, John's version of the passion narrative is read on Good Friday, with the other three Gospels alternating on Palm Sunday. Ironically, this places John, with his tendency to generalize from specific individuals to "the Jews," in a position of maximum exposure. The liturgical expert, Father Gerard S. Sloyan, has suggested one possible solution to the problem: that "brief selections from all four Gospels be read and extended homilies given on the mystery of salvation, rather than that the present situation continue of a twenty-minute reading and no homily" (*Face to Face*, vol. 2, 1976). Unlike the Protestant tradition, Father Sloyan points out, the Catholic Lectionary has always freely selected from and ended readings to bring out "the point which its framers think is that of greatest impact." This solution is in many ways a happy one, since it advocates no changes in the text itself and provides for desperately needed explanation. Many of the readings and prayers during the later part of Lent and Holy Week (such as the Reproaches) can easily lead to misunderstandings about Jews and Judaism, and homilies and catechetical classes alone cannot overcome their deep emotional impact.

The liturgy is the most effective teaching mechanism in the Church. Because of what is known today, one can say without disrespect that the liturgy desperately needs revision. Otherwise, our efforts to improve textbooks and sermons will continue to be undercut by the more powerful appeal of the anti-Jewish attitudes interwoven in Holy Week celebrations.

Happily, it can be reported that a group of biblical and theological experts has been commissioned by the American bishops to work on this difficult problem. This gives real cause for hope. Perhaps alternate biblical readings and prayers, such as passages from Romans 9–11, can be inserted into the ritual in such a way as to foster positive attitudes in place of the harsh negatives. We have the precedent of Pope John XXIII's removal of the phrase "perfidious Jews" as an example of what can be done.

## 4. Para-liturgical Celebrations

### (a) "Thy Kingdom Come"

In the meantime, popular devotions and para-liturgies can be developed to celebrate the great strides in understanding already taking place as a result of Vatican II. As an example, I have developed the following celebration. It can be used either in church or at home, and either by Catholics alone or at meetings attended by Catholics and Jews together.

"THY KINGDOM COME"

*Leader:* Since the time of Christ, we Christians have tended to deny our birthright. Though Judaism is our root and our continuing source, we have at times attacked it and sought to make it serve our own pride. Though Jesus was a Jew, we have oppressed his people. Today, we wish to repent openly of all such errors, past and present. Today, we wish to say with the Jews: Never again! In this spirit, let us pray:

*All:* O Lord, we are conscious today that many centuries of blindness have cloaked our eyes, so that we no longer see the beauty of your chosen people. We realize that the mark of Cain stands on our foreheads. Across the centuries our brother Abel has lain in blood which we drew, or shed tears which we caused, forgetting your love. Heavenly Father, forgive us.

*Leader:* With St. Paul, we are deeply pained by the division between Christians and Jews.

*1st Reading:* Romans 9:1–5; 11:1–2, 16–18.

*Response:* Blessed are you, Lord our God, King of the universe.

*Leader:* Mindful of what unites us as well as what divides, we listen with Judaism to the *Shema*, a central prayer of the Jewish service.

*2nd Reading:* Deuteronomy 6:4–9.

*Response:*   Blessed are you, Lord our God, King of the Universe.

*Leader:*   Though we Christians hold that Jesus is the Savior, the Messiah, we are united with Jews the world over in awaiting the coming of the messianic Kingdom of God. We see that peace and justice have yet to be established in the world. We are one with Judaism in hope as well as belief. With Jews, then, we can join hands to pray three great prayers central to our two traditions: the Our Father, the Alenu, and the Kaddish.

*All:*   (joining hands to form circle)

Our Father, who art in heaven, hallowed be thy name.

Thy kingdom come. Thy will be done on earth as it is in heaven.

Give us this day our daily bread.

And forgive us our trespasses as we forgive those who trespass against us.

And lead us not into temptation, but deliver us from evil.

*All:*   (raising hands toward the sky)

Glorified and sanctified be God's great name throughout the world which he has created according to his will.

May he establish his Kingdom in your lifetime and during your days, and within the life of the entire house of Israel, speedily and soon. And say, Amen! (from the *Kaddish*)

We hope, therefore, Lord our God, soon to see your majestic glory,

when the abominations shall be removed from the earth;

when the world shall be perfected under the reign of God,

and all humanity will call upon your name,

and all the wicked of the earth will be turned toward you.

May all the inhabitants of the earth realize and know that to you every knee must bend, every tongue must vow allegiance....

May they all accept the yoke of your kingdom, and do you reign over them speedily and forever.

For the kingdom is yours, and to all eternity you will reign in glory, as it is written....

"On that day the Lord shall be one, and his name one."

(from the *Alenu*)

*Leader:* Now take the hands which we have raised in worship and use them to proclaim the mercy of God, by giving God a huge round of applause!

*Kiss of Peace:* The celebration concludes with all giving each other the Kiss of Peace as a sign of reconciliation and an affirmation of unity.

### (b) A Way of the Cross for Special Occasions

Many popular devotions can be rather easily adapted to meet the needs of historical truth and ecumenical amity. This suggested version of the Stations of the Cross is but one example. (Note that the Stations, which are a powerful evocation of the passion, should probably not be used with younger children at least until the intermediate grades, when adequate preparation is possible.)

The following Stations are designed, not for general use, but within the context of a unit dealing with the theme of improving Jewish/Christian relations. Other Stations could be developed, bringing out other important themes such as world justice and peace, etc.

## A Way of the Cross

### Opening Prayer

Jesus, you made this journey for me. You challenge me to die to my own prejudices, and to live with you a faith free of stereotypes and bigotry.

### 1. Jesus Is Condemned by Pilate

Jesus, you died a victim of the oppression of Jews by Roman imperialism, a sign of all downtrodden people. May I join with all persons of good will to make human liberation a reality.

### 2. Jesus Bears His Cross

Jesus, teach me to live a life for others, accepting the biblical command you reminded me of: to love my neighbor as myself. Help me to remember that "neighbor" means everybody — not just other Christians.

### 3. Jesus Falls

Jesus, one of the lessons of history is that triumphs are never complete, defeats never final. Help me to rise again and again to make justice flow like a living stream in a world racked with brutality.

### 4. Jesus Meets His Mother

Jesus, your mother raised you to be an observant Jew. May I be as faithful to Christianity as you were to Judaism.

### 5. Jesus Is Helped by Simon

Jesus, may I struggle to lift the burden of oppression from others, as Simon shared yours.

### 6. Jesus and Veronica

Jesus, your image exists for us today in the living tradition of your people, the Jews. Help me to respect that tradition and those of others even though I may not share them fully.

### 7. Jesus Falls Again

Jesus, may I learn to delight in the differences between people rather than trying to make all humanity into my own image. Teach me the lesson of pluralism: humility of vision.

### 8. Jesus and the Women of Jerusalem

Jesus, help me to understand the results of sexism in my own life, and to oppose the oppression of women everywhere.

### 9. Jesus Falls a Third Time

Jesus, after hundreds of years of mistrust, Christians are seeking honest dialogue with members of other faith communities. Help me to see my role in this historic task.

### 10. Jesus Is Stripped of His Garments

Jesus, strip me of the fears that lead to prejudice, the insecurity that leads to hatred, and the envy that leads to violence.

### 11. Jesus Is Nailed to the Cross

Jesus, in this century we have seen the worst horrors ever perpetrated against women, men and children: the death camps of Auschwitz, Bergen-Belsen, Buchenwald and the rest, an alphabet of terror. With the survivors, let me pray: Never again!

### 12. Jesus Dies

Jesus, from the cross you prayed: "My God, why have you forsaken me?" In this age of the noise of war and the silence of God, help me to see your presence in every living being.

### 13. Jesus Is Taken from the Cross

Jesus, take me down from my phony pedestal — the one that makes me think that I am "better" because I am different. Help me to see all people as you see them.

### 14. Jesus Is Laid in the Tomb

Jesus, your resurrection gives me hope that justice can overcome injustice, that peace can overwhelm the lust for war. Because of you, I have a dream. Help me to make it a reality.

### 5. Classroom Activities

This list of activities is meant to set the wheels of creativity in motion rather than to be an exhaustive list of all possibilities. Though age levels are suggested, most of them can be easily adapted for us in upper grades or lower grades as needed. Many could also be used with adults or in a family-centered religious education program.

*(a) Role Plays: (1) The Lunch Room.* (Sixth grade and up) This is based on a real incident. Have three or four children sit at a table. Explain that they are eating lunch and that they are Jewish. They are students in a large public high school where the majority of the students are non-Jewish. One child plays the role of a Catholic whose best friends are out sick that day and who therefore has no one to eat with. He/she decides to try to eat with the Jewish children whom he/she knows slightly. Two or three other kids come up and begin to make wisecracks about "those" people. They tell the Catholic student: "Don't you know 'they' are pushy and uppity? They're all rich and trying to run everything. My mother says we shouldn't play with them because they're trying to own all the banks, etc."

Be careful to note the various spontaneous stereotypes that may pop up in this role play, and deal with each. Ask the children who played the Jewish kids how they felt at being excluded.

*(2) You Killed Jesus!* (Intermediate and up) Two children are playing, one Jewish, one Catholic. Suddenly a third comes up and accuses the Jewish child of having killed Jesus. What does his/her Catholic friend do? Two to four other children overhear and choose sides. Let this be spontaneous, i.e., let the children

themselves choose sides. Be sure to de-brief their feelings with them. (A moving account of a Jewish child's response to such a situation can be found in Chaim Potok's novel, *The Chosen* (Simon & Schuster, 1967). This could be read to the children after the exercise.

*(b)* Have a group or committee *list all the Jewish holidays,* beginning with the Jewish New Year, and then draw up a comparable list of Catholic feasts and practices. Let the class first draw any conclusions it can about differences or similarities — and then carry out research to test theories. (This and the following three activities are taken from the Anti-Defamation League's book, *Image of the Jews: Teachers Guide to Jews and Their Religion* [New York: KTAV, 1970], pp. 125–130, which contains excellent background and many such activities.)

*(c)* Have the students *write a poem, story or playlet* that retells the story of the Exodus, or that uses it as a springboard for dealing with the theme of "from slavery to freedom" in a modern context. Parallels between the experience of the ancient Jews in Egypt and the black experience in this country can be drawn based on the lyrics of Negro spirituals. The Passover story can also be related to the immigrant experience of various European groups in this country.

*(d)* Ask students (any age) to *compose short prayers* that could be said by young Jewish people as well as by them, expressing the following central ideas: repentance, forgiveness, hope, concern about the state of the world.

*(e)* *Build a sukkah* in the classroom or wherever, and have a meal or a snack in it. There are pre-fabricated ones available from stores which deal with Jewish items (bookstores, etc.). Then discuss the experience of the Jews living in tents, the meaning of the harvest, parallels with Thanksgiving in our country, etc. Perhaps you could invite a Jewish family to come in to help build the sukkah and to explain how they celebrate Sukkoth as a family.

*(f)* Arrange a model Friday evening home service, Passover seder, etc., including if possible a meal of Jewish foods. Visit a synagogue, preferably for a religious service.

*(g)* As a beginning to the study of Jews (sixth grade and up), ask each child to write down the first word he/she thinks of when you say the word "Jew." Write these on the board and discuss. Hopefully both negative and positive reactions will come out. These will give you a great deal of insight into their attitudes and

help you develop future lessons. The same technique can be used with reactions to words such as "Pharisee," etc. Older children could be asked to list their own questions and attitudes about Jews and Judaism. These can be collected and the more salient copied on the chalkboard or newsprint.

(h) American Jews and Catholics share an immigrant background. Together we virtually make up the "ethnics" in this country, with similar experiences in being outsiders and trying to "make it" in America without losing our own unique identities. Have the students write or tell of their families' backgrounds, concerns, etc. You might have them interview their parents or grandparents to get these stories (the cities they are from, involvement in labor movement, problems in being assimilated, language, "funny" names, etc.). Then show a filmstrip dealing with Jewish immigrant experience and history in this country, like the ADL's sound filmstrip *Jews in America*. The ADL also has a good strip on *Italians in America* that can be used to show the parallels.

(i) *Sample discussion starters.* These are provocative questions for the upper grades that can be used to start discussions or lead to research projects:

— Can we speak of the Jewish American in the exact same way we speak of the Catholic American? Yes or no, and why?

— What would you have done if you were in Germany in 1939? (You might have the students read *Diary of Anne Frank* as a background for this one.)

— What would you do if you were refused admission to the public park (or skating rink or swimming pool, etc.) just because you are a Catholic?

— Do you have any Jewish friends?

— If the students have seen the movie *Jesus Christ Superstar*, a discussion of its numerous inaccuracies and historical distortions could make clear how prejudice pre-determines our understanding of the New Testament passion accounts.

— On the other hand, viewing and discussing such movies as *Night and Fog* (40 minutes), *Fiddler on the Roof* (full length feature) and *Exodus* will provide positive experiences.

— The best filmstrip to date on Jewish-Christian relations from a Christian point of view is: "Christians and Jews: A Troubled Brotherhood," Alba House Communications, Canfield, Ohio 44406. The filmstrip comes in two parts and covers the history of our relations as well as understandings of dialogue. The set is complete with script and discussion questions. (For junior high to adult.)

*(j) The ADL Attitude Survey.* The book *Adolescent Prejudice* (Harper & Row, 1975) reports the results of a study, made by Charles Glock and sponsored by the Anti-Defamation League, of the attitudes of high school students in three schools in California. The results were intriguing. You might wish to have your students take the same survey and compare the results with those found by Glock and his team. The questions used can also be used as discussion starters or as ideas for role plays. The questionnaire set up the scene first of a "lower class" Jewish teenager coming into your school for the first time. He/she was described as "a student who is white, Jewish and getting failing grades." The same question was repeated but describing the Jewish teenager as "white, Jewish and getting B's." The question was asked whether the students would be willing to:

Sit next to this person in class?

Work on a committee at school with this person?

Have this person as one of your speaking acquaintances?

Go to a party to which this person was invited? Eat lunch with this person at school?

Have this person as a close personal friend? Invite this person home to dinner?

Have this person date your brother/sister?

(Note, the ADL study found that positive responses declined as one goes down the list in this order. That is, the more intimate the relationship called for, the greater the resistance to it.)

Another test done by the same team sought to measure acceptance of stereotypes. Some of the questions, which could be asked of your students, with the results compared, asked whether they agreed or disagreed with the following:

Jewish teenagers are likely to be selfish — concerned only for themselves and their own group.

Jewish teenagers are unfriendly, do not mix with others, go around only with their own group.

Jewish teenagers often dress in a loud and flashy way.

Jews are more loyal to Israel than to America.

Jews are just not as honest as others when it comes to business.

Jewish teenagers think they are better than other people.

Jewish teenagers try to push into groups where they are not really wanted. Jewish teenagers are loud and show-offy and try to grab attention for themselves.

Jewish teenagers are often in trouble with school authorities and police. Jewish teenagers are not very law-abiding.

# CHAPTER SEVEN

# Christian Teaching and Judaism Today: A Study of Religion Texts

In the early 1950s, the American Jewish Committee initiated a long-range effort aimed at bringing the light of objective scholarship to bear on the sensitive question of the treatment of intergroup relations in religious textbooks. To ensure against any bias on the part of the researchers, the projects were wisely conceived as self-studies, with Catholics, Jews and Protestants each studying their own curriculum materials and following research designs suited to those materials. The Catholic study was done at St. Louis University, the Jewish study at The Dropsie College for Hebrew and Cognate Learning, and the Protestant study at Yale University.

In April 1960, the first fruits of these self-studies were announced in a symposium published in the journal of the Religious Education Association (vol. LV, no. 2, 109–138). Sr. Rose Thering's doctoral study of then currently-used Catholic religion texts revealed discouraging results in terms of the treatment of Jews and Judaism. The infamous deicide charge, for example, which has precipitated so much violence against Jews over the centuries, was still to be found throughout the series studied (see *Catechetics and Prejudice* by Fr. John Pawlikowski, Paulist Press, 1973). These results, however, were given to the bishops during the Second Vatican Council, and they had a great impact on the Council's statement on the Jews which finally laid this charge to rest.

In the 1960s, the American Jewish Committee initiated studies of Roman Catholic textbooks published in Europe between 1950 and 1965. The results, reported in *How Catholics Look at Jews* by Claire Huchet Bishop (Paulist Press, 1974) also revealed a high proportion of negative statements concerning Jews and Judaism.

Thus, when I came to do my own study of Catholic religion materials currently in use in the United States, I had a rich background of findings upon which to draw for comparison. My study, completed in 1976 as a dissertation for New York University, covered sixteen major religion series currently in use on the grade and high school levels. The 161 student texts and 113 teachers' manuals were published between 1967 and 1975.

In general, the results of my American study are encouraging, though negative aspects still persist. Using the 1975 Vatican Guidelines and the statements of the American bishops as criteria, I found that American Catholic religion materials are significantly more positive toward Judaism than they were before the Vatican Council. They are also more positive and historically accurate than the earlier European textbooks studied by Bishop. Table 1 gives the series included in the studies and their overall scores.

The "Preoccupation" scores in the first column on the right simply give the percentage of references to Jews in each series. For example, if there were 100 units in the series, and 25 of these contained a reference to Jews and Judaism, the "Preoccupation" score would be 25%.

The "Imbalance" score gives the percentage between positive and negative references. If all the statements in a given series are positive or at least neutral toward the Jews, the imbalance would be "+1.0" and so on. (The formula is: where "p" = the total number of positive statements and "n" = the total number of negative statements, the Imbalance is "p-n/p+n." Other statistics were also applied, but not discussed here.)

These scores reveal some interesting facts. In 1961, the average percent of preoccupation was 23%. For elementary (Grades 1–8) texts today, it is nearly 42%. This means that some reference to Jews or Judaism is made in just about every other lesson! Jews, because of the recent emphasis on the use of Sacred Scripture, are talked about far more than any other non-Catholic group. It is therefore vital that teachers, parents, lectors and all active Christians have a solid understanding of Judaism if the increased use of Scripture today is to provide the word that heals rather than leads to misunderstandings.

Interestingly, only some 17% of the lessons in our high school level textbooks contain references to Jews or Judaism. There is

**TABLE 1**

| Series: | Secondary | Preoccupation | Gen'l Imbalance |
|---|---|---|---|
| 01. | Allyn & Bacon, *Pearl & Seed* (1971) | 25% | +1.0 |
| 02. | Argus Comm., *Choose Life* (1969) | 10% | − .030 |
| 03. | Wm. C. Brown, *To Live Is Christ* (1967–74) | 45% | + .842 |
| 04. | Christian Brothers, *Christian Awareness* (1969) | 25% | + .545 |
| 05. | Daughters of St. Paul, *Divine Master* (1969) | 11% | + .328 |
| 06. | Paulist, *Discovery* (1969–71) | 3% | +1.0 |
| 07. | Silver Burdett, *Concern* (1970–71) | 4% | +1.0 |
| 08. | Winston, *Conscience & Concern* (1969–73) | 19% | + .785 |
| 09. | Winston, *Infinity* (1972–73) | 14% | + .292 |
| 10. | Winston, *Inquire & Believe* (1974) | 15% | +1.0 |
| **Series:** | **Elementary** | **Preoccupation** | **Gen'l Imbalance** |
| 11. | Winston, *Joy* (1972–73) | 45% | + .360 |
| 12. | Sadlier, *New Life* (1973) | 50% | + .634 |
| 13. | Silver Burdett (1969–74) | 43% | + .410 |
| 14. | Benziger, *Word Is Life* (1973) | 40% | + .305 |
| 15. | Daughters. of St. Paul, *Way, Truth, Life* (1968–74) | 42% | + .219 |
| 16. | Paulist, *Come to the Father* (1972–75) | 30% | + .303 |

less use of Scripture at these age levels than in the lower grades. This may be because so many other topics, such as social morality, personhood and Church history, are dealt with in the secondary years.

Even more intriguing is the discrepancy found in the imbalance scores. Like a detective faced with a seemingly insoluble crime, the dry statistics of a study such as this come to life when the unexpected happens. Because of the impact of Vatican II's declaration and more recent episcopal statements, it was expected that textbooks today would be more positive toward Judaism than those written before the Council. This proved to be true for the high school texts, whose average score went up from +.432 to +.674. But the elementary texts contained the surprise.

These actually went down! They averaged only about +.367, reflecting a higher percentage of negative statements than in 1961. What can account for this?

As we shall see, the critical area for Jewish-Christian relations as revealed in the study lies in our treatment of New Testament themes and events. How do we view the Pharisees? The relation of Jesus and his people? The crucifixion? Since the elementary-level textbooks use the New Testament much more now than before the Council, these key problem areas come up more frequently. Almost all of the negative references to Jews and Judaism occur in statements dealing with New Testament themes. It is only natural, then, to find an increase in negative statements, since the problem areas are treated more often.

Great progress has been made in following the mandates of Vatican II concerning the Jews. The most blatant accusations against them, such as "Christ killers" or "deicides," have been eliminated, but much remains to be done. Vestiges of the old polemics still remain, and, in the view of the author, the teachers' manuals fail to give an adequate background for the correct interpretation of difficult New Testament passages, such as those in Matthew and John. The period and theme categories attempted to pinpoint precisely where negative statements were most likely to be found in today's textbooks.

## The Period Categories

The table below gives the percentage of statements concerning a particular period to the total number of references to Jews and Judaism. In a separate column for both secondary and elementary series, it also gives an imbalance score, indicating the frequency of negative statements in each period. The closer to "+1.0" the score, the more positive the treatment of Jews and Judaism for that period.

In every category *except* the New Testament period, the treatment of Jews and Judaism is overwhelmingly positive. This is in marked contrast to earlier studies, which showed negative treatments in all periods. For the elementary series, however, the table shows that almost half of the statements about Jews are negative. It has only a slightly positive imbalance of +.122.

The table reveals another significant fact. There are almost no references to Jews or Judaism between the close of the New Testa-

**TABLE 2**
**PERIOD CATEGORIES**

|  | SECONDARY SERIES | | ELEMENTARY SERIES | |
|---|---|---|---|---|
|  | Preoccupation | Imbalance | Preoccupation | Imbalance |
| Hebrew Scriptures | 24% | + .960 | 46% | + .811 |
| New Testament | 35% | + .339 | 52% | + .122 |
| Rabbinic Judaism | 2.4% | +1.0 | .6% | +1.0 |
| Middle Ages | 3.1% | +3.75 | — | — |
| Reformation | .9% | +1.0 | — | — |
| Twentieth Century | 14% | +1.0 | 2.7% | +1.0 |
| General or Today | 27% | + .939 | 20% | + .888 |

ment period and the twentieth century. Such a gap is unfortunate, since it can reinforce in the students the idea that Judaism ceased to be religiously vital after the coming of Christ. As we have seen, the 1975 Vatican Guidelines specifically rebut such a view. Needed, then, are lessons dealing with the history of the Jews during the rabbinic and medieval periods. One excellent source by a Catholic historian is Frederick M. Schweitzer, *A History of the Jews* (Macmillan, 1971, $1.95).

## The Theme Categories

These ten categories zeroed in on critical areas on Jewish/ Christian concern today. How often do they arise in our cat- echesis? How are they treated? The table gives the results for both high school and elementary series. Each deserves special comment.

### *Jesus as a Jew*

This was one of the areas of greatest improvement. Note that the "imbalance" scores for both show that nearly all of the state- ments are positive or neutral. No less than 109 clear references to Jesus' Jewishness are made in the sixteen series. By contrast, earlier studies and the European studies found almost no refer- ences of this type. This change reflects recent Church teaching, as we have seen. The following statement, for one example, would have been impossible only a few years ago:

> Jesus experienced life and expressed himself as the man he was, a very bright, very charismatic, very energetic, culturally condi- tioned Jewish male (Wm. C. Brown Co., *The Jesus Book*, p. 52).

TABLE 3
THEME CATEGORIES

| | SECONDARY SERIES | | ELEMENTARY SERIES | |
|---|---|---|---|---|
| | Preoccupation | Imbalance | Preoccupation | Imbalance |
| Jesus as a Jew | 9% | + .952 | 12% | + .875 |
| Jesus and the Jews | 10% | − .026 | 12% | − .543 |
| The Pharisees | 8% | − .472 | 9% | − .784 |
| The Crucifixion | 10% | + .026 | 12% | − .385 |
| Divine Retribution | 0.7% | +1.0 | 0.2% | +1.0 |
| The Holocaust | 9% | +1.0 | 1.7% | +1.0 |
| Modern Israel | 4% | +1.0 | 2.7% | + .800 |
| Covenant (DT v NT) | 26% | + .707 | 36% | − .245 |
| Crusades | .7% | +1.0 | — | — |
| Inquisition | .7% | + .500 | — | — |

### Divine Retribution

Happily, the study discovered that entirely eliminated from our teaching today is the spurious notion that Jewish suffering is the result of God's punishment for the alleged crime of deicide. Such statements were occasionally found in Catholic teaching materials in the United States prior to Vatican Council II and are still present in some European texts. However, the only references to this idea in our texts today in this country clearly condemn the notion.

### The Holocaust

The Nazi attempt to exterminate the Jewish people is, in most series, handled with great sensitivity. This is in contrast to the European and earlier American materials, where no references were found at all. An excellent treatment of the history of anti-Semitism that can be recommended to all is found in Allyn and Bacon's *The Pearl and the Seed, Booklet 4* in the chapter and manual on "Bishop Sheil Acts Against Anti-Semitism." Also showing what can be done is a chapter in Silver Burdett's *Concern* series booklet on *World Religions* (pp. 28–30).

### Crusades, Inquisition

Only three references to the violence against the Jews occasioned by the Crusades and the Inquisition are found in the sixteen series. Two of them clearly condemn Christian misdeeds, but one falls into rationalization:

> Its (the Inquisition's) goal was to protect the newly united country against the plot of Muslims (Moors) and secret Jews (pretending to be Christians) to overthrow both the government and the Christian faith (Daughters of St. Paul, *The Church's Amazing Story,* p. 77).

This treatment rather seriously misrepresents a complex historical fact. Pedagogically, it is far better to treat the Inquisition honestly than it is to try to cover up errors and allow the children to find out the truth on their own at a later time.

## Modern Israel

Fr. Edward Flannery, former head of the bishops' Secretariat for Catholic/Jewish Relations in Washington, D.C., points out that the Jews "see Israel as central to Judaism itself and essential not only to Israeli but also Jewish survival, and therefore as an ecumenical and a religious consideration which should be included in the dialogue." The question here, then, is whether Catholics are being adequately prepared for dialogue, not whether there is any mistreatment. Only four out of the ten secondary series mention Israel or Zionism, and one series, Wm. C. Brown's *To Live Is Christ,* accounts for nine of the total sixteen references for this age level. Further, only fourteen elementary *lessons* mention the modern state of Israel. Given the increasingly high profile of Israel/Arab relations in the daily news reports, here might be a good opportunity for a balanced approach to the subject, especially in our high school lessons.

## General or Today

Almost all of the 235 statements which referred to Judaism in general terms are found to be either positive or neutral. Again, this shows great progress since before the Council. Many of these statements are specifically designed to correct previous misunderstandings and show the tremendous good will of the textbook publishers today. For example:

> The Torah is often misunderstood by Christians.... But then we learn from the rabbis their conviction that the accomplishment of

any one command in a perfect manner secures salvation. Viewed thus, God is not being oppressive, but rather beneficent in "multiplying" commands. Thereby he is multiplying the likelihood that something will be commanded that the struggling individual can accomplish with total purity of heart.... Again, the Jew was to have the same fondness for the Torah which a young man feels for his new bride.... Such a Torah is surely not a curse; rather it is a joy supreme (Paulist, *Come to the Father,* Grade 7, p. 22).

### *Jesus, the Jews, and the Crucifixion*

Many of the same series which include such highly positive views of Judaism as the above tend to have difficulties when dealing with the relationship between Jesus and his people and the events of Jesus' passion. At one point, for example, the Sadlier *New Life* program has this:

Advent is also a fitting time to tell children about the Jews, to teach them to esteem and love this people as God does. Anti-Jewish prejudice should be presented by calling attention to God's love for the Jews.... Explain (to the students) that Jesus is a Jew (Grade 2, CCD Manual, p. 105).

A later manual in the same series, however, has:

Now Pilate knew the real reason why the people wanted Jesus to die — because Jesus claimed to be the Son of God.... They want no king but Caesar. This is their final apostasy, their final rejection of God (Grade 3, CCD Manual, pp. 92–93).

Often, the descriptions of Christ's passion are unnecessarily vivid in depicting Jesus' agonies, especially in the earlier grades. Besides being pedagogically unsound to subject young children to such vivid scenes of violence, it is also unwise to link "the people," "the Jews," or even "the leaders of the people" with these events in such a way as to play down the role of Pilate and Rome.

### *The Pharisees*

Throughout the series, the Pharisees are painted in dark, evil colors. The danger here lies not only in a distortion of history. Deeper is the fact that negative traits ascribed to the Pharisees are likely to be imputed to the Jews as a whole by the uncritical reader or teacher. Legalism, hypocrisy and craftiness are all stereotypes of Jews which owe their origins to a negative portrait of the Pharisees.

At times, correctives are attempted. The sixth grade Benziger text, for example, introduces the Pharisees in this way:

> Some people among the Jews were not so interested in political power.... They were concerned more with keeping God's Law ... to serve God well.... These men were called the Pharisees (pp. 189–190).

The same text, however, immediately continues:

> They were strict with the people but often did not live up to God's laws in their own hearts. So the people went through the motions of practicing their religion.... They were the people of God in name. But many were not the people of God in their hearts (p. 190).

Like sexism and anti-black racism, the negative stereotypes about Jews seem to be so deeply embedded in our culture that it takes a great deal of care to identify and root them out. The teacher's manual to the Paulist Grade 7 text, for example, contains excellent background for teachers on the Pharisees (p. 148). This piece corrects the "caricature" of the Pharisees commonly accepted until a short time ago. It notes the "rabbi-like nature of Jesus' work" as we have done, and it shows how Jesus was at one with "the vast majority of Pharisees" in his beliefs, practices and teachings.

### The Relationship Between the Covenants

The approaches to this crucial topic cover the whole range of current Catholic thinking, from the very negative to the most positive. Many are remarkably advanced:

> As followers of Jesus, we believe that we have a new (or additional) covenant with God in Christ proclaimed by Jesus at the Last Supper (Wm. C. Brown Co., *Understanding Christian Worship*, p. 64).

> St. Paul... reminds us that the Jewish people always remain very dear to God. For, as he said, God never takes back his promises, and the Jews are always the chosen people whom God loves (Paulist, *Come to the Father*, Grade 6, p. 81).

While these follow the 1975 Vatican Guidelines and the stance of the American bishops, others had to be scored as negative according to those criteria — for example:

> This covenant lasted until the coming of Christ.... What is new
> about his Law is that love has replaced fear (Sadlier, *New Life,*
> Grade 6, School Manual, p. 151).

Some even adopt the tactic of taking basic Jewish tenets from the
Hebrew Scriptures, subsuming them into Christianity, and then
using them to "prove" that Christianity is superior to the Judaism
which gave birth to those ideas. For example:

> For a certain man, in a certain place, in a certain environment,
> Judaism may be the best religion for him at the moment....
> However, Christianity remains the best objectively for three rea-
> sons: 1. Christianity is built on love, not fear. 2. Christianity teaches
> that the whole man is good, both the body and the spirit. 3. Chris-
> tianity teaches that each man is free to be uniquely himself (Win-
> ston, *Conscience and Concern* series, "Who Cares?" p. 3).

The first idea can be found in the Hebrew Bible in Deuteronomy
6:5, the second in Genesis 1, and the third in Genesis 4:7, Joshua
24: 15, and many other places.

### Update of Textbook Studies: The 1992 Cunningham Study

In January of 1992, Catholic religious educator Philip Cunningham submitted to Boston College a Ph.D. dissertation updating my own content analysis reported in this chapter (see
"Resources" for cite). By the time he came to do the study, Cunningham was already well known in the field, having published
such excellent texts as *Jewish Apostle to the Gentiles: Paul as He
Saw Himself* (Twenty-Third Publications, 1986). Here, I will only
indicate the general results of Cunningham's analysis of 1990s
Catholic grade and high school religion series, urging the reader
to obtain his own more complete reports of his results when these
are published, hopefully in the non too distant future.

Briefly, Cunningham reports significant progress in primary
grade series in the fifteen years since the completion of my own
study, as I had in the fifteen years since the Thering study. This is
true even in the areas that remain today most problematic as they
were when I did my study: Jesus and the Jews, The Pharisees, The
Crucifixion, and Covenant. These went from very heavy negative
imbalances ($-.57$, $-.79$, $-.42$ and $-.24$, respectively) to marginally
negative imbalances $-.04$, $-.23$, $-.03$, and $-.06$). In other words,
there were a lot more attempts at positive and corrective portray-

als even in these most difficult categories than there were in the 1970s. But at least as much needs to be done as has been done before one can say that the problems which have plagued our teaching traditionally have been adequately resolved.

Interestingly, it is precisely these four categories that receive the major attention of the 1985 Vatican "Notes on the Correct Way to Present the Jews and Judaism in Preaching and Catechesis in the Roman Catholic Church." So there is reason to expect yet further progress when the next textbook study is done.

Another interesting note raised by Cunningham is that the textbook series which came out worst (i.e. most negative toward Jews and Judaism) in my study comes out best today in its most recent revision. This should give some solace to those of us working in this field who are sometimes tempted to feel that our efforts remain, as I have heard some say "those of an elite" and do not "reach the grass roots." Well, all the efforts by scholars and dialoguers all these years since the Council does indeed pay off where it counts, in our classrooms.

For the remainder of the period and theme categories, the results were similar to my own results (which were already quite encouraging, of course), producing a similar profile, only higher in the positive scale. Analyzing recent materials, Cunningham also points out that my concern with the lacuna of treatment of Jews and Judaism in the centuries in between the New Testament and World War II may be ameliorated by two factors: First, the texts provide very little Catholic history either, so it is not as if they are unfairly ignoring Jewish history. Second, the treatment of contemporary Jews and Judaism is invariable very positive, which is likely to be what sticks in the minds of students in any event.

For secondary texts, which I had discovered to be more positive than primary level texts in the 1970s, Cunningham found "relatively little change" in the overall profiles in the 90s. In the four key categories cited above, "Jesus and the Jews" and the "Pharisees" improved measurably but not greatly (from $-.23$ and $-.61$ to $-.16$ and $-.38$). The Covenant Relationship category, while receiving far less attention in current textbooks than before, continued to have an essentially positive ($+.52$) imbalance.

The Crucifixion category, however, dropped both in terms of percentage of treatment and rather precipitously toward the negative (from $+.03$ to $-.09$), a phenomenon which Cunningham quite rightly highlights as "particularly disturbing." Cunningham does note, however, that most of the negative references came in rather glancing references that were essentially paraphrases or citations from the passion narratives or Acts. Where there was a more conscious treatment, it was usually quite corrective and responsible, so the issue may be more carelessness than what Cunningham aptly calls "the libelous language found in the earliest textbook studies." And the fact that there were fewer negative statements even in this category should also be noted.

In sum, one can say that the system is working, if slowly. Things are improving, if more slowly than we might like. Dr. Cunningham's analysis is a great gift to all of us, pinpointing as it does with precision what needs to be done as well as what has already been accomplished.

## Conclusion

The positive changes since Vatican Council II are almost overwhelming in their honesty and integrity of vision. The Spirit has indeed come among us to open us to new relationships and new understandings of our parent religion, Judaism.

Much has been accomplished, but much remains to be done. The statements of the Council, of the Vatican, and of the American bishops are designed to lead us into an ever-renewed dialogue with Judaism. Jesus was a Jew and his teachings presume an audience intimate with the tenets of Judaism. If we are to read the New Testament intelligently, if we are to be open to the Word of God speaking to us through the Jewish people in the Sacred Scriptures and today in the dialogue, we must always be open to the spirit of truth. Jesus told the Samaritan woman that "salvation is from the Jews." This is as true today as it was when he uttered it. We must be open to it, though that saving dialogue may take us in directions which we cannot now predict. In union with the rest of the Christian community, journey beckons to us.

# APPENDICES

# APPENDIX A

# Guidelines for the Evaluation of the Treatment of Jews and Judaism in Catechetical Materials

## I. Official Sources for the Criteria Developed Here

1. The Second Vatican Council, "Declaration on Non-Christian Religions" (*Nostra Aetate,*) Section 4, October 28, 1965.

2. "Guidelines for Catholic-Jewish Relations," Secretariat for Catholic-Jewish Relations, National Conference of Catholic Bishops of the United States, 1967.

3. "Pastoral Orientations on the Attitude of Christians to Judaism," Episcopal Committee of the Roman Catholic Bishops of France, April 1973.

4. "Statement of the United States Catholic Conference of Bishops (USA) on the Middle East," November 13, 1973.

5. "Guidelines and Suggestions for Implementing the Conciliar Declaration Nostra Aetate," Vatican Commission for Religious Relations with the Jews, January 2, 1975.

6. "Statement on Catholic-Jewish Relations," NCCB, November 20, 1975.

## II. The Criteria

### A. The Hebrew Scriptures

1. Does the catechesis affirm the value of the *whole* Bible? Does it show that, far from being rendered void by the New Testament, the Hebrew covenant remains in fact the root, the source, the foundation and the promise of the new covenant?

2. Are the inspiration and validity of the Hebrew Scriptures recognized in their own right?

3. Do lessons picture the Hebrew Bible as a source of inspiration for Jesus, the New Testament authors and later Christian writers? Do the materials show the Hebrew Scriptures to be *the* Scripture of the New Testament Church?

4. Do lessons set the Hebrew Scriptures and the Jewish tradition rounded on it against the New Testament in a false way? — i.e., are the Hebrew Scriptures pictured as constituting a religion of only justice, fear and legalism, with no appeal to the love of God and neighbor? (Cf. Deut. 6:5 and Lev. 19:18 as the source of Jesus' "law of love.")

5. Is the fact noted that the phrase "Old Testament" is seen-by Jews as an insult to the continuing validity of the Hebrew Bible?

6. Is the religion of the Hebrew Scriptures presented as dynamic and currently valid or is it seen as dead and anachronistic, merely a precursor of the religion of the New Testament?

7. How are the personalities of the Hebrew Scriptures treated? Is their Jewishness noted or are they pictured as "hidden" Christians?

8. Are the Hebrew Scriptures used in such a way that the children can identify with Hebrew biblical figures such as Abraham as models of faith? Or is the story told in such a way that the "fickleness" of the people is stressed?

## B. Judaism in New Testament Times

1. Does lesson material indicate that the Judaism which gave birth to Christianity was dynamic and vital? Or is it falsely presented as degenerate, legalistic and materialistic?

2. Is attention paid to the multiplicity of sects and groups within Judaism in Jesus' time? Are these described fully developed or only in negative stereotypes?

3. Is the full range of Jewish beliefs regarding the Messiah adequately presented? Or are Jewish messianic expectations reduced to the notion of awaiting, a purely materialistic, earthly king?

4. Is mention made of the achievements of Judaism during New Testament times? (e.g., the development of the synagogue, the literature of the period, Qumran, rabbinic works)?

## C. The Pharisees

1. Are the Pharisees treated fairly or only as a negative stereotype? As legalistic? As all the same (e.g., see the different Pharisaic movements such as the schools of Hillel and Shammai)?

2. Are the negative images ascribed to the Pharisees then applied to "the Jews" as a whole?

3. Are the revolutionary religious and social achievements of the Pharisees and their role as preservers of Judaism after the destruction of the temple explained?

4. Is mention made of positive relations between Jesus and the Pharisees (e.g., Lk. 11:37–44, 13:31; Jn. 9:13; Nicodemus) and between the Pharisees and the early Church (e.g., Acts 5:34–39; 23:6–9)?

## D. Jesus and the Jews

1. Is the Jewishness of Jesus clearly stated and used where appropriate to explain his behavior? His understanding of and adherence to the Jewish Law? That he considered himself a faithful Jew?

2. Do the lessons state or imply that "the Jews" rejected Jesus, despite the fact that most Jews could never have heard of him in his lifetime? And that the apostles and early disciples were all Jews?

3. When phrases like "some Jews" or "some Jewish leaders" are used, is adequate teacher background given in the manuals so that teachers will know *why* these terms are used and be able to prepare students for encounters with usages of the term "the Jews" in John's Gospel and elsewhere at Sunday Mass?

4. Is Jesus pictured as opposing or denouncing the Judaism of his time? Or is he seen in context — as a Jew — who thought and debated within the Jewish milieu, teaching quite often in the manner of the Pharisees?

## E. The Crucifixion

1. Is it made clear that "what happened at his passion cannot be blamed upon all the Jews then living, without distinction, nor upon the Jews of today" (Vatican II).

2. Are the results of recent biblical scholarship, showing the historical complexities of the New Testament portrayals of the trial and crucifixion, used in the text and especially in the teachers' manuals?

3. Is the role of Pilate whitewashed? Is it made clear that crucifixion was a Roman method of execution? That the chief priest was a Roman appointee?

4. Is it shown that the New Testament does not mention the Pharisees as being involved in his arrest, trial or death?

5. Is guilt for the crucifixion consistently placed where it belongs theologically — on all humanity? Or are "the Jewish leaders" actually blamed in concrete descriptions of the passion?

6. Is the notion that Jewish suffering is the result of divine retribution for their alleged rejection of Jesus explicitly condemned — or at least never mentioned or in any way implied?

## F. Rabbinic and Medieval Judaism

1. Does the treatment of Judaism cease with the New Testament period?

2. Are Jews mentioned in Church history only as victims of persecution? Or are the significant Jewish contributions to Western, "Christian" history treated and fairly developed?

3. Is there mention of the great religious significance of the Mishnah and the Talmud? Of the medieval Jewish communities of Europe? Of the role of Spanish Jewry in developing medieval Scholastic philosophy and Arabic thought for Christian Europe?

4. Is the story of Europe only the story of "Christendom?" Is the influence of Jewish intellectual and theological thought on Christian thought (e.g., Maimonides on Aquinas, Spinoza on Pascal, Jewish linguistic and biblical studies on Erasmus, etc.) presented? Jewish mysticism?

5. Is medieval Jewish "ghetto" life seen in all its vitality and creativity? Jewish emancipation beginning with the French Enlightenment in 1790?

6. In short, is Jewish history treated only as a passive backwater of Christian history, or is the true role of Judaism in post-biblical history portrayed in a positive manner? Is it treated at all?

7. If not treated, so that there is a long silence between the New Testament and the Holocaust in the twentieth century except as victims of persecution, is there an underlying message that there is somehow a link between the last appearance of the Jews as "Christ killers" and their next appearance as suffering victims?

## G. Reformation to Twentieth Century

1. Is the contribution of Jewish thought and culture to the Reformation (both Protestant and Catholic) and to the Enlightenment presented?

2. Is the role of Jewry in European economic development in this period made clear, without false stereotype? The role of Jews in the discovery and growth of America? Involvement in the growth of trade unions?

3. Is there any presentation of profound Jewish religious movements such as Hasidism? Jewish philosophy and poetry that influenced current thought such as Heinrich Heine, Martin Buber, and Franz Rosenzweig? Are great scientists such as Freud and Einstein portrayed as Jews?

4. Is there an appreciation for the development of and differences between Reform, Orthodox and Conservative Jewry, especially in the United States? The development of Zionism in this country (Brandeis, etc.)?

5. Any reference to the Hebraic and biblical origins of much of the thought of early American colonists like the Puritans as well as that of the framers of the Constitution?

## H. Christian Persecution of the Jews

1. Do texts treating of Church history honestly admit to Christian mistreatment of the Jews during various periods in history? Do they urge repentance?

2. Are the "excesses" of the Crusades and the Inquisition treated with candor or is an attempt made to cover over or even justify these events?

3. Is the history of Christian anti-Semitism clearly traced, along with its consequences in pogroms, ghettos, etc.?

4. On the other hand, are the efforts of some of the popes, such as Gregory the Great, to stop the practice of forced conversion and protect the Jews mentioned as models of a more Christian practice?

## I. The Holocaust

1. Are the implications of this event for traditional Christian understandings clearly dealt with, at least in the upper grade levels?

2. Is the fact that the destruction of six million Jews took place in supposedly Christian countries admitted?

3. Are Christian heroes like Franz Jagerstatter who died at the hands of Hitler praised for their courage?

4. Is the Church's silence regarding the death camps handled in a balanced and fair manner?

5. Are the more recent forms of anti-Semitism such as "anti-Zionism" analyzed and clearly condemned?

6. Is the Holocaust literature written by Jewish survivors of the death camps used where appropriate (liturgies, etc.)? Are the authors presented as Jewish (e.g., Anne Frank, Elie Wiesel, Viktor Frankl, etc.)?

## J. The Modern State of Israel

1. Is the Jewish concept of peoplehood fully explained — i.e., "a peoplehood that is not solely racial, ethnic or religious but in a sense a composite of all three" (NCCB, November 1975)?

2. Do the texts help students to understand "the link between land and people which Jews have expressed in their writings and worship throughout two millennia as a longing for the homeland, holy Zion" (NCCB, November 1975)?

3. Are students prepared to understand with sympathy the view of American Jews with regard to the state of Israel in such a way that they will be able to enter into dialogue with Jews even if they do not themselves accept the biblical/theological rationale?

4. Is the validity of the existence of the Jewish state of Israel clearly affirmed along with an affirmation of the rights of the Palestinians (NCCB, November 1975)?

5. If mention is made of current Israeli-Arab conflicts, is an adequate background for both sides of the issue presented?

6. Is an attempt made to explain Zionism as a movement for liberation in reaction to both European and Moslem oppression?

## K. The Relationship Between the Covenants

1. Is it made clear that the Jewish covenant with God was not abrogated with the establishment of the Christian covenant in Christ? That we are the "wild shoots" which have been "grafted" unto Israel (Rom. 11)?

2. Is the point clearly made that still today "God holds the Jews most dear" and that "he does not repent of the gifts he makes or of the calls he issues" *(Nostra/Aetate;* of. Romans 11)? Is the permanent and continuing election of the Jewish people, i.e., the on-going role of Judaism in the divine plan, clearly seen as an essential aspect of a valid Christian theological understanding of Judaism (cf. French bishops, 1973; Vatican II, *De Ecclesia, n.* 16)?

3. Is an attempt made to see this continuing salvific role of Judaism in the world on Jewish as well as Christian terms — for example, as the "sanctification of the name" (French bishops, 1973)?

4. Even if not fully developed, is an attempt made to frame a positive theological understanding of Jewish-Christian relations for today based on the above biblical and official sources while avoiding indifferentism?

5. Are adequate activities, information and attitudinal approaches developed appropriate to each age level by which Christians can have the opportunity, as the Vatican Guidelines stipulate, "to learn by what essential traits the Jews define themselves in the light of their own religious experience"?

## III. General and Technical Aspects

1. Does the overall scope and age sequence of the series attempt to integrate understandings of Jews and Judaism throughout the lessons, where appropriate? Or are all positive references to Jewish history, beliefs and customs in the post-biblical period concentrated in a single chapter of a single text?

2. How do the pictures, photos and other illustrations image Jews? Do pictures which involve clearly distinguishable Jewish figures show them as "bad guys" or "good guys" — or a mixture of both?

3. Are Jesus, Mary and the apostles pictured as Jewish? Any illustrations of Jesus with forelocks or wearing a prayer shawl, perhaps? Phylacteries?

4. Does the text or series tend to be overwhelmingly negative in its statements, or is it simply silent on crucial issues, periods and themes? (If the latter, supplementary material can easily be supplied on such themes as the history of Judaism after the New Testament period, the modern state of Israel, Jewish feasts and festivals, the Holocaust, etc.)

5. Do high school texts attempt to overcome previous distortions?

6. Does the series on whatever level try to replace the negative myths with a positive approach to Jews and Judaism or does it merely try to avoid negatives?

7. Is background given to teachers and students for understanding possible misconceptions derived from biblical passages used in the liturgy, e.g., is sound historical background for Jesus' passion introduced when treating of Holy Week themes?

8. Are the Judaic origins of sacraments such as the Eucharist and baptism made clear throughout the series and fully explained in the manuals for teachers? Are Jewish feasts and customs explained or used as examples of prayer and celebration?

9. Are the teachings of the Second Vatican Council and subsequent documents such as the Guidelines of the American bishops referred to and explained in the teachers' manuals, and embodied in the texts?

10. Are Jewish sayings and tales, such as those of the Talmud, the Midrash and the Hasidim, used in appropriate places and correctly identified?

# APPENDIX B

# Documents of the Holy See and Pope John Paul II

**ECUMENICAL COUNCIL VATICAN II:**
**"Declaration on the Relationship of the Church**
**to Non-Christian Religions,"** *Nostra Aetate* **(no. 4)**
**(October 28, 1965)**

As this sacred Synod searches into the mystery of the Church, it recalls the spiritual bond linking the people of the New Covenant with Abraham's stock.

For the Church of Christ acknowledges that, according to the mystery of God's saving design, the beginnings of her faith and her election are already found among the patriarchs, Moses, and the prophets. She professes that all who believe in Christ. Abraham's sons according to faith (cf. *Ga* 3:7), are included in the same patriarch's call, and likewise that the salvation of the Church was mystically foreshadowed by the chosen people's exodus from the land of bondage.

The Church, therefore, cannot forget that she received the revelation of the Old Testament through the people with whom God in His inexpressible mercy deigned to establish the Ancient Covenant. Nor can she forget that she draws sustenance from the root of that good olive tree onto which have been grafted the wild olive branches of the Gentiles (cf. *Rm* 11:17–24). Indeed, the Church believes that by His cross Christ, our Peace, reconciled Jew and Gentile, making them both one in Himself (cf. *Ep* 2:14–16).

Also, the Church ever keeps in mind the words of the Apostle about his kinsmen, who have the adoption as sons, and the glory and the covenant and the legislation and the worship and the promise; who have the fathers, and from whom is Christ according to the flesh (*Rm* 9:4-5), the son of the Virgin Mary. The Church recalls too that from the Jewish people sprang the apostles, her foundation stones and pillars, as well as most of the early disciples who proclaimed Christ to the world.

As holy Scripture testifies, Jerusalem did not recognize the time of her visitation (cf. *Lk* 19:44), nor did the Jews in large number accept the gospel; indeed, not a few opposed the spreading of it (cf. *Rm* 11:28). Nevertheless, according to the Apostle, the Jews still remain most dear to God because of their fathers, for He does not repent of the gifts He makes nor of the calls He issues (cf. *Rm* 11:28–29). In company with the prophets and the same Apostle, the Church awaits that day, known to God alone, on which all peoples will address the Lord in a single voice and "serve Him with one accord" (*Soph* 3:9; cf. *Is* 66:23; *Ps* 65:4; *Rm* 11:11–32).

Since the spiritual patrimony common to Christians and Jews is thus so great, this sacred Synod wishes to foster and recommend that mutual understanding and respect which is the fruit above all of biblical and theological studies, and of brotherly dialogues.

True, authorities of the Jews and those who followed their lead pressed for the death of Christ (cf. *Jn* 19:6); still, what happened in His passion cannot be blamed upon all the Jews then living, without distinction, nor upon the Jews of today. Although the Church is the new people of God, the Jews should not be presented as repudiated or cursed by God, as if such views followed from the holy Scriptures. All should take pains, then, lest in catechetical instruction and in the preaching of God's Word they teach anything out of harmony with the truth of the gospel and the spirit of Christ.

The Church repudiates all persecutions against any man. Moreover, mindful of her common patrimony with the Jews, and motivated by the gospel's spiritual love and by no political considerations, she deplores the hatred, persecutions, and displays of anti-Semitism directed against the Jews at any time and from any source.

Besides, as the Church has always held and continues to hold, Christ in His boundless love freely underwent His passion and death because of the sins of all men, so that all might attain salvation. It is, therefore, the duty of the Church's preaching to proclaim the cross of Christ as the sign of God's all-embracing love and as the fountain from which every grace flows.

## COMMISSION FOR RELIGIOUS RELATIONS WITH THE JEWS:
### "Guidelines and Suggestions for Implementing the Conciliar Declaration *Nostra Aetate* (no. 4)" (December 1, 1974).

### *Introductory Note*

The document is published over the signature of Cardinal Willebrands, in his capacity as President of the new Commission for the Catholic Church's religious relations with the Jews, instituted by Paul VI on 22 October 1974. It comes out a short time after the ninth anniversary of the promulgation of *Nostra Aetate*, the Second Vatican Council's Declaration on the Church's relations with non-Christian religions.

The "Guidelines and Suggestions," which refer to no. 4 of the Declaration, are notable for their almost exclusively practical nature and for their sobriety.

This deliberately practical nature of the text is justified by the fact that it concerns a pragmatic document.

It does not propose a Christian theology of Judaism. Such a theology certainly has an interest for specialist research and reflection, but it still needs considerable study. The new Commission for Religious Relations with the Jews should be able to play a part in the gradual fruition of this endeavour.

The *first part* of the Document recalls the principal teachings of the Council on the condemnation of anti-Semitism and of all discrimination, and the obligation of reciprocal understanding and of renewed mutual esteem. It also hopes for a better knowledge on the part of Christians of the essence of the religious tradition of Judaism and of the manner in which Jews identify themselves.

The text then proposes a series of concrete suggestions.

The section dedicated to *dialogue* calls for fraternal dialogue and the establishment of deep doctrinal research. Prayer in common is also proposed as a means of encounter.

With regard to the *liturgy,* mention is made of the links between the Christian liturgy and the Jewish liturgy and of the caution which is needed in dealing with commentaries on biblical texts, and with liturgical explanations and translations.

The part concerning *teaching* and *education* allows the relations between the two touched upon and stress is laid on the note of expectation which characterizes both the Jewish and the Christian religion. Specialists are invited to conduct serious research and the establishment of chairs of Hebrew studies is encouraged where it is possible, as well as collaboration with Jewish scholars.

The final section deals with the possibilities of *common social action* in the context of a search for social justice and for peace.

The *conclusion* touches on, among other things, the ecumenical aspect of the problem of relations with Judaism, the initiatives of local churches in this area, and the essential lines of the mission of the new Commission instituted by the Holy See.

The great sobriety of the text is noted also in the concrete suggestions which it puts forward. But it would certainly be wrong to interpret such sobriety as being indicative of a limiting programme of activities. The document does propose limited suggestions for some key sectors, but it is a document meant for the universal Church, and as such it cannot take account of all the individual situations. The suggestions put forward are intended to give ideas to those who were asking themselves how to start on a local level that dialogue which the text invites them to begin and to develop. These suggestions are mentioned because of their value as examples. They are made because it seems that they could find ample application and that their proposal at the same time constitutes an apt programme for aiding local churches to organize their own activities, in order to harmonize with the general movement of the universal Church in dialogue with Judaism.

The Document can be considered from a certain point of view as the Commission's first step for the realization of religious relations with Judaism. It will devolve on the new Commission to prepare and put forward, when necessary., the further developments which may seem necessary in order that the initiative of the Second Vatican Council in this important area may continue to bear fruit on a local and on a worldwide level, for the benefit of peace of heart and harmony of spirit of all who work under the protection of the one Almighty God.

The Document, which gives the invitation to an effort of mutual understanding and collaboration, coincides with the opening of the Holy Year, which is consecrated to the theme of reconciliation. It is impossible not to perceive in such a coincidence an invitation to study and to apply in concrete terms throughout the whole world the suggestions which the Document proposes. Likewise one cannot fail to hope that our Jewish brothers too may find in it useful indications for their participation in a commitment which is common.

•

## PREAMBLE

The Declaration *Nostra Aetate,* issued by the Second Vatican Council on 28 October 1965, "on the relationship of the Church to non-Christian religions" (no. 4), marks an important milestone in the history of Jewish-Christian relations.

Moreover, the step taken by the Council finds its historical setting in circumstances deeply affected by the memory of the persecution and massacre of Jews which took place in Europe just before and during the Second World War.

Although Christianity sprang from Judaism. taking from it certain essential elements of its faith and divine cult, the gap dividing them was deepened more and more, to such an extent that Christian and Jew hardly knew each other.

After two thousand years, too often marked by mutual ignorance and frequent confrontation, the Declaration *Nostra Aetate* provides an opportunity to open or to continue a dialogue with a view to better mutual understanding. Over the past nine years, many steps in this direction have been taken in various countries. As a result, it is easier to distinguish the conditions under which a new relationship between Jews and Christians may be worked out and developed. This seems the right moment to propose, following the guidelines of the Council, some concrete suggestions born of experience, hoping that they will help to bring into actual existence in the life of the Church the intentions expressed in the conciliar document.

While referring the reader back to this document, we may simply restate here that the spiritual bonds and historical links binding the Church to Judaism condemn (as opposed to the very spirit of Christianity) all forms of anti-Semitism and discrimination, which in any case the dignity of the human person alone would suffice to condemn. Further still, these links and relationships render obligatory a better mutual understanding and renewed mutual esteem. On the practical level in particular, Christians must therefore strive to acquire a better knowledge of the basic components of the religious tradition of Judaism; they must strive to learn by what essential traits Jews define themselves in the light of their own religious experience.

With due respect for such matters of principle, we simply propose some first practical applications in different essential areas of the Church's life, with a view to launching or developing sound relations between Catholics and their Jewish brothers.

## I. Dialogue

To tell the truth, such relations as there have been between Jew and Christian have scarcely ever risen above the level of monologue. From now on, real dialogue must be established.

Dialogue presupposes that each side wishes to know the other, and wishes to increase and deepen its knowledge of the other. It constitutes a particularly suitable means of favouring a better mutual knowledge and, especially in the case of dialogue between Jews and Christians, of probing the riches of one's own tradition. Dialogue demands respect for the other as he is; above, all respect for his faith and his religious convictions.

In virtue of her divine mission, and her very nature, the Church must preach Jesus Christ to the world (*Ad Gentes,* 2). Lest the witness of Catholics to Jesus Christ should give offence to Jews, they must take care to live and spread their Christian faith while maintaining the strictest respect for religious liberty in line with the teaching of the Second Vatican Council (Declaration *Dignitatis Humanae*). They will likewise strive to understand the difficulties which arise for the Jewish soul — rightly imbued with an extremely high, pure notion of the divine transcendence — when faced with the mystery of the incarnate Word.

While it is true that a widespread air of suspicion, inspired by an unfortunate past, is still dominant in this particular area, Christians, for their part, will be able to see to what extent the responsibility is theirs and deduce practical conclusions for the future.

In addition to friendly talks, competent people will be encouraged to meet and to study together the many problems deriving from the fundamental convictions of Judaism and of Christianity. In order not to hurt (even involuntarily) those taking part, it will be vital to guarantee, not only tact, but a great openness of spirit and diffidence with respect to one's own prejudices.

In whatever circumstances as shall prove possible and mutually acceptable, one might encourage a common meeting in the presence of God, in prayer and silent meditation, a highly efficacious way of finding that humility, that openness of heart and mind, necessary prerequisites for a deep knowledge of oneself and of others. In particular, that will be done in connection with great causes such as the struggle for peace and justice.

## II. Liturgy

The existing links between the Christian liturgy and the Jewish liturgy will be borne in mind. The idea of a living community in the service of God, and in the service of men for the love of God, such as it is realized in the liturgy, is just as characteristic of the Jewish liturgy as it is of the Christian one. To improve Jewish-Christian relations, it is important to take cognizance of those common elements of the liturgical life (formulas, feasts, rites, etc.) in which the Bible holds an essential place.

An effort will be made to acquire a better understanding of whatever in the Old Testament retains its own perpetual value (cf. *Dei Verbum*, 14–15), since that has not been cancelled by the later interpretation of the New Testament. Rather, the New Testament brings out the full meaning of the Old, while both Old and New illumine and explain each other (cf. *ibid.*, 16). This is all the more important since liturgical reform is now bringing the text of the Old Testament ever more frequently to the attention of Christians.

When commenting on biblical texts, emphasis will be laid on the continuity of out faith with that of the earlier Covenant, in the perspective of the promises, without minimizing those elements of Christianity which are original. We believe that those promises were fulfilled with the first coming of Christ. But it is none the less true that we still await their perfect fulfilment in his glorious return at the end of time.

With respect to liturgical readings, care will be taken to see that homilies based on them will not distort their meaning, especially when it is a question of passages which seem to show the Jewish people as such in an unfavourable light. Efforts will be made so to instruct the Christian people that they will understand the true interpretation of all the texts and their meaning for the contemporary believer.

Commissions entrusted with the task of liturgical translation will pay particular attention to the way in which they express those phrases and passages which Christians, if not well informed, might misunderstand because of prejudice. Obviously, one cannot alter the text of the Bible. The point is that, with a version destined for liturgical use, there should be an overriding preoccupation to bring out explicitly the meaning of a text,[1] while taking scriptural studies into account.

The preceding remarks also apply to introductions to biblical readings, to the Prayer of the Faithful, and to commentaries printed in missals used by the laity.

## III. Teaching and Education

Although there is still a great deal of work to be done, a better understanding of Judaism itself and its relationship to Christianity has been achieved in recent years thanks to the teaching of the Church, the study and research of scholars, as also to the beginning of dialogue.

In this respect, the following facts deserve to be recalled:

— It is the same God, "inspirer and author of the books of both Testaments" (*Dei Verbum, 16,*) who speaks both in the old and new Covenants.

— Judaism in the time of Christ and the Apostles was a complex reality, embracing many different trends, many spiritual, religious, social and cultural values.

— The Old Testament and the Jewish tradition rounded upon it must not be set against the New Testament in such a way that the former seems to constitute a religion of only justice, fear and legalism, with no appeal to the love of God and neighbour (*cf. Dt* 6:5; *Lv* 19:18; *Mt* 22:34–40).

— Jesus was born of the Jewish people, as were his Apostles and a large number of his first disciples. When he revealed himself as the Messiah and Son of God (d. *Mt* 16:16), the bearer of the

---

1. Thus the formula "the Jews," in St. John, sometimes according to the context means "the leaders of the Jews," or "'the adversaries of Jesus," terms which express better thought of the evangelist and avoid appearing to arraign the Jewish people as such. Another example is the use of the words "pharisee" and "pharisaism" which have taken on a largely pejorative meaning.

new Gospel message, he did so as the fulfilment and perfection of the earlier Revelation. And, although his teaching had a profoundly new character, Christ, nevertheless, in many instances, took his stand on the teaching of the Old Testament. The New Testament is profoundly marked by its relation to the Old. As the Second Vatican Council declared: "God, the inspirer and author of the books of both Testaments, wisely arranged that the New Testament be hidden in the Old and the Old be made manifest in the New" (*Dei Verbum*, 16). Jesus also used teaching methods similar to those employed by the rabbis of his time.

— With regard to the trial and death of Jesus, the Council recalled that "what happened in his passion cannot be blamed upon all the Jews then living, without distinction, nor upon the Jews of today" (*Nostra Aetate*, 4).

— The history of Judaism did not end with the destruction of Jerusalem, but rather went on to develop a religious tradition. And, although we believe that the importance and meaning of that tradition were deeply affected by the coming of Christ, it is still nonetheless rich in religious values.

— With the prophets and the apostle Paul, "the Church awaits the day, known to God alone, on which all peoples will address the Lord in a single voice and 'serve Him with one accord' (*Soph* 3:9)" (*Nostra Aetate*, 4).

Information concerning these questions is important at all levels of Christian instruction and education. Among sources of information, special attention should be paid to the following:

— catechism and religious textbooks;

— history books;

— the mass-media (press, radio, cinema, television).

The effective use of these means presupposes the thorough formation of instructors and educators in training schools, seminaries and universities.

Research into the problems bearing on Judaism and Jewish-Christian relations will be encouraged among specialists, particularly in the fields of exegesis, theology, history and sociology. Higher institutions of Catholic research, in association if possible with other similar Christian institutions and experts, are invited to contribute to the solution of such problems. Wherever possible, chairs of Jewish studies will be created, and collaboration with Jewish scholars encouraged.

## IV. Joint Social Action

Jewish and Christian tradition, rounded on the Word of God, is aware of the value of the human person, the image of God. Love of the same God must show itself in effective action for the good of mankind. In the spirit of the prophets, Jews and Christians will work willingly together, seeking social justice and peace at every level — local, national and international.

At the same time, such collaboration can do much to foster mutual understanding and esteem.

## Conclusion

The Second Vatican Council has pointed out the path to follow in promoting deep fellowship between Jews and Christians. But there is still a long road ahead.

The problem of Jewish-Christian relations concerns the Church as such, since it is when "pondering her own mystery" that she encounters the mystery of Israel. Therefore, even in areas where no Jewish communities exist, this remains an important problem. There is also an ecumenical aspect to the question: the very return of Christians to the sources and origins of their faith, grafted on to the earlier Covenant, helps the search for unity in Christ, the cornerstone.

In this field, the bishops will know what best to do on the pastoral level, within the general disciplinary framework of the Church and m line with the common teaching of her magisterium. For example, they will create some suitable commissions or secretariats on a national or regional level, or appoint some competent person to promote the implementation of the conciliar directives and the suggestions made above.

On 22 October 1974, the Holy Father instituted for the universal Church this Commission for Religious Relations with the Jews, joined to the Secretariat for Promoting Christian Unity. This special Commission, created to encourage and foster religious relations between Jews and Catholics — and to do so eventually in collaboration with other Christians — will be, within the limits of its competence, at the service of all interested organizations, providing information for them, and helping them to pursue their task in conformity with the instructions of the Holy See.

The Commission wishes to develop this collaboration in order to implement, correctly and effectively, the express intentions of the Council.

Given at Rome, 1 December 1974.

✠JOHANNES Card. WILLEBRANDS
*President of the Commission*

Pierre-Marie de Contenson, OP
*Secretary of the Commission*

## JOHN PAUL II:
*Address to Jewish Representatives,* **Mainz (November 17, 1980).**

Shalom!
Ladies and Gentlemen, Dear Brothers and Sisters!
I thank you for your friendly and sincere words of greeting. This meeting was a deep need for me in the framework of this apostolic journey, and I thank you for fulfilling it. May God's blessing accompany this hour!

1. If Christians must consider themselves brothers of all men and behave accordingly, this holy obligation is all the more binding when they find themselves before members of the Jewish people! In the "Declaration on the relationship of the Church with Judaism" in April of this year, the Bishops of the Federal Republic of Germany put this sentence at the beginning: "Whoever meets Jesus Christ, meets Judaism." I would like to make these words mine too. The faith of the Church in Jesus Christ, the son of David and the son of Abraham (cf. *Mt* 11:1) actually contains what the Bishops call in that declaration "the spiritual heritage of Israel for the Church" (par. 11), a living heritage, which must be understood and preserved in its depth and richness by us Catholic Christians.

2. The concrete brotherly relations between Jews and Catholics in Germany assume a quite particular value against the grim background of the persecution and the attempted extermination of Judaism in this country. The innocent victims in Germany and elsewhere, the families destroyed or dispersed, the cultural values

or art treasures destroyed forever, are a tragic proof where dis-crimination and contempt of human dignity can lead, especially if they are animated by perverse theories on a presumed differ-ence in the value of races or on the division of men into men of "high worth," "worthy of living," and men who are "worthless," "unworthy of living." Before God all men are of the same value and importance.

In this spirit, during the persecution, Christians likewise com-mitted themselves, often at the risk of their lives, to prevent or relieve the sufferings of their Jewish brothers and sisters. I would like to express recognition and gratitude to them at this moment. And also to those people who, as Christians, affirming they be-longed to the Jewish people, travelled along the *via crucis* of their brothers and sisters to the end — like the great Edith Stein, called in her religious institute Teresa Benedikta of the Cross, whose memory is rightly held in great honour.

I would further like to mention also Franz Rosenzweig and Martin Buber, who, through their creative familiarity with the Jewish and German languages, constructed a wonderful bridge for a deeper meeting of both cultural areas.

You yourselves stressed, in your words of greeting, that in the many efforts to build up a new common life with Jewish citizens in this country, Catholics and the Church have made a decisive contribution. This recognition and the necessary collaboration on your part fills me with joy. For my part, I wish to express grateful admiration also for your initiatives in this connection, including the recent foundation of your Heidelberg University.

3. The depth and richness of our common heritage are re-vealed to us particularly in friendly dialogue and trusting collab-oration. I rejoice that, in this country, conscious and zealous care is dedicated to all this. Many public and private initiatives in the pastoral, academic, and social field serve this purpose, as on very solemn occasions such as the recent one at the Katholikentag in Berlin. Also an encouraging sign was the meeting of the Inter-national Liaison Committee between the Roman Catholic Church and Judaism in Regensburg last year.

It is not just a question of correcting a false religious view of the Jewish people, which in the course of history was one of the causes that contributed to misunderstanding and persecution, but above all of the dialogue between the two religions which —

with Islam — gave the world faith in the One, ineffable God who speaks to us, and which desire to serve Him on behalf of the whole world.

The first dimension of this dialogue, that is, the meeting between the people of God of the Old Covenant, never revoked by God (cf. *Rm* 11:29), and that of the New Covenant, is at the same time a dialogue within our Church, that is to say, between the first and the second part of her Bible. In this connection the directives for the application of the conciliar Declaration *Nostra Aetate* say: "The effort must be made to understand better everything in the Old Testament that has its own, permanent value ... since this value is not wiped out by the later interpretation of the New Testament, which, on the contrary, gave the Old Testament its full meaning, so chat it is a question rather of reciprocal enlightenment and explanation" (no. 11).

A second dimension of our dialogue — the true and central one — is the meeting between the present-day Christian Churches and the present-day people of the Covenant concluded with Moses. It is important here that Christians — so continue the postconciliar directives — should aim at understanding better the fundamental elements "of the religious tradition of Judaism," and learn what fundamental lines are essential for the religious reality lived by the Jews, according to their own understanding (Introduction). The way for this mutual knowledge is dialogue. l thank you, venerated brothers and sisters, for carrying it out, you too, with that "openness and breadth of spirit," with that "tact" and with that "prudence" which are recommended to us Catholics by the above-mentioned directives. A fruit of this dialogue and an indication for its fruitful continuation, is the declaration of German bishops quoted at the beginning "on the relationship between the Church and Judaism" in April of this year. It is my eager desire that this declaration should become the spiritual property of all Catholics in Germany!

I would also like to refer briefly to a third dimension of our dialogue. The German bishops dedicate the concluding chapter of their declaration to the tasks which we have in common. Jews and Christians, as children of Abraham, are called to be a blessing for the world (cf. *Gn* 12:2ff.), by committing themselves together for peace and justice among all men and peoples, with the fullness and depth that God himself intended us to have, and with the readiness for sacrifices that this high goal may demand. The more our meeting is imprinted with this sacred duty, the more it becomes a blessing also for ourselves.

4. In the light of this promise and call of Abraham's, I look with you to the destiny and role of your people among the peoples. I willingly pray with you for the fullness of Shalom for all your brothers, in nationality and in faith, and also for the land to which Jews look with particular veneration. Our century saw the first pilgrimage of a Pope to the Holy Land. In conclusion, I wish to repeat Paul VI's words on entering Jerusalem: "Implore with us, in your desire and in your prayer, respect and peace upon this unique land, visited by God! Let us pray here together for the grace of a real and deep brotherhood between all men, between all peoples!... May they who love you be blessed. Yes, may peace dwell in your walls, prosperity in your palaces. I pray for peace for you. I desire happiness for you" (cf. *Ps* 122:6–9).

May all peoples in Jerusalem soon be reconciled and blessed in Abraham! May He, the Ineffable, of whom His creation speaks to us: He, who does not force mankind to goodness, but guides it: He, who manifests himself in our fate and is silent; He, who chooses all of us as His people; may He guide us along His ways to His future!

Praised be His Name! Amen.

## COMMISSION FOR RELIGIOUS RELATIONS WITH THE JEWS:
### "Notes on the correct way to present the Jews and Judaism in preaching and catechesis in the Roman Catholic Church" (June 24, 1985)

*Preliminary Considerations*

On March 6th, 1982, Pope John Paul II told delegates of episcopal conferences and other experts, meeting in Rome to study relations between the Church and Judaism:

> ...you yourselves were concerned, during your sessions, with Catholic teaching and catechesis regarding Jews and Judaism.... We should aim, in this field, that Catholic teaching at its different levels, in catechesis to children and young people, presents Jews and Judaism, not only in an honest and objective manner,

free from prejudices and without any offences, but also with full awareness of the heritage common to Jews and Christians.

In this passage, so charged with meaning, the Holy Father plainly drew inspiration from the Council Declaration *Nostra Aetate*, 4, which says:

All should take pains, then, lest in catechetical instruction and in the preaching of God's Word they teach anything out of harmony with the truth of the Gospel and the spirit of Christ; as also from these words: Since the spiritual patrimony common to Christians and Jews is thus so great, this sacred Synod wishes to foster and recommend mutual understanding and respect....

In the same way, the *Guidelines and Suggestions for implementing the Conciliar declaration Nostra Aetate (no. 4)* ends its chapter III, entitled "Teaching and education," which lists a number of practical things to be done, with this recommendation:

Information concerning these questions is important at all levels of Christian instruction and education. Among sources of information, special attention should be paid to the following:

— catechisms and religious textbooks;

— history books;

— the mass media (press, radio, cinema, television).

The effective use of these means presupposes the thorough formation of instructors and educators in training schools, seminaries and universities" (*AAS* 77 [1975] 73).

The paragraphs which follow are intended to serve this purpose.

## I. Religious Teaching and Judaism

1. In *Nostra Aetate*, 4, the Council speaks of the "spiritual bonds linking" Jews and Christians and of the "great spiritual patrimony" common to both and it further asserts that "the Church of Christ acknowledges that, according to the mystery of God's saving design, the beginning of her faith and her election are already found among the patriarchs, Moses and the prophets."

2. Because of the unique relations that exist between Christianity and Judaism "linked together at the very level of their identity" (John Paul II, 6th March, 1982) — relations "founded

on the design of the God of the Covenant" (*ibid.*), the Jews and Judaism should not occupy an occasional and marginal place in catechesis: their presence there is essential and should be organically integrated.

3. This concern for Judaism in Catholic teaching has not merely a historical or archeological foundation. As the Holy Father said in the speech already quoted, after he had again mentioned the "common patrimony" of the Church and Judaism as "considerable": "To assess it carefully in itself and with due awareness of the faith and religious life of the Jewish people *as they are professed and practiced still today,* can greatly help us to understand better certain aspects of the life of the Church" (underlining added). It is a question then of *pastoral* concern for a still living reality closely related to the Church. The Holy Father has stated this permanent reality of the Jewish people in a remarkable theological formula, in his allocution to the Jewish community of West Germany at Mainz, on November 17th, 1980: " ... the people of God of the Old Covenant, which has never been revoked. ... "

4. Here we should recall the passage in which the *Guidelines and Suggestions,* 1, tried to define the fundamental condition of dialogue: "respect for the other as he is," knowledge of the "basic components of the religious tradition of Judaism" and again learning "by what essential traits the Jews define themselves in the light of their own religious experience" (*Introd.*).

5. The singular character and the difficulty of Christian teaching about Jews and Judaism lies in this, that it needs to balance a number of pairs of ideas which express the relation between the two economies of the Old and New Testament:

Promise and Fulfilment

Continuity and Newness

Singularity and Universality

Uniqueness and Exemplary Nature.

This means that the theologian and the catechist who deals with the subject needs to show in his practice of teaching that:

— promise and fulfilment throw light on each other;

— newness ties in a metamorphosis of what was there before;

— the singularity of the people of the Old Testament is not exclusive and is open, in the divine vision, to a universal extension;

— the uniqueness of the Jewish people is meant to have the force of an example.

6. Finally, "work that is of poor quality and lacking in precision would be extremely detrimental" to Judaeo-Christian dialogue (John Paul II, speech of March 6th, 1982). But it would be above all detrimental — since we are talking of teaching and education — to Christian identity (*ibid.*).

7. "In virtue of her divine mission, the Church" which is to be "the all-embracing means of salvation" in which alone "the fullness of the means of salvation can be obtained" (*(Unitatis Redintegratio,* 3), "must of her nature proclaim Jesus Christ to the world" (cf. *Guidelines and Suggestions,* I). Indeed we believe that it is through Him that we go to the Father (cf. *Jn* 14:6) "and this is eternal life, that they know Thee the only true God and Jesus Christ whom Thou hast sent" (*Jn* 17:3).

Jesus affirms (*ibid.* 10:16) that "there shall be one flock and one shepherd." Church and Judaism cannot then be seen as two parallel ways of salvation and the Church must witness to Christ as the Redeemer for all, "while maintaining the strictest respect for religious liberty in line with the teaching of the Second Vatican Council (Declaration *Dignitatis Humanae*" (Guidelines and Suggestions, 1).

8. The urgency and importance of precise, objective and rigorously accurate teaching on Judaism for our faithful follows too from the danger of anti-Semitism which is always ready to reappear under different guises. The question is not merely to uproot from among the faithful the remains of anti-Semitism still to be found here and there, but much rather to arouse in them, through educational work, an exact knowledge of the wholly unique "bond" (*Nostra Aetate,* 4) which joins us as a Church to the Jews and to Judaism. In this way, they would learn to appreciate and love the latter, who have been chosen by God to prepare the coming of Christ and have preserved everything that was progressively revealed and given in the course of that preparation, notwithstanding their difficulty in recognizing in Him their Messiah.

## II. Relations Between the Old and New Testament[1]

1. Our aim should be to show the unity of Biblical Revelation (O.T. and N.T.) and of the divine plan, before speaking of each historical event, so as to stress that particular events have meaning when seen in history as a whole — from creation to fulfilment. This history concerns the whole human race and especially believers. Thus the definitive meaning of the election of Israel does not become clear except in the light of the complete fulfilment (*Rm* 9–11) and election in Jesus Christ is still better understood with reference to the announcement and the promise (cf. *Heb* 4:1–11).

2. We are dealing with singular happenings which concern a singular nation but are destined, in the sight of God who reveals His purpose, to take on universal and exemplary significance.

The aim is moreover to present the events of the Old Testament not as concerning only the Jews but also as touching us personally. Abraham is truly the father of our faith (cf. *Rm* 4:11–12; Roman Canon: *patriarchae nostri Abrahae*). And it is said (*1 Co* 10:1): "*Our* fathers were all under the cloud, and all passed through the sea." The patriarchs, prophets and other personalities of the Old Testament have been venerated and always will be venerated as saints in the liturgical tradition of the Oriental Church as also of the Latin Church.

3. From the unity of the divine plan derives the problem of the relation between the Old and New Testaments. The Church already from apostolic times (cf. *I Co* 10:11; *Heb* 10:1) and then constantly in tradition resolved this problem by means of typology, which emphasises the primordial value that the Old Testament must have in the Christian view. Typology, however, makes many people uneasy and is perhaps the sign of a problem unresolved.

4. Hence, in using typology, the teaching and practice which we have received from the Liturgy and from the Fathers of the Church, we should be careful to avoid any transition from the Old to the New Testament which might seem merely a rupture. The Church, in the spontaneity of the Spirit which animates her,

---

1. We continue to use the expression *Old Testament* because it is traditional (cf. already 2 *Co* 3:14) but also because "Old" does not mean "out of date" or "outworn." In any case, it is the *permanent* value of the O.T. as a source of Christian Revelation that is emphasised here (cf. *Dei Verbum*, 3).

has vigorously condemned the attitude of Marcion[2] and always opposed his dualism.

5. It should also be emphasised that typological interpretation consists in reading the Old Testament as preparation and, in certain aspects, outline and foreshadowing of the New (cf., e.g., *Heb* 5:5–10, etc.). Christ is henceforth the key and point of reference to the Scriptures: "the rock *was* Christ" (*1 Co* 10:4).

6. It is true then, and should be stressed, that the Church and Christians read the Old Testament in the light of the event of the dead and risen Christ and that on these grounds there is a Christian reading of the Old Testament which does not necessarily coincide with the Jewish reading. Thus Christian identity and Jewish identity should be carefully distinguished in their respective reading of the Bible. But this detracts nothing from the value of the Old Testament in the Church and does nothing to hinder Christians from profiting discerningly from the traditions of Jewish reading.

7. Typological reading only manifests the unfathomable riches of the Old Testament, its inexhaustible content and the mystery of which it is full, and should not lead us to forget that it retains its own value as Revelation that the New Testament often does no more than resume (cf. *Mk* 12:29–31). Moreover, the New Testament itself demands to be read in the light of the Old. Primitive Christian catechesis constantly had recourse to this (cf., e.g., *1 Co* 5:6–8; 10:1–11).

8. Typology further signifies reaching towards the accomplishment of the divine plan, when "God will be all in all" (*1 Cor* 15:28). This holds true also for the Church which, realised already in Christ, yet awaits its definitive perfecting as the Body of Christ. The fact that the Body of Christ is still tending towards its full stature (cf. *Ep* 4:12–19) takes nothing from the value of being a Christian. So also the calling of the patriarchs and the Exodus from Egypt do not lose their importance and value in God's design from being at the same time intermediate stages (cf., e.g., *Nostra Aetate*, 4).

9. The Exodus, for example, represents an experience of salvation and liberation that is not complete in itself, but has in it, over and above its own meaning, the capacity to be developed further.

---

2. A man of gnostic tendency who in the second century rejected the Old Testament and part of the New as the work of an evil god, a demiurge. The Church reacted strongly against this heresy (cf. Irenaeus).

Salvation and liberation are already accomplished in Christ and gradually realised by the sacraments in the Church. This makes way for the fulfilment of God's design, which awaits its final consummation with the return of Jesus as Messiah, for which we pray each day. The Kingdom, for the coming of which we also pray each day, will be finally established. With salvation and liberation the elect and the whole of Creation will be transformed in Christ (*Rm* 8:19–23).

10. Furthermore, in underlining the eschatological dimension of Christianity we shall reach a greater awareness that the people of God of the Old and the New Testament are tending towards a like end in the future: the coming or return of the Messiah — even if they start from two different points of view. It is more clearly understood that the person of the Messiah is not only a point of division for the people of God but also a point of convergence (cf. *Sussidi per l'ecumenismo* of the diocese of Rome, n. 140). Thus it can be said that Jews and Christians meet in a comparable hope, rounded on the same promise made to Abraham (cf. *Gn* 12:1–3; *Heb* 6:13–18).

11. Attentive to the same God who has spoken, hanging on the same word, we have to witness to one same memory and one common hope in Him who is the master of history. We must also accept our responsibility to prepare the world for the coming of the Messiah by working together for social justice, respect for the rights of persons and nations and for social and international reconciliation. To this we are driven, Jews and Christians, by the command to love our neighbour, by a common hope for the Kingdom of God and by the great heritage of the Prophets. Transmitted soon enough by catechesis, such a conception would teach young Christians in a practical way to cooperate with Jews, going beyond simple dialogue (cf. *Guidelines*, IV).

### III. Jewish Roots of Christianity

12. Jesus was and always remained a Jew, his ministry was deliberately limited the lost sheep of the house of Israel" (*Mt* 15:24). Jesus is fully a man of his time, and of his environment — the Jewish Palestinian one of the first century, the anxieties and hopes of which he shared. This cannot but underline both the reality of the Incarnation and the very meaning of the history of salvation, as it has been revealed in the Bible (cf. *Rm* 1:3–4; *Ga* 4:4–5).

13. Jesus' relations with biblical law and its more or less traditional interpretations are undoubtedly complex and he showed great liberty towards it (cf. the "antitheses" of the Sermon on the Mount: *Mt* 5:21–48, bearing in mind the exegetical difficulties; his attitude to rigorous observance of the Sabbath: *Mk* 3:1–6, etc.).

But there is no doubt that he wished to submit himself to the law (cf. *Ga* 4:4), that he was circumcised and presented in the Temple like any Jew of his time (cf. *Lk* 2:21, 22–24), that he was trained in the law's observance. He extolled respect for it (cf. *Mt* 5:17–20) and invited obedience to it (cf. *Mt* 8:4). The rhythm of his life was marked by observance of pilgrimages on great feasts, even from his infancy (cf. *Lk* 2:41–50; *Jn* 2:13; 7–10, etc.). The importance of the cycle of the Jewish feasts has been frequently underlined in the Gospel of John (cf. 2:13; 5:1; 7:2.10.37; 10:22; 12:1; 13:1; 18:28; 19:42, etc.).

14. It should be noted also that Jesus often taught in the Synagogues (cf. *Mt* 4:23; 9:35; *Lk* 4:15–18; *Jn* 18:20, etc.) and in the Temple (cf. *Jn* 18:20, etc.), which he frequented as did the disciples even after the Resurrection (cf., e.g., *Ac* 2:46; 3:1; 21:26, etc.). He wished to put in the context of synagogue worship the proclamation of his Messiahship (cf. *Lk* 4:16–21). But above all he wished to achieve the supreme act of the gift of himself in the setting of the domestic liturgy of the Passover, or at least of the paschal festivity (cf. *Mk* 14:1.12 and parallels; *Jn* 18:28). This also allows of a better understanding of the "memorial" character of the Eucharist.

15. Thus the Son of God is incarnate in a people and a human family (cf. *Ga* 4:4; *Rm* 9:5). This takes away nothing, quite the contrary, from the fact that he was born for all men (Jewish shepherds and pagan wise men are found at his crib: *Lk* 2:8–20; *Mt* 2:1–12) and died for all men (at the foot of the cross there are Jews, among them Mary and John: *Jn* 19:25–27, and pagans like the centurion: *Mk* 15:39 and parallels). Thus he made two peoples one in his flesh (cf. *Ep* 2:14–17). This explains why with the *Ecclesia ex gentibus* we have, in Palestine and elsewhere, an *Ecclesia ex circumcisione*, of which *Eusebius* for example speaks (*H.E.*, IV, 5).

16. His relations with the Pharisees were not always or wholly polemical. there are many proofs:

— It is Pharisees who warn Jesus of the risks he is running *(Lk* 13:31);

— Some Pharisees are praised — e.g., "the scribe" of *Mk* 12:34;

— Jesus eats with Pharisees *(Lk* 7:36; 14:1).

17. Jesus shares, with the majority of Palestinian Jews of that time, some pharisaic doctrines: the resurrection of the body; forms of piety, like aims-giving, prayer, fasting (cf. *Mt* 6:1–18) and the liturgical practice of addressing God as Father; the priority of the commandment to love God and our neighbour (cf. *Mk* 12:28–34). This is so also with Paul (cf. *Ac* 23:8), who always considered his membership of the Pharisees as a title of honour (cf. *ibid.*, 23:6; 26:5; *Ph* 3:5).

18. Paul also, like Jesus himself, used methods of reading and interpreting Scripture and of teaching his disciples which were common to the Pharisees of their time. This applies to the use of parables in Jesus' ministry, as also to the method of Jesus and Paul of supporting a conclusion with a quotation from Scripture.

19. It is noteworthy too that the Pharisees are not mentioned in accounts of the Passion. Gamaliel (*Ac* 5:34–39) defends the apostles in a meeting of the Sanhedrin. An exclusively negative picture of the Pharisees is likely to be inaccurate and unjust (cf. *Guidelines*, note 1; cf. *AAS*, p. 76). If in the Gospel and elsewhere in the New Testament there are all sorts of unfavourable references to the Pharisees, they should be seen against the background of a complex and diversified movement. Criticisms of various types of Pharisees are moreover not lacking in rabbinical sources (cf. the *Babylonian Talmud*, the *Sotah* treatise 22b, etc.). "Phariseeism" in the pejorative sense can be rife in any religion. It may also be stressed that, if Jesus shows himself severe towards the Pharisees, it is because he is closer to them than to other contemporary Jewish groups (cf. *supra* no. 17).

20. All this should help us to understand better what St. Paul says (*Rm* 11:16ff) about the "root" and the "branches." The Church and Christianity, for all their novelty, find their origin in the Jewish milieu of the first century of our era, and more deeply still in the "design of God" (*Nostra Aetate*, 4), realised in the Patriarchs, Moses and the Prophets (*ibid.*), down to its consummation in Christ Jesus.

## IV. The Jews in the New Testament

21. The *Guidelines* already say (note 1) that "the formula 'the Jews' sometimes, according to the context, means 'the leaders of the Jews' or 'the adversaries of Jesus,' terms which express better

the thought of the evangelist and avoid appearing to arraign the Jewish people as such."

An objective presentation of the role of the Jewish people in the New Testament should take account of these various facts:

*A)* The Gospels are the outcome of long and complicated editorial work. The dogmatic constitution *Dei Verbum,* following the Pontifical Biblical Commission's Instruction *Sancta Mater Ecclesia,* distinguished three stages: "The sacred authors wrote the four Gospels, selecting some things from the many which had been handed on by word of mouth or in writing, reducing some of them to a synthesis, explicating some things in view of the situation of their Churches, and preserving the form of proclamation, but always in such fashion that they told us the honest truth about Jesus" (no. 19).

Hence it cannot be ruled out that some references hostile or less than favourable to the Jews have their historical context in conflicts between the nascent Church and the Jewish community. Certain controversies reflect Christian-Jewish relations long after the time of Jesus.

To establish this is of capital importance if we wish to bring out the meaning of certain Gospel texts for the Christians of today.

All this should be taken into account when preparing catechesis and homilies for the last weeks of Lent and Holy Week (cf. already *Guidelines* II, and now also *Sussidi per l'ecumenismo nella diocesi di Roma,* 1982, 144b).

*B)* It is clear on the other hand that there were conflicts between Jesus and certain categories of Jews of his time, among them Pharisees, from the beginning of his ministry (cf. *Mk* 2:1–11.24; 3:6, etc.).

*C)* There is moreover the sad fact that the majority of the Jewish people and its authorities did not believe in Jesus — a fact not merely of history but of theological bearing, of which St. Paul tries hard to plumb the meaning (*Rm* chap. 9–11).

*D)* This fact, accentuated as the Christian mission developed, especially among the pagans, led inevitably to a rupture between Judaism and the young Church, now irreducibly separated and divergent in faith, and this stage of affairs is reflected in the texts of the New Testament and particularly in the Gospels. There is no question of playing down or glossing over this rupture; that could only prejudice the identity of either side. Nevertheless it certainly does not cancel the spiritual "bond" of which the Council speaks ((*Nostra Aetate,* 4) and which we propose to dwell on here.

E) Reflecting on this in the light of Scripture, notably of the chapters cited from the epistle to the Romans, Christians should never forget that the faith is a free gift of God (cf. *Rm* 9:12) and that we should never judge the consciences of others. St. Paul's exhortation "do not boast" in your attitude to "the root" (*Rm* 11:18) has its full point here.

F) There is no putting the Jews who knew Jesus and did not believe in him, or those who opposed the preaching of the apostles, on the same plane with Jews who came after or those of today. If the responsibility of the former remains a mystery hidden with God (cf. *Rm* 11:25), the latter are in an entirely different situation. Vatican II in the declaration on *Religious Liberty* teaches that "all men are to be immune from coercion...in such wise that in matters religious no one is to be forced to act in a manner contrary to his own beliefs. Nor...restrained from acting in accordance with his own beliefs" (no. 2). This is one of the bases — proclaimed by the Council-on which Judaeo-Christian dialogue rests.

22. The delicate question of responsibility for the death of Christ must be looked at from the standpoint of the conciliar declaration *Nostra Aetate,* 4 and of *Guidelines and Suggestions* (§III): "What happened in (Christ's) passion cannot be blamed upon all the Jews then living without distinction nor upon the Jews of today," especially since "authorities of the Jews and those who followed their lead pressed for the death of Christ." Again, further on: "Christ in his boundless love freely underwent his passion and death because of the sins of all men, so that all might attain salvation" (*Nostra Aetate,* 4). The *Catechism* of the Council of Trent teaches that Christian sinners are more to blame for the death of Christ than those few Jews who brought it about — they indeed "knew not what they did" (cf. *Lk* 23:34) and we know it only too well (Pars I, caput V, Quaest. XI). In the same way and for the same reason, "the Jews should not be presented as repudiated or cursed by God, as if such views followed from the holy Scriptures" (*Nostra Aetate,* 4), even though it is true that "the Church is the new people of God" (*ibid.*).

## V. The Liturgy

23. Jews and Christians find in the Bible the very substance of their liturgy: for the proclamation of God's word, response to it, prayer of praise and intercession for the living and the dead, recourse to the divine mercy. The Liturgy of the word in its own structure originates in Judaism. The prayer of Hours and other liturgical texts and formularies have their parallels in Judaism as do the very formulas of our most venerable prayers, among them the Our Father. The eucharistic prayers also draw inspiration from models in the Jewish tradition. As John Paul II said (Allocution of March 6th, 1982): "... the faith and religious life of the Jewish people as they are professed and practised still today, can greatly help us to understand better certain aspects of the life of the Church. Such is the case of liturgy...."

24. This is particularly evident in the great feasts of the liturgical year, like the Passover. Christians and Jews celebrate the Passover: the Jews, the historic Passover looking towards the future; the Christians, the Passover accomplished in the death and resurrection of Christ, although still in expectation of the final consummation (cf. *supra* no. 9). It is still the "memorial" which comes to us from the Jewish tradition, with a specific content different in each case. On either side, however, there is a like dynamism: for Christians it gives meaning to the eucharistic celebration (cf. the antiphon *O sacrum convivium*), a paschal celebration and as such a making present of the past, but experienced in the expectation of what is to come.

## VI. Judaism and Christianity in History

25. The history of Israel did not end in 70 A.D. (cf. *Guidelines*, II). It continued, especially in a numerous Diaspora which allowed Israel to carry to the whole world a witness — often heroic — of its fidelity to the one God and to "exalt Him in the presence of all the living" (*Tobit* 13:4), while preserving the memory of the land of their forefathers at the heart of their hope (Passover *Seder*).

Christians are invited to understand this religious attachment which finds its roots in Biblical tradition, without however making their own any particular religious interpretation of this relationship (cf. *Declaration* of the US Conference of Catholic Bishops, November 20, 1975).

The existence of the State of Israel and its political options should be envisaged not in a perspective which is in itself religious, but in their reference to the common principles of international law.

The permanence of Israel (while so many ancient peoples have disappeared without trace) is a historic fact and a sign to be interpreted within God's design. We must in any case rid ourselves of the traditional idea of a people *punished,* preserved as a *living argument* for Christian apologetic. It remains a chosen people, "the pure olive on which were grafted the branches of the wild olive which are the gentiles" (John Paul II, 6th March, 1982, alluding to *Rm* 11:17–24). We must remember how much the balance of relations between Jews and Christians over two thousand years has been negative. We must remind ourselves how the permanence of Israel is accompanied by a continuous spiritual fecundity, in the rabbinical period, in the Middle Ages and in modern times, taking its start from a patrimony which we long shared, so much so that "the faith and religious life of the Jewish people as they are professed and practised still today, can greatly help us to understand better certain aspects of the life of the Church" (John Paul II, March 6th, 1982). Catechesis should on the other hand help in understanding the meaning for the Jews of the extermination during the years 1939–1945, and its consequences.

26. Education and catechesis should concern themselves with the problem of racism, still active in different forms of anti-Semitism. The Council presented it thus: "Moreover, (the Church) mindful of her common patrimony with the Jews and motivated by the Gospel's spiritual love and by no political considerations, deplores the hatred, persecutions and displays of anti-Semitism directed against the Jews at any time and from any source" (*Nostra Aetate,* 4). The *Guidelines* comment: "The spiritual bonds and historical links binding the Church to Judaism condemn (as opposed to the very spirit of Christianity) all forms of anti-Semitism and discrimination, which in any case the dignity of the human person alone would suffice to condemn" (*Guidelines,* Preamble).

## Conclusion

27. Religious teaching, catechesis and preaching should be a preparation not only for objectivity, justice, tolerance but also for understanding and dialogue. Our two traditions are so related

that they cannot ignore each other. Mutual knowledge must be encouraged at every level. There is evident in particular a painful ignorance of the history and traditions of Judaism, of which only negative aspects and often caricature seem to form part of the stock ideas of many Christians.

That is what these notes aim to remedy. This would mean that the Council text and *Guidelines and Suggestions* would be more easily and faithfully put into practice.

JOHANNES Cardinal WILLEBRANDS
*President*

PIERRE DUPREY
*Vice-President*

JORGE MEJÍA
*Secretary*

## JOHN PAUL II:
*Allocution in the Great Roman Synagogue* (April 13, 1986)

Dear Chief Rabbi of the Jewish community in Rome,
Dear President of the Union of Italian Jewish communities,
Dear President of the community in Rome,
Dear Rabbis,
Dear Jewish and Christian friends and brethren taking part in this historic celebration,

1. First of all, I would like, together with you, to give thanks and praise to the Lord who stretched out the heavens and laid the foundations of the earth (cf. *Is* 51:16) and who chose Abraham in order to make him father of a multitude of children, as numerous "as the stars of heaven and as the sand which is on the seashore" (*Gn* 22:17; cf. *Is* 15:5) — to give thanks and praise to Him because it has been His good pleasure, in the mystery of His Providence, that this evening there should be a meeting in this your "Major Temple" between the Jewish community that has been living in this city since the times of the ancient Romans and the Bishop of Rome and universal Pastor of the Catholic Church.

I likewise feel it is my duty to thank the Chief Rabbi, Professor Elio Toaff, who from the first moment accepted with joy the idea that I should make this visit, and who is now receiving me with great openness of heart and a profound sense of hospitality; and in addition to him I also thank all those members of the Jewish community in Rome who have made this meeting possible and who in so many ways have worked to ensure that it should be at one and the same time a reality and a symbol.

> Many thanks therefore to you all.
> *Toda râbbâ* (Many thanks).

2. In the light of the Word of God that has just been proclaimed and that lives for ever (cf. *Is* 30:8), I would like us to reflect together, in the presence of the Holy One-may He be blessed! (as your liturgy says) — on the fact and the significance of this meeting between the Bishop of Rome, the Pope, and the Jewish community that lives and works in this city which is so dear to you and to me.

I had been thinking of this visit for a long time. In fact, the Chief Rabbi was kind enough to come and see me, in February 1981, when I paid a pastoral visit to the nearby Parish of San Carlo ai Catinari. In addition, a number of you have been more than once to the Vatican, on the occasion of the numerous audiences that I have been able to have with representatives of Italian and world Jewry, and still earlier, in the time of my predecessors Paul VI, John XXIII and Pius XII. I am likewise well aware that the Chief Rabbi. on the night before the death of Pope John, did not hesitate to go to Saint Peter's Square; and accompanied by members of the Jewish faithful, he mingled with the crowd of Catholics and other Christians, in order to pray and keep vigil, as it were bearing witness, in a silent but very effective way, to the greatness of soul of that Pontiff, who was open to all people without distinction, and in particular to the Jewish brethren.

The heritage that I would now like to take up is precisely that of Pope John, who on one occasion, as he passed by here — as the Chief Rabbi has just mentioned — stopped the car so that he could bless the crowd of Jews who were coming out of this very Temple. And I would like to take up his heritage at this very moment, when I find myself not just outside, but, thanks to your generous hospitality, inside the Synagogue of Rome.

3. This gathering in a way brings to a close, after the Pontificate of John XXIII and the Second Vatican Council, a long

period which we must not tire of reflecting upon in order to draw from it the appropriate lessons. Certainly, we cannot and should not forget that the historical circumstances of the past were very different from those that have laboriously matured over the centuries. The general acceptance of a legitimate plurality on the social, civil and religious levels has been arrived at with great difficulty. Nevertheless, a consideration of centuries-long cultural conditioning could not prevent us from recognizing that the acts of discrimination, unjustified limitation of religious freedom, oppression also on the level of civil freedom in regard to the Jews were, from an objective point of view, gravely deplorable manifestations. Yes, once again, through myself, the Church, in the words of the well-known Declaration *Nostra Aetate* (no. 4), "deplores the hatred, persecutions and displays of anti-Semitism directed against the Jews at any time and by anyone"; I repeat: "by anyone."

I would like once more to express a word of abhorrence for the genocide decreed against the Jewish people during the last War, which led to the *holocaust* of millions of innocent victims.

When I visited on 7 June 1979 the concentration camp at Auschwitz and prayed for the many victims from various nations, I paused in particular before the memorial stone with the inscription in Hebrew and thus manifested the sentiments of my heart: "This inscription stirs the memory of the People whose sons and daughters were destined to total extermination. This People has its origin in Abraham, who is our father in faith" (cf. *Rm* 4:12), as Paul of Tarsus expressed it. Precisely this people, which received from God the commandment: "Thou shalt not kill," has experienced in itself to a particular degree what killing means. Before this inscription it is not permissible for anyone to pass by with indifference" (*Insegnamenti*, 1979, p. 1484).

The Jewish community of Rome too paid a high price in blood.

And it was surely a significant gesture that in those dark years of racial persecution the doors of our religious houses, of our churches, of the Roman Seminary, of buildings belonging to the Holy See and of Vatican City itself were thrown open to offer refuge and safety to so many Jews of Rome being hunted by their persecutors.

4. Today's visit is meant to make a decisive contribution to the consolidation of the good relations between our two commu-

nities, in imitation of the example of so many men and women who have worked and who are still working today, on both sides, to overcome old prejudices and to secure ever wider and fuller recognition of that "bond" and that "common spiritual patrimony" that exists between Jews and Christians.

This is the hope expressed in the fourth paragraph of the Council's Declaration *Nostra Aetate,* which I have just mentioned, on the relationship of the Church to non-Christian religions. The decisive turning-point in relations between the Catholic Church and Judaism, and with individual Jews, was occasioned by this brief but incisive paragraph.

We are all aware that, among the riches of this paragraph no. 4 of *Nostra Aetate, three points* are especially relevant. I would like to underline them here, before you, in this truly unique circumstance.

The *first* is that the Church of Christ discovers her "bond" with Judaism by "searching into her own mystery" (cf. *Nostra Aetate, ibid.*) The Jewish religion is not "extrinsic" to us, but in a certain way is "intrinsic" to our own religion. With Judaism therefore we have a relationship which we do not have with any other religion. You are our dearly beloved brothers and, in a certain way, it could be said that you are our eider brothers.

The *second* point noted by the Council is that no ancestral or collective blame can be imputed to the Jews as a people for "what happened in Christ's passion" (cf. *Nostra Aetate, ibid.*) Not indiscriminately to the Jews of that time, nor to those who came afterwards, nor to those of today. So any alleged theological justification for discriminatory measures or, worse still, for acts of persecution is unfounded. The Lord will judge each one "according to his own works," Jews and Christians alike (cf. *Rm* 2:6).

The *third* point that I would like to emphasize in the Council's Declaration is a consequence of the second. Notwithstanding the Church's awareness of her own identity, it is not lawful to say that the Jews are "repudiated or cursed," as if this were taught or could be deduced from the Sacred Scriptures of the Old or the New Testament (cf. *Nostra Aetate, ibid.*). Indeed, the Council had already said in this same text of *Nostra Aetate,* but also in the Dogmatic Constitution *Lumen Gentium,* no. 16, referring to Saint Paul in the Letter to the Romans (11:28–29), that the Jews are beloved of God, who has called them with an irrevocable calling.

5. On these convictions rest our present relations. On the occasion of this visit to your Synagogue, I wish to reaffirm them and to proclaim them in their perennial value.

For this is the meaning which is to be attributed to my visit to you, to the Jews of Rome.

It is not of course because the differences between us have now been overcome that I have come among you. We know well that this is not so.

First of all, each of our religions, in the full awareness of the many bonds which unite them to each other, and in the first place that "bond" which the Council spoke of, wishes to be recognized and respected in its own identity, beyond any syncretism and any ambiguous appropriation.

Furthermore, it is necessary to say that the path undertaken is still at the beginning, and therefore a considerable amount of time will still be needed, notwithstanding the great efforts already made on both sides, to remove all forms of prejudice, even subtle ones, to readjust every manner of self-expression and therefore to present always and everywhere, to ourselves and to others, the true face of the Jews and of Judaism, as likewise of Christians and of Christianity, and this at every level of outlook, teaching and communication.

In this regard, I would like to remind my brothers and sisters of the Catholic Church, also those living in Rome, of the fact that the guidelines for implementing the Council in this precise field are already available to everyone in the two documents published respectively in 1974 and in 1985 by the Holy See's Commission for Religious Relations with Judaism. It is only a question of studying them carefully, of immersing oneself in their teachings and of putting them into practice.

Perhaps there still remain between us difficulties of the practical order waiting to be overcome on the level of fraternal relations: these are the result of centuries of mutual misunderstanding, and also of different positions and attitudes, not easily settled, in complex and important matters.

No one is unaware that the fundamental difference from the very beginning has been the attachment of us Catholics to the person and teaching of Jesus of Nazareth, a son of your People, from which were also born the Virgin Mary, the Apostles who were the "foundations and pillars of the Church" and the greater part of the first Christian community. But this attachment is located in the order of faith, that is to say in the free assent of the mind and heart guided by the Spirit, and it can never be the object of exterior pressure, in one sense or the other. This is the reason why we wish to deepen dialogue in loyalty and friendship, in respect for one another's intimate convictions, taking as a fundamental basis the elements of the Revelation which we have in common, as a "great spiritual patrimony" (cf. *Nostra Aetate, 4*).

6. It must be said, then, that the ways opened for our collaboration, in the light of our common heritage drawn from the Law and the Prophets, are various and important. We wish to recall first of all a collaboration in favour of man, his life from concept[on until natural death, his dignity, his freedom, his rights, his self-development in a society which is not hostile but friendly and favourable, where justice reigns and where, in this nation, on the various continents and throughout the world, it is peace that rules, the *shalom* hoped for by the lawmakers, prophets and wise men of Israel.

More in general, there is the problem of morality, the great field of individual and social ethics. We are all aware of how acute the crisis is on this point in the age in which we are living. In a society which is often lost in agnosticism and individualism and which is suffering the bitter consequences of selfishness and violence, Jews and Christians are the trustees and witnesses of an ethic marked by the Ten Commandments, in the observance of which man finds his truth and freedom. To promote a common reflection and collaboration on this point is one of the great duties of the hour.

And finally I wish to address a thought to this City in which there live side by side the Catholic community with its Bishop, and the Jewish community with its authorities and its Chief Rabbi.

Let this not be a mere "co-existence," a kind of juxtaposition, interspersed with limited and occasional meetings, but let it be animated by-fraternal love.

7. The problems of Rome are many. You know this well. Each one of us, in the light of that blessed heritage to which I alluded earlier, is conscious of an obligation to work together, at least to some degree, for their solution. Let us seek, as far as possible, to do so together; from this visit of mine and from the harmony and

serenity which we have attained may there flow forth a fresh and health-giving spring like the river that Ezekiel saw gushing from the eastern gate of the Temple of Jerusalem (cf. *Ez* 47:1ff.), which will help to heal the wounds from which Rome is suffering.

In doing this, I venture to say, we shall each be faithful to our most sacred commitments, and also to that which most profoundly unites and gathers us together: faith in the One God who "loves strangers and "renders justice to the orphan and the widow" (cf. *Dt* 10:18), commanding us too to love and help them (cf. *ibid.*, and *Lv* 19:18.34). Christians have learned this desire of the Lord from the Torah, which you here venerate, and from Jesus, who took to its extreme consequences the love demanded by the Torah.

8. All that remains for me now, as at the beginning of my address, is to turn my eyes and my mind to the Lord, to thank Him and praise Him for this joyful meeting and for the good things which are already flowing from it, for the rediscovered brotherhood and for the new and more profound understanding between us here in Rome, and between the Church and Judaism everywhere, in every country, for the benefit of all.

Therefore I would like to say with the Psalmist, in his original language which is also your own inheritance:

> Hodû la-Adonai ki tob
> ki le-olam hasdô
> yomar-na Yisrael
> ki le-olam hasdô
> yomerû-na yir'è Adonai
> ki le-olam hasdô (*Ps* 118:1–2.4).

> O give thanks to the Lord for He is good,
> His steadfast love endures for ever
> Let Israel say,
> His steadfast love endures for ever!
> Let those who fear the Lord say,
> "His steadfast love endures for ever!"

# APPENDIX C

# Documents of the National Conference of Catholic Bishops

## 1975 Statement on Catholic-Jewish Relations

Ten years have passed since the Second Vatican promulgated its statement on the Jewish people *Nostra Aetate,* no. 4). This decade has been a period unique in Catholic-Jewish relations. The vantage point ten years later provides a timely opportunity for the Church in the United States to recall, reaffirm reflect on the principles and teachings of the conciliar, and to evaluate their implementation in our country.

For this task we welcome the new *Guidelines and for Implementing Nostra Aetate,* no. 4 issued in January of this year by the Commission for Religious Relations with the Jews recently established the Holy See. And we are reminded of the still applicable very programs recommended by the *Guidelines for Catholic-Jewish Relations* which our National Conference of Catholic Bishops issued in 1967. We are gratified that the latter have been highly regarded, especially in the Jewish community, and that some of their recommendations anticipated portions of the new *Guidelines* of the Holy See and also of several diocesan documents.

These two documents, themselves fruits of *Nostra Aetate,* no. 4, elucidate the conciliar declaration, considerably extend its perspectives and broaden the paths it opened. Both are eloquent testimonies to the new horizons the Second Vatican Council succeeded in bringing into Catholic view.

These ten years make it clear that *Nostra Aetate,* no. 4 initiated a new era in Catholic-Jewish affairs. Calling for "fraternal dialogue and biblical studies" with Jews, it ended a centuries-long silence between Church and Synagogue. An age of dialogue was begun. Conversations between Catholics and Jews proliferated rapidly in many forms. Productive meetings took place on every level, from the highest intellectual exchanges to the most popular types of social gatherings, often referred to as "living room dialogues." Our own Bishops' Conference was among the first to form a national commission which sought to implement the Council document. Even before the close of the Second Vatican Council in 1965, the United States Bishops had decided to establish a commission in the National Conference of Catholic Bishops to promote Catholic-Jewish understanding, and in 1967 the first full-time Secretariat for Catholic-Jewish relations was in operation.

Since that time the Secretariat has maintained fruitful contact with the major groups within the Jewish community and has been in regular communication with the dioceses of the country. Many dioceses have followed the example of our Conference and have established Commissions or Secretariats for Jewish-Catholic relations. Numerous projects have been undertaken, including, for example, a careful and systematic analysis of Catholic teaching texts in order to eliminate offensive references to Jews and replace them with materials showing Judaism in a positive light. Numerous theological discussions have been undertaken and Catholic collaboration with the Jewish community has resulted in a variety of social action programs. We are pleased to observe that many of these initiatives have been emulated on the unofficial level by many individuals and groups across the country who have shown admirable sensitivity, dedication and expertise in promoting Catholic-Jewish amity.

We do not wish to convey the impression that all our problems are behind us. There still exist areas of disagreement and misunderstanding which create tensions in both communities. We hope that the difficulties can be resolved to some degree in amicable discussion. Certainly the Catholic view on aid to non-public schools should be the subject of serious dialogue and concern. We are pleased that this and other exchanges have already been held on important subjects of disagreement, and it is our hope that progress will be made in mutual understanding by furthering this dialogic method.

Recalling past centuries, invites a sobering evaluation of our progress and warns against becoming overconfident about an early end to remaining problems. Those were centuries replete with alienation, misunderstanding and hostility between Jews and Christians. While we rejoice that there are signs that anti-Semitism is declining in our country, conscience compels us to confront with candor the unhappy record of Jewish sufferings both past and present. We make our own the statement of *Nostra Aetate*, " ... for the sake of her common patrimony with the Jews, the Church decries hatred, persecutions, displays of anti-Semitism staged against Jews at whatever time in history and by whomsoever" and we reaffirm with the new Vatican *Guidelines* that "the spiritual bonds and historical links binding the Church to Judaism condemn (as opposed to the very spirit of Christianity) all forms of anti-Semitism...." We urge all in the Church who work in the area of education, whether in the seminary, the school or the pulpit, not only to avoid any presentation that might tend to disparage Jews or Judaism but also to emphasize those aspects of our faith which bear witness to our common patrimony and our spiritual ties with Jews.

Much of the alienation between Christian and Jew found its origins in a certain anti-Judaic theology which over the centuries has led not only to social friction with Jews but often to their oppression. One of the most hopeful developments in our time, powerfully assisted by *Nostra Aetate*, has been the decline of the old anti-Judaism and the reformation of Christian theological expositions of Judaism along more constructive lines.

The first major step in this direction was the repudiation of the charge that Jews were and are collectively guilty of the death of Christ. *Nostra Aetate* and the new *Guidelines* have definitely laid to rest this myth which has caused so much suffering to the Jewish people. There remains however the continuing task of ensuring that nothing which in any way approaches the notion of Jewish collective guilt should be found in any Catholic medium of expression or communication. Correctly viewed, the disappearance of the charge of collective guilt of Jews pertains as much to the purity of the Catholic faith as it does to the defense of Judaism.

The Council's rejection of this charge against Jews has been interpreted by some commentators as an "exoneration" of the Jewish people. Such a view of the matter still persists. The truth is that the Council acknowledged that the Jewish people never were, nor are they now, guilty of the death of Christ.

*Nostra Aetate* was a new beginning in Catholic-Jewish relations and, as with all beginnings, we are faced with the task of revising some traditional understandings and judgments. The brief suggestions of the Council document have been taken up by some theologians, but their implications for theological renewal have not yet been fully explored. We therefore make a few recommendations in line with two themes of the document: the Jewish origins of the Church and the thought of St. Paul.

Christians have not fully appreciated their Jewish roots. Early in Christian history a de-Judaizing process dulled our awareness of our Jewish beginnings. The Jewishness of Jesus, of his mother, his disciples, of the primitive Church, was lost from view. That Jesus was called Rabbi; that he was born, lived and died under the Law; that He and Peter and Paul worshipped in the Temple — these facts were blurred by the controversy that alienated Christians from the Synagogue. How Jewish the Church was toward mid-point of the first century is dramatically reflected in the description of the "Council of Jerusalem" (Acts Ch. 15). The question at issue was whether Gentile converts to the Church had to be circumcised and observe the Mosaic Law? The obligation to obey the Law was held so firmly by the Jewish Christians of that time that miraculous visions accorded to Peter and Cornelius (Acts Ch. 10) were needed to vindicate the contrary contention that Gentile Christians were not so obliged. By the third century, however, a de-Judaizing process had set in which tended to undervalue the Jewish origins of the Church, a tendency that has surfaced from time to time in devious ways throughout Christian history. Some catechists, homilists, and teachers still convey little appreciation of the Jewishness of that heritage and rich spirituality which we derive from Abraham, Moses, the prophets, the psalmists, and other spiritual giants of the Hebrew Scriptures.

Most essential concepts in the Christian creed grew at first in Judaic soil. Uprooted from that soil, these basic concepts cannot be perfectly understood. It is for reasons such as these that *Nostra Aetate* recommends joint "theological and biblical studies" with Jews. The Vatican *Guidelines* of 1975 encourage Catholic specialists to engage in new research into the relations of Judaism and Christianity and to seek out "collaboration with Jewish scholars." The renewal of Christian faith is the issue here, for renewal always entails to some extent a return to one's origins.

The Council document cites St. Paul, particularly in chapters 9 to 11 of his letter to the Romans. We find in these rediscovered, precious chapters Paul's love for his kinsmen and a firm basis for Christian reverence for the Jewish people. Admittedly, Paul's theology of Judaism has its more negative aspects; they have been adequately emphasized over the centuries in Catholic teaching. It would be well today to explore and emphasize the positive elements of Paul's thought that have received inadequate attention.

In these chapters Paul reveals his deep love of the Jewish people. He tells of his willingness to accept damnation itself for the sake of his kinsmen (9:3), even though he also expresses his painful disappointment and incomprehension at Israel's failure to accept Jesus as its Messiah. Crucial to an understanding of his admiration of the Jewish people and to a Christian understanding of their situation is the following text. Written at the midpoint of the first century, Paul refers to his "kinsmen according to the flesh who are Israelites, who have the adoption as sons, and the glory and the covenants and the legislation and the worship and the promises; who have the fathers, and from whom is the Christ according to the flesh" (9:3–5), thus making clear the continuing validity of Israel's call. Paul, moreover, insists that God has by no means rejected his people. "Is it possible that God has rejected his people? Of course not. I, an Israelite descended from Abraham through the tribe of Benjamin, could never agree that God has rejected his people, the people he chose specially long age" (11:1–2). What proof does Paul offer for the enduring validity of Israel's relationship to God even after the rounding of the Church? "God never takes back his gifts or revokes his choice" (11:29).

Paul warns fellow Christians against showing contempt for the Jewish people by reminding them that they (Christians) are wild branches grafted into the olive tree itself to share its life. "...Remember that you do not support the root: it is the root that supports you" (11:18). And he invites his listeners to a love of the Jews, since they are "still loved by God for the sake of their ancestors" (11:28).

In effect, we find in the Epistle to the Romans (Ch. 9–11) long-neglected passages which help us to construct a new and positive attitude toward the Jewish people. There is here a task incumbent on theologians, as yet hardly begun, to explore the continuing relationship of the Jewish people with God and their spiritual bonds with the New Covenant and the fulfillment of God's plan for both Church and Synagogue.

To revere only the ancient Jewish patriarchs and prophets is not enough. The all too common view of Judaism as a legalistic and decadent form of religion that lost all significance with the coming of Christ and all vitality after the destruction of the Temple has lingered on in the Christian centuries. The 1975 *Guidelines* put us on guard against such a view and urge us to see post-biblical Judaism as rich in religious values and worthy of our sincere respect and esteem. The *Guidelines* in fact discourage us from attempting to define the Jews in exclusively Christian terms, explicitly stating, "Dialogue demands respect for the other as he is" (Part 1). Again, "Christians must therefore strive to acquire a better knowledge of the basic components of the religious tradition of Judaism; they must strive to learn by what essential traits the Jews define themselves in the light of their own religious experience" (Introduction).

In dialogue with Christians, Jews have explained that they do not consider themselves as a church, a sect, or a denomination, as is the case among Christian communities, but rather as a peoplehood that is not solely racial, ethnic or religious, but in a sense a composite of all these. It is for such reasons that an overwhelming majority of Jews see themselves bound in one way or another to the land of Israel. Most Jews see this tie to the land as essential to their Jewishness. Whatever difficulties Christians may experience in sharing this view they should strive to understand this link between land and people which Jews have expressed in their writings and worship throughout two millennia as a longing for the homeland, holy Zion. Appreciation of this link is not to give assent to any particular religious interpretation of this bond. Nor is this affirmation meant to deny the legitimate rights of other parties in the region, or to adopt any political stance in the controversies over the Middle East, which lie beyond the purview of this statement.

On this tenth anniversary of *Nostra Aetate* we reaffirm our wholehearted commitment to the principles of that document as well as to the directives of the *Guidelines* of 1975. Aware of the magnitude of the task before us and of the excellence of the many practical guidelines and suggestions contained in the documents, we urge that special attention be given to the following exhortations:

1. That all dioceses, according to their needs and circumstances, create and support whatever instrument or agency is appropriate for carrying out the recommendations of *Nostra Aetate, no. 4,* the Vatican *Guidelines* of 1975 and the American Bishops' *Guidelines for Catholic-Jewish Relations* of 1967.

2. That homilists and liturgists pay special attention to the presentation and interpretation of scripture so as to promote among the Catholic people a genuine appreciation of the special place of the Jewish people as God's first-chosen in the history of salvation and in no way slight the honor and dignity that is theirs.

3. That Catholic scholars address themselves in a special way to the theological and scriptural issues raised by those documents which deal with the relationships of the Church with Judaism.

We are firm in our faith that the God of Abraham, Isaac and Jacob and He whom we consider Israel's fairest Son will sustain us in this holy endeavor.

## God's Mercy Endures Forever:
## Bishop's Committee on the Liturgy
## Guidelines on the Presentation of Jews and Judaism
## in Catholic Preaching (1988)

In the Fall of 1988, the Administrative Committee approved the document, *God's Mercy Endures Forever* as a statement of the Bishops' Committee on the Liturgy of the National Conference of Catholic Bishops. It is the first such official document devoted entirely to the liturgical implications of the reconciliation between the church and the Jewish people begun by the Second Vatican Council. It is reprinted here with permission of the USCC Office of Publishing and Promotion Services, and is available directly from them in individual orders or in bulk (Publication No. 247-0; Phone: 800-235-USCC). We include here also the bibliography of "Suggested Readings" recommended by the Bishops' Committee on the Liturgy.

*God's Mercy Endures Forever* draws in a remarkable way upon the scholarly sources represented in this volume, as well as upon the numerous official statements of the church mentioned in its "Documentation" section. It both reflects and refracts these rich materials, providing a focus for all that has been said above and, in the process, a vision for the future.

As such, it provides a fitting conclusion for this volume, as well as a trenchant summary of the challenges raised for us by our contributors.

## Preface

*Even in the twentieth century, the age of the Holocaust, the Shoah, the "Scouring Wind," God's mercy endures forever.*

*The Holocaust drew its fiery breath from the ancient, some times latent, but always persistent anti-Semitism which, over the centuries, found too large a place within the hearts of too many Christian men and women. Yet, since the Holocaust and since the Second Vatican Council, Christians have struggled to learn the reasons for such irrational and anti-Christian feelings against the special people for whom "God's mercy endures forever," to deal with those feelings, and to overcome them through knowledge, understanding, dialogue, and love.*

*For the past fifteen years, the Bishops' Committee on the Liturgy and its Secretariat have attempted to respond to the decree of* Nostra Aetate *and to the various documents issued by the Holy See's Commission for Religious Relations with the Jews, to see to it that our liturgical celebrations never again become occasions for that anti-Semitic or anti-Jewish sentiment that sometimes marred the liturgy in the past. Working with the Bishops' Committee for Ecumenical and Interreligious Affairs and the Anti-Defamation League of B'nai B'rith, the Committee on the Liturgy and its Secretariat have suggested pastoral ways to deal with such matters as Christians gathering for a seder in Holy Week, the proper understanding of the* Improperia *on Good Friday, and the proclamation of the passion narratives in Holy Week, particularly on Good Friday.*

*The present statement and guidelines are also offered in response to* Nostra Aetate *and especially to the latest guidelines issued in 1985 by the Commission for Religious Relations with the Jews. These guidelines are intended to offer assistance to Catholic preachers so that Jews and Judaism are correctly and rightly presented in homilies and other forms of preaching. For preaching to be of the Spirit, the heart of the preacher must be converted. These guidelines are also meant to offer preachers assistance in their own understanding of Jews and Judaism and, if necessary, to be a help in their own conversion.*

*The preparation and publication of* God's Mercy Endures Forever *was made possible only because of the participation and insight of a number of men and women who are scholars of the Bible, of Christian and Jewish liturgy, or of Judaism. The Liturgy Committee and Secretariat owe a special debt of gratitude to the Anti-Defamation League of B'nai B'rith and to the NCCB Secretariat for Catholic-Jewish Relations for their support and assistance at every turn in the preparation of this document, which takes its title from that hesed, that enduring merciful love of God for all who are faithful to the Law.*

> Most Rev. Joseph P. Delaney
> Bishop of Fort Worth
> Chairman
> Bishops' Committee on Liturgy

### Introduction

On June 24, 1985, the solemnity of the Birth of John the Baptist, the Holy See's Commission for Religious Relations with the Jews issued its *Notes on the Correct Way to Present Jews and Judaism in Preaching and Catechesis of the Roman Catholic Church* (hereafter, 1985 *Notes*; USCC Publication No. 970). The 1985 *Notes* rested on a foundation of previous church statements, addressing the tasks given Catholic homilists by the Second Vatican Council's *Declaration on the Relationship of the Church to Non-Christian Religions* (*Nostra Aetate*), no. 4.

On December 1, 1974, for example, the Holy See had issued *Guidelines and Suggestions far Implementing the Conciliar Declaration "Nostra Aetate," no. 4* (hereafter, 1974 *Guidelines*). The second and third sections of this document placed central emphasis upon the important and indispensable role of the homilist in ensuring that God's Word be received without prejudice toward the Jewish people or their religious traditions, asking "with respect to liturgical readings," that "care be taken to see that homilies based on them will not distort their meaning, especially when it is a question of passages which seem to show the Jewish people as such in unfavorable light" (1974 *Guidelines*, no. 2).

In this country, the National Conference of Catholic Bishops, in 1975, similarly urged catechists and homilists to work together to develop among Catholics increasing "appreciation of the Jewishness of that heritage and rich spirituality which we derive from Abraham, Moses, the prophets, the psalmists, and other spiritual giants of the Hebrew Scriptures" (*Statement on Catholic-Jewish Relations*, November 20, 1975, no. 12).

Much progress has been made since then. As it continues,

sensitivities will need even further sharpening, rounded on the Church's growing understanding of biblical and rabbinic Judaism.

It is the purpose of these present *Guidelines* to assist the homilist in these continuing efforts by indicating some of the major areas where challenges and opportunities occur and by offering perspectives and suggestions for dealing with them.

## *Jewish Roots of the Liturgy*

1. "Our common spiritual heritage [with Judaism] is considerable. To assess it carefully in itself and with due awareness of the faith and religious life of the Jewish people as they are professed and practiced still today, can greatly help us to understand better certain aspects of the life of the Church. Such is the case with the liturgy, whose Jewish roots remain still to be examined more deeply, and in any case should be better known and appreciated by the faithful" (Pope John Paul II, March 6, 1982).

2. Nowhere is the deep spiritual bond between Judaism and Christianity more apparent than in the liturgy. The very concepts of a liturgical cycle of feasts and the *lectio continua* principle of the lectionary that so mark Catholic tradition are adopted from Jewish liturgical practice. Easter and Pentecost have historical roots in the Jewish feasts of Passover and Shavuoth. Though their Christian meaning is quite distinct, an awareness of their original context in the story of Israel is vital to their understanding, as the lectionary readings themselves suggest. Where appropriate, such relationships should be pointed out. The homilist, as a "mediator of meaning" (NCCB Committee on Priestly Life and Ministry, *Fulfilled in Your Hearing,* 1982) interprets for the liturgical assembly not only the Scriptures but their liturgical context as well.

3. The central action of Christian worship, the eucharistic celebration, is likewise linked historically with Jewish ritual. The term for Church, *ecclesia,* like the original sense of the word *synagogue,* is an equivalent for the Hebrew term *keneset* or *kenessiyah* (assembly). The Christian understanding of *ecclesia* is based on the biblical understanding of *qahal* as the formal "gathering" of the people of God. The Christian *ordo* (order of worship) is an exact rendering of the earliest rabbinic idea of prayer, called a *seder,* that is, an "order" of service. Moreover, the Christian *ordo* takes its form and structure from the Jewish *seder:* the Liturgy of the

Word, with its alternating biblical readings, doxologies, and blessings; and the liturgical form of the Eucharist, rooted in Jewish
meal liturgy, with its blessings over bread and wine. Theologically, the Christian concept of *anamnesis* coincides with the Jewish
understanding of *zikkaron* (memorial reenactment). Applied to
the Passover celebration, the *zikkaron* refers to the fact that God's
saving deed is not only recalled but also relived through the ritual meal. The synoptic gospels present Jesus as instituting the
Eucharist during a Passover *seder* celebrated with his followers,
giving to it a new and distinctly Christian "memory."

4. In addition to the liturgical seasons and the Eucharist, numerous details on prayer forms and ritual exemplify the Church's
continuing relationship with the Jewish people throughout the
ages. The liturgy of the hours and the formulas of many of the
Church's most memorable prayers, such as the "Our Father,"
continue to resonate with rabbinic Judaism and contemporary
synagogue prayers.

## Historical Perspectives and Contemporary Proclamation

5. The strongly Jewish character of Jesus' teaching and that
of the primitive Church was culturally adapted by the growing Gentile majority and later blurred by controversies alienating
Christianity from emerging rabbinic Judaism at the end of the first
century. "By the third century, however, a de-Judaizing process
had set in which tended to undervalue the Jewish origins of the
Church, a tendency that has surfaced from time to time in devious
ways throughout Christian history" (*Statement on Catholic-Jewish
Relations*, no. 12).

6. This process has manifested itself in various ways in Christian history. In the second century, Marcion carried it to its absurd
extreme, teaching a complete opposition between the Hebrew
and Christian Scriptures and declaring that different Gods had inspired the two Testaments. Despite the Church's condemnation
of Marcion's teachings, some Christians over the centuries continued to dichotomize the Bible into two mutually contradictory
parts. They argued, for example, that the New Covenant "abrogated" or "superseded" the Old, and that the Sinai Covenant was
discarded by God and replaced with another. The Second Vatican
Council, in *Dei Verbum* and *Nostra Aetate*, rejected these theories
of the relationship between the Scriptures. In a major address

in 1980, Pope John Paul II linked the renewed understanding of the Scripture with the Church's understanding of its relationship with the Jewish people, stating that the dialogue, as "the meeting between the people of God of the Old Covenant, never revoked by God, is at the same time a dialogue within our Church, that is to say, a dialogue between the first and second part of its Bible" (Pope John Paul II, Mainz, November 17, 1980).

7.  Another misunderstanding rejected by the Second Vatican Council was the notion of collective guilt, which charged the Jewish people *as a whole* with responsibility for Jesus' death (cf. nos. 21–25 below, on Holy Week). From the theory of collective guilt, it followed for some that Jewish suffering over the ages reflected divine retribution on the Jews for an alleged "deicide." While both rabbinic Judaism and early Christianity saw in the destruction of the Jerusalem Temple in A.D. 70 a sense of divine punishment (see Lk 19:42–44), the theory of collective guilt went way beyond Jesus' poignant expression of his love as a Jew for Jerusalem and the destruction it would face at the hands of Imperial Rome. Collective guilt implied that because "the Jews" had rejected Jesus, God had rejected them. With direct reference to Luke 19:44, the Second Vatican Council reminded Catholics that "nevertheless, now as before, God holds the Jews most dear for the sake of their fathers; he does not repent of the gifts he makes or of the calls he issues," and established as an overriding hermeneutical principle for homilists dealing with such passages that "the Jews should not be represented as rejected by God or accursed, as if this followed from Holy Scripture" (*Nostra Aetate*, no. 4; cf. 1985 *Notes*, VI:33).

8. Reasons for increased sensitivity to the ways in which Jews and Judaism are presented in homilies are multiple. First, understanding of the biblical readings and of the structure of Catholic liturgy will be enhanced by an appreciation of their ancient sources and their continuing spiritual links with Judaism. The Christian proclamation of the saving deeds of the One God through Jesus was formed in the context of Second Temple Judaism and cannot be understood thoroughly without that context. It is a proclamation that, at its heart, stands in solidarity with the continuing Jewish witness in affirming the One God as Lord of history. Further, false or demeaning portraits of a repudiated Israel may undermine Christianity as well. How can one confidently affirm the truth of God's covenant with all humanity and

creation in Christ (see Rom. 8:21) without at the same time affirming God's faithfulness to the Covenant with Israel that also lies at the heart of the biblical testimony?

9. As Catholic homilists know, the liturgical year presents both opportunities and challenges. One can show the parallels between the Jewish and Catholic liturgical cycles. And one can, with clarity, confront misinterpretations of the meaning of the lectionary readings, which have been too familiar in the past. Specifically, homilists can guide people away from a triumphalism that would equate the pilgrim Church with the Reign of God, which is the Church's mission to herald and proclaim. Likewise, homilists can confront the unconscious transmission of anti-Judaism through cliches that derive from an unhistorical overgeneralization of the self-critical aspects of the story of Israel as told in the Scriptures (e.g., "hardheartedness" of the Jews, "blindness," "legalism," "materialism," "rejection of Jesus," etc.). From Advent through Passover/Easter, to Yom Kippur and Rosh Hashana, the Catholic and Jewish liturgical cycles spiral around one another in a stately progression of challenges to God's people to repent, to remain faithful to God's call, and to prepare the world for the coming of God's Reign. While each is distinct and unique, they are related to one another. Christianity is engrafted on and continues to draw sustenance from the common root, biblical Israel (Rom. 11:13–24).

10. In this respect, the 1985 *Notes,* stressing "the unity of the divine plan" (no. 11), caution against a simplistic framing of the relationship of Christianity and Judaism as "two parallel ways of salvation" (no. 7). The Church proclaims the universal salvific significance of the Christ-event and looks forward to the day when "there shall be one flock and one shepherd" (Jn 10:16; cf. Is 66:2; Zep 3:9; Jer 23:3; Ez 11:17; see also no. 31e below). So intimate is this relationship that the Church "encounters the mystery of Israel" when "pondering her own mystery" (1974 *Guidelines,* no. 5).

### Advent: The Relationship Between the Scriptures

11. The lectionary readings from the prophets are selected to bring out the ancient Christian theme that Jesus is the "fulfillment" of the biblical message of hope and promise, the inauguration of the "days to come" described, for example, by the daily

Advent Masses, and on Sundays by Isaiah in cycle A and Jeremiah in cycle C for the First Sunday of Advent. This truth needs to be framed very carefully. Christians believe that Jesus is the promised Messiah who has come (see Lk 4:22), but also know that his messianic kingdom is not fully realized. The ancient messianic prophecies are not merely temporal predictions but profound expressions of eschatological hope. Since this dimension can be misunderstood or even missed altogether, the homilist needs to raise clearly the hope found in the prophets and heightened in the proclamations of Christ. This hope includes trust in what is promised but not yet seen. While the biblical prophecies of an age of universal *shalom* are "fulfilled" (i.e., irreversibly inaugurated) in Christ's coming, the fulfillment is not yet completely worked out in each person's life or perfected in the world at large (1974 *Guidelines*, no. 2). It is the mission of the Church, as also that of the Jewish people, to proclaim and to work to prepare the world for the full flowering of God's reign, which is, but is "not yet" (cf. 1974 *Guidelines*, II). Both the Christian "Our Father" and the Jewish *Kaddish* exemplify this message. Thus, both Christianity and Judaism seal their worship with a common hope: "Thy kingdom come!"

12. Christians proclaim that the Messiah has indeed come and that God's Reign is "at hand." With the Jewish people we await the complete realization of the messianic age.

> In underlining the eschatological dimension of Christianity, we shall reach a greater awareness that the people of God of the Old and the New Testament are tending toward a like end in the future: the coming or return of the Messiah — even if they start from two different points of view (1985 *Notes*, nos. 18–19).

13. Other difficulties may be less theologically momentous but can still be troublesome. For example, the reading from Baruch in cycle C or from Isaiah in cycle A for the Second Sunday of Advent can leave the impression that pre-Jesus Israel was wholly guilt-ridden and in mourning, and Judaism virtually moribund. In fact, in their original historical settings, such passages reveal Judaism's remarkable capacity for self-criticism. While Israel had periods of deep mourning (see Lamentations) and was justly accused of sinfulness (e.g., see Jeremiah), it also experienced periods of joy, return from Exile, and continuing *teshuvah*, turning back to God in faithful repentance. Judaism was and is incredibly com-

plex and vital, with a wide variety of creative spiritual movements vying for the people's adherence.

14. The reform of the liturgy initiated by the Second Vatican Council reintroduced regular readings from the Old Testament into the lectionary. For Catholics, the Old Testament is that collection that contains the Hebrew Scriptures and the seven deuterocanonical books. Using postbiblical Jewish sources, with respect for the essential differences between Christian and Jewish traditions of biblical interpretation, can enliven the approach to the biblical text (cf. nos. 31a and 31i below). The opportunity also presents a challenge for the homilist. Principles of selection of passages vary. Sometimes the readings are cyclic, providing a continuity of narrative over a period of time. At other times, especially during Advent and Lent, a reading from the prophets or one of the historical books of the Old Testament and a gospel pericope are "paired," based on such liturgical traditions as the *sensus plenior* (fuller meaning) or, as is especially the case in Ordinary Time, according to the principle of *typology*, in which biblical figures and events are seen as "types" prefiguring Jesus (see no. 31e below).

15. Many of these pairings represent natural associations of similar events and teachings. Others rely on New Testament precedent and interpretation of the messianic psalms and prophetic passages. Matthew 1:23, for example, quotes the Septuagint, which translates the Hebrew *almah* (young woman) as the Greek for *virgin* in its rendering of Isaiah 7:14. The same biblical text, therefore, can have more than one valid hermeneutical interpretation, ranging from its original historical context and intent to traditional Christological applications. The 1985 *Notes* describe this phenomenon as flowing from the "unfathomable riches" and "inexhaustible content" of the Hebrew Bible. For Christians, the unity of the Bible depends on understanding all Scripture in the light of Christ. Typology is one form, rooted in the New Testament itself, of expressing this unity of Scripture and of the divine plan (see no. 31e below). As such, it "should not lead us to forget that it [the Hebrew Bible] retains its own value as Revelation that the New Testament often does no more than resume" (1985 *Notes*, no. 15; cf. *Dei Verbum*, 14–18).

## Lent: Controversies and Conflicts

16. The Lenten lectionary presents just as many challenges. Prophetic texts such as Joel (Ash Wednesday), Jeremiah's "new covenant" (cycle B, Fifth Sunday), and Isaiah (cycle C, Fifth Sunday) call the assembly to proclaim Jesus as the Christ while avoiding negativism toward Judaism.

17. In addition, many of the New Testament texts, such as Matthew's references to "hypocrites in the synagogue" (Ash Wednesday), John's depiction of Jesus in the Temple (cycle B, Third Sunday), and Jesus' conflicts with the Pharisees (e.g., Lk, cycle C, Fourth Sunday) can give the impression that the Judaism of Jesus' day was devoid of spiritual depth and essentially at odds with Jesus' teaching. References to earlier divine punishments of the Jews (e.g., 1 Cor, cycle C, Third Sunday) can further intensify a false image of Jews and Judaism as a people rejected by God.

18. In fact, however, as the 1985 *Notes* are at pains to clarify (sec. III and IV), Jesus was observant of the Torah (e.g., in the details of his circumcision and purification given in Lk 2:21–24), he extolled respect for it (see Mt 5:17–20), and he invited obedience to it (see Mt 8:4). Jesus taught in the synagogues (see Mt 4:23 and 9:35; Lk 4:15–18; Jn 18:20) and in the Temple, which he frequented, as did the disciples even after the Resurrection (see Acts 2:46; 3:1ff). While Jesus showed uniqueness and authority in his interpretation of God's word in the Torah — in a manner that scandalized some Jews and impressed others — he did not oppose it, nor did he wish To abrogate it.

19. Jesus was perhaps closer to the Pharisees in his religious vision than to any other group of his time. The 1985 *Notes* suggest that this affinity with Pharisaism may be a reason for many of his apparent controversies with them (see no. 27). Jesus shared with the Pharisees a number of distinctive doctrines: the resurrection of the body; forms of piety such as almsgiving, daily prayer, and fasting; the liturgical practice of addressing God as Father; and the priority of the love commandment (see no. 25). Many scholars are of the view that Jesus was not so much arguing against "the Pharisees" as a group, as he was condemning excesses of some Pharisees, excesses of a sort that can be found among some Christians as well. In some cases, Jesus appears to have been participating in internal Pharisaic debates on various points of interpretation of God's law. In the case of divorce (see Mk 10:2–12),

an issue that was debated hotly between the Pharisaic schools of Hillel and Shammai, Jesus goes beyond even the more stringent position of the House of Shammai. In other cases, such as the rejection of a literal interpretation of the *lex talionis* ("An eye for an eye . . ."), Jesus' interpretation of biblical law is similar to that found in some of the prophets and ultimately adopted by rabbinic tradition as can be seen in the *Talmud*.

20. After the Church had distanced itself from Judaism (see no. 5 above), it tended to telescope the long historical process whereby the gospels were set down some generations after Jesus' death. Thus, certain controversies that may actually have taken place between church leaders and rabbis toward the end of the first century were "read back" into the life of Jesus:

> Some [New Testament] references hostile or less than favorable to Jews have their historical context in conflicts between the nascent Church and the Jewish community. Certain controversies reflect Christian-Jewish relations long after the time of Jesus. To establish this is of capital importance if we wish to bring out the meaning of certain gospel texts for the Christians of today. All this should be taken into account when preparing catechesis and homilies for the weeks of Lent and Holy Week (1985 *Notes*, no. 29; see no. 26 below).

## *Holy Week: The Passion Narratives*

21. Because of the tragic history of the "Christ-killer" charge as providing a rallying cry for anti-Semites over the centuries, a strong and careful homiletic stance is necessary to combat its lingering effects today. Homilists and catechists should seek to provide a proper context for the proclamation of the passion narratives. A particularly useful and detailed discussion of the theological and historical principles involved in presentations of the passions can be found in *Criteria for the Evaluation of Dramatizations of the Passion* issued by the Bishops' Committee for Ecumenical and Interreligious Affairs (March 1988).

22. The message of the liturgy in proclaiming the passion narratives in full is to enable the assembly to see vividly the love of Christ for each person, despite their sins, a love that even death could not vanquish. "Christ in his boundless love freely underwent his passion and death because of the sins of all so that all might attain salvation" (*Nostra Aetate*, no. 4). To the extent that

Christians over the centuries made Jews the scapegoat for Christ's death, they drew themselves away from the paschal mystery. For it is only by dying to one's sins that we can hope to rise with Christ to new life. This is a central truth of the Catholic faith stated by the *Catechism* of the Council of Trent in the sixteenth century and reaffirmed by the 1985 *Notes* (no. 30).

23. It is necessary to remember that the passion narratives do not offer eyewitness accounts or a modern transcript of historical events. Rather, the events have had their meaning focused, as it were, through the four theological "lenses" of the gospels. By comparing what is shared and what distinguishes the various gospel accounts from each other, the homilist can discern the core from the particular optics of each. One can then better see the significant theological differences between the passion narratives. These differences also are part of the inspired Word of God.

24. Certain historical essentials are shared by all four accounts: a growing hostility against Jesus on the part of some Jewish religious leaders (note that the Synoptic gospels do not mention the Pharisees as being involved in the events leading to Jesus' death, but only the "chief priest, scribes, and eiders"); the Last Supper with the disciples; betrayal by Judas; arrest outside the city (an action conducted covertly by the Roman and Temple authorities because of Jesus' popularity among his fellow Jews); interrogation before a high priest (not necessarily a Sanhedrin trial); formal condemnation by Pontius Pilate (cf. the Apostles' and Nicene Creeds, which mention *only* Pilate, even though some Jews were involved); crucifixion by Roman soldiers; affixing the title "King of the Jews" on the cross; death; burial; and resurrection. Many other elements, such as the crowds shouting "His blood be on us and on our children" in Matthew, or the generic use of the term "the Jews" in John, are unique to a given author and must be understood within the context of that author's overall theological scheme. Often, these unique elements reflect the perceived needs and emphases of the author's particular community at the end of the first century, *after* the split between Jews and Christians was well underway. The bitterness toward synagogue Judaism seen in John's gospel (e.g., Jn 9:22; 16:2) most likely reflects the bitterness felt by John's own community after its "parting of the ways" with the Jewish community, and the martyrdom of St. Stephen illustrates that verbal disputes could, at times, lead to violence by Jews against fellow Jews who believed in Jesus.

25. Christian reflection on the passion should lead to a deep sense of the need for reconciliation with the Jewish community today. Pope John Paul II has said:

> Considering history in the light of the principles of faith in God, we must also reflect on the catastrophic event of the *Shoah*....
>
> Considering this mystery of the suffering of Israel's children, their witness of hope, of faith, and of humanity under dehumanizing outrages, the Church experiences ever more deeply her common bond with the Jewish people and with their treasure of spiritual riches in the past and in the present" (*Address to Jewish Leadership*, Miami, September 1987).

## The Easter Season

26. The readings of the Easter season, especially those from the book of Acts, which is used extensively throughout this liturgical period, require particular attention from the homilist in light of the enduring bond between Jews and Christians. Some of the readings from Acts (e.g., cycles A and B for the Third and Fourth Sundays of Easter) can leave an impression of collective Jewish responsibility for the crucifixion ("You put to death the author of life..." Acts 3:15). In such cases, the homilist should put before the assembly the teachings of *Nostra Aetate* in this regard (see no. 22 above), as well as the fact noted in Acts 3:17 that what was done by some individual Jews was done "out of ignorance" so that no unwarranted conclusion of collective guilt is drawn by the hearers. The Acts may be dealing with a reflection of the Jewish-Christian relationship as it existed toward the end of the first century (when Acts was composed) rather than with the actual attitudes of the post-Easter Jerusalem Church. Homilists should desire to convey the spirit and enthusiasm of the early Church that marks these Easter season readings. But in doing so, statements about Jewish responsibility have to be kept in context. This is part of the reconciliation between Jews and Christians to which we are all called.

## Pastoral Activity During Holy Week and the Easter Season

27. Pope John Paul II's visit to the Chief Rabbi of Rome on Good Friday, 1987, gives a lead for pastoral activities during Holy Week in local churches. Some dioceses and parishes, for example,

have begun traditions such as holding a "Service of Reconciliation" with Jews on Palm Sunday, or inviting Holocaust survivors to address their congregations during Lent.

28. It is becoming familiar in many parishes and Catholic homes to participate in a Passover Seder during Holy Week. This practice can have educational and spiritual value. It is wrong, however, to "baptize" the Seder by ending it with New Testament readings about the Last Supper or, worse, turn it into a prologue to the Eucharist. Such mergings distort both traditions. The following advice should prove useful:

> When Christians celebrate this sacred feast among themselves, the rites of the *haggadah* for the seder should be respected in all their integrity. The seder...should be celebrated in a dignified manner and with sensitivity to those to whom the seder truly belongs. The primary reason why Christians may celebrate the festival of Passover should be to acknowledge common roots in the history of salvation. Any sense of "restaging" the Last Supper of the Lord Jesus should be avoided.... The rites of the Triduum are the [Church's] annual memorial of the events of Jesus' dying and rising (Bishops' Committee on the Liturgy *Newsletter,* March 1980, p. 12).

Seders arranged at or in cooperation with local synagogues are encouraged.

29. Also encouraged are joint memorial services commemorating the victims of the *Shoah* (Holocaust). These should be prepared for with catechetical and adult education programming to ensure a proper spirit of shared reverence. Addressing the Jewish community of Warsaw, Pope John Paul II stressed the uniqueness and significance of Jewish memory of the *Shoah:* "More than anyone else, it is precisely you who have become this saving warning. I think that in this sense you continue your particular vocation, showing yourselves to be still the heirs of that election to which God is faithful. This is your mission in the contemporary world before...all of humanity" (Warsaw, June 14, 1987). On the Sunday closest to *Yarn ha Shoah,* Catholics should pray for the victims of the Holocaust and their survivors. The following serve as examples of petitions for the general intercessions at Mass:

- For the victims of the Holocaust, their families, and all our Jewish brothers and sisters, that the violence and hatred they experienced may never again be repeated, we pray to the Lord.

- For the Church, that the Holocaust may be a reminder to us that we can never be indifferent to the sufferings of others, we pray to the Lord.

- For our Jewish brothers and sisters, that their confidence in the face of long-suffering may spur us on to a greater faith and trust in God, we pray to the Lord.

## Preaching Throughout the Year

30. The challenges that peak in the seasons of Advent, Lent, and Easter are present throughout the year in the juxtaposition of the lectionary readings. There are many occasions when it is difficult to avoid a reference either to Jews or Judaism in a homily based upon a text from the Scriptures. For all Scripture, including the New Testament, deals with Jews and Jewish themes.

31. Throughout the year, the following general principles will be helpful:

a) Consistently affirm the value of the whole Bible. While "among all the Scriptures, even those of the New Testament, the Gospels have a special preeminence" (*Dei Verbum*, 18), the Hebrew Scriptures are the word of God and have validity and dignity in and of themselves (ibid., 15). Keep in view the intentions of the biblical authors (ibid., 19).

b) Place the typology inherent in the lectionary in a proper context, neither overemphasizing nor avoiding it. Show that the meaning of the Hebrew Scriptures for their original audience is not limited to nor diminished by New Testament applications (1985 *Notes*, II).

c) Communicate a reverence for the Hebrew Scriptures and avoid approaches that reduce them to a propaedeutic or background for the New Testament. It is God who speaks, communicating himself through divine revelation (*Dei Verbum*, 6).

d) Show the connectedness between the Scriptures. The Hebrew Bible and the Jewish tradition rounded on it must not be set against the New Testament in such a way that the former seems to constitute a religion of only retributive justice, fear, and legalism, with no appeal to love of God and neighbor (cf. Dt 6:5; Lv 19:18, 32; Hos 11:1–9; Mt 22:34–40).

e) Enliven the eschatological hope, the "not yet" aspect of the *kerygma*. The biblical promises are realized in Christ. But the Church awaits their perfect fulfillment in Christ's glorious return when all creation is made free (1974 *Guidelines*, II).

f) Emphasize the Jewishness of Jesus and his teachings and highlight the similarities of the teachings of the Pharisees with those of Christ (1985 *Notes*, III and IV).

g) Respect the continuing validity of God's covenant with the Jewish people and their responsive faithfulness, despite centuries of suffering, to the divine call that is theirs (1985 *Notes*, VI).

h) Frame homilies to show that Christians and Jews together are "trustees and witnesses of an ethic marked by the Ten Commandments, in the observance of which humanity finds its truth and freedom" (John Paul II, Rome Synagogue, April 13, 1986).

i) Be free to draw on Jewish sources (rabbinic, medieval, and modern) in expounding the meaning of the Hebrew Scriptures and the apostolic writings. The 1974 *Guidelines* observe that "the history of Judaism did not end with the destruction of Jerusalem, but went on to develop a religious tradition ... rich in religious values." The 1985 *Notes* (no. 14) thus speak of Christians "profiting discerningly from the traditions of Jewish readings" of the sacred texts.

32. The 1985 *Notes* describe what is central to the role of the homilist: "Attentive to the same God who has spoken, hanging on the same word, we have to witness to one same memory and one common hope in him who is master of history. We must also accept our responsibility to prepare the world for the coming of the Messiah by working together for social justice, respect for the rights of persons and nations, and for social and international reconciliation. To this we are driven, Jews and Christians, by the command to love our neighbor, by a common hope for the Kingdom of God, and by the great heritage of the prophets" (1985 *Notes*, no. 19; see also Lv 19:18, 32).

### Criteria for the Evaluation of Dramatizations of the Passion, Bishops' Committee for Ecumenical and Interreligious Affairs (1988)

*Preliminary Considerations*

On June 24, 1985, the Vatican Commission for Religious Relations with the Jews issued *Notes on the Correct Way to Present the Jews and Judaism in Preaching and Catechesis of the Roman Catholic Church* (USCC Office of Publishing and Promotion Services, 1985). That document, like its predecessor, *Guidelines and Suggestions for*

*Implementing the Conciliar Declaration "Nostra Aetate" (n. 4)* (December 1, 1974), drew its inspiration from the Second Vatican Council and was intended to be an offering on the part of the Holy See to Catholics on how the Conciliar mandate can properly be fulfilled "in our time."

The present document, in its turn, seeks to specify the catechetical principles established in the *Notes* with reference to depictions and presentations of the events surrounding the passion and death of Jesus, including but not limited to dramatic, staged presentations of Jesus' death most popularly known as "passion plays." The principles here invoked are applicable as the *Guidelines* suggest (ch. III) to "all levels of Christian instruction and education," whether written (textbooks, teachers' manuals, etc.) or oral (preaching, the mass media).

Specifically, the present document aims to provide practical applications regarding such presentations as they flow from the more general principles of the *Guidelines* and of sections III and IV of the *Notes* concerning the "Jewish Roots of Christianity" and the portrayal of "Jews in the New Testament." These principles (sec. A, below) lead to both negative and positive criteria (sec. B) for the evaluation of the many ways in which the Christian community throughout the world seeks, with commendable and pious intent, to remind itself of the universal significance and eternal spiritual challenge of the Savior's death and resurrection. A final section (C) acknowledges the many difficulties facing those attempting to dramatize the gospel narratives. It is hoped that this section will be helpful in providing perspectives on the many complex questions that can arise.

It has been noted by scholars that dramatizations of the passion were among the very last of the forms of "miracle" or "morality" plays to be developed in the Middle Ages. This hesitancy on the part of our ancestors in the faith can today only be regarded as most seemly, for the Church's primary reflection on the meaning of Jesus' death and resurrection takes place during Holy Week, as the high point of the liturgical cycle, and touches upon the most sacred and central mysteries of the faith.

It is all the more important, then, that extraliturgical depictions of the sacred mysteries conform to the highest possible standards of biblical interpretation and theological sensitivity. What is true of Catholic teaching in general is even more crucial with regard to depictions of Jesus' passion. In the words of Pope John Paul II as cited at the beginning of the *Notes:* "We should aim, in this field, that Catholic teaching at its different levels ... presents Jews and Judaism, not only in an honest and objective manner, free from prejudices and without any offenses, but also with full awareness of the heritage common [to Jews and Christians]."

## A. The Mystery of the Passion

1. The overall aim of any depiction of the passion should be the unambiguous presentation of the doctrinal understanding of the event in the light of faith, that is, of the Church's traditional interpretation of the meaning of Christ's death for all humanity. *Nostra Aetate* states this central gospel truth quite clearly: "Christ in his boundless love freely underwent his passion and death because of the sins of all, so that all might attain salvation" (cf. *Notes* IV, 30).

Therefore, any presentations that explicitly or implicitly seek to shift responsibility from human sin onto this or that historical group, such as the Jews, can only be said to obscure a core gospel truth. It has rightly been said that "correctly viewed, the disappearance of the charge of collective guilt of Jews pertains as much to the purity of the Catholic faith as it does to the defense of Judaism" (*Statement* of the National Conference of Catholic Bishops, November 20, 1975).

2. The question of *theological* responsibility for Jesus' death is a long settled one. From the theological perspective, the *Catechism* of the Council of Trent (cited in the *Notes* IV, 30) articulated without hesitancy what should be the major dramatic or moral focus of any dramatization of the event for Christians — a profound self-examination of our own guilt, through sin, for Jesus' death:

> In this guilt are involved all those who fall frequently into sin; for, as our sins consigned Christ the Lord to the death of the cross, most certainly those who wallow in sin and iniquity crucify to themselves again the Son of God. ... This guilt seems more enormous in us than in the Jews since, if they had known it, they would never have crucified the Lord of glory; while we, on the contrary, professing to know him, yet denying him by our actions, seem in some sort to lay violent hands on him (*Catechism* of the Council of Trent).

3. The central creeds of the Church focus precisely on this theological message, without reference to the extremely complex

historical question of reconstructing what various individuals might have done or not done. Only Pilate is mentioned, as the person with sole legal responsibility for the case: "He was also crucified for us, suffered under Pontius Pilate and was buried" (Nicene Creed). This fact gives a certain hermeneutical guidance for the use of various materials from the gospel passion narratives in a dramatic context (cf. sec. C, below).

4. In the development and evaluation of passion performances, then, the central criterion for judgment must be what the *Guidelines* called "an overriding preoccupation to bring out explicitly the *meaning* of the [gospel] text while taking scriptural studies into account" (II, emphasis added). Anything less than this "overriding preoccupation" to avoid caricaturing the Jewish people, which history has all too frequently shown us, will result almost inevitably in a violation of the basic hermeneutical principle of the Council in this regard: "the Jews should not be presented as rejected or accursed by God as if tiffs followed from Sacred Scripture" (*Nostra Aetate*).

5. The 1985 *Notes* also provide a model for the positive understanding of the relationship between the Church and the Jewish people that should form a key element of the vision underlying presentations of the passion. As the *Notes* state: "The question is not merely to uproot from among the faithful the remains of anti-Semitism still to be found here and there, but much rather to arouse in them, through educational work, an exact knowledge of the wholly unique 'bond' (*Nostra Aetate*, 4) which joins us as a Church to the Jews and to Judaism" (I, 8; cf. II, 10–11).

## B. Avoiding Caricatures and False Oppositions

1. Any depiction of the death of Jesus will, to a greater or lesser extent, mix theological perspectives with historical reconstructions of the event based with greater or lesser fidelity on the four gospel accounts and what is known from extrabiblical records.

The nature of such mixtures leaves the widest possible latitude for artistic creativity and insight, but also for abuses and prejudices. What the *Notes* state in their conclusion regarding Christian-Jewish relations generally is equally, and perhaps especially, true of the history of the development of passion plays in their various forms: "There is evident, in particular, a painful ignorance of the history and traditions of Judaism, of which only negative aspects and often caricature seem to form part of the stock ideas of many Christians."

2. Judaism in the first century, especially, incorporated an extraordinarily rich and diverse set of groups and movements. Some sought a certain accommodation with Hellenic/Roman culture in the Diaspora and in the Land of Israel. Others vigorously opposed any cultural compromise, fearing ultimate religious assimilation. Some argued for armed rebellion against Rome (Zealots), others for peaceful but firm resistance to cultural oppression (some Pharisees) and a few, such as the Temple priesthood and its party (Sadducees) acted in the eyes of the people as collaborators with Rome.

Emotions and hopes (both practical and spiritual) ran high, and rhetoric often higher. Thus, along the lines of great issues of the day, anal reacting to the pressure of Roman occupation, there moved a variety of groups, each with its own wide range of internal diversity: Sadducees, Zealots, apocalypticists, Pharisees (of varying dispositions, especially the two major schools of Hillel and Shammai), Herodians, Hellenists, scribes, sages, and miracle workers of all sorts. Scripture was understood variously: literally, mystically, allegorically, and through mediating principles of interpretation.

Jesus and his teachings can only be understood within this fluctuating mixture of Jewish trends, and movements. In point of fact, various groups and leaders of Jesus' time (perhaps especially certain Pharisees) would have espoused many of Jesus, ideas, such as the nearness of the kingdom of God, resurrection of the body, opposition to the policies of the Temple, and so forth. The gospels reflect only some of this diversity. Succeeding generations of Christians, perhaps misconstruing the theological thrust of St. John's use of the term *Ioudaioi* ("the Jews" or "Judeans"), tended to flatten it into a monolithic, usually negative stereotype. Thus, caricature came to form the basis of the pejorative "stock ideas" rejected so forcefully by the *Notes*. Presentations of the passion, on the contrary, should strive to present the diversity of Jewish communities in Jesus' time, enabling viewers to understand that many of Jesus' major concerns (e.g., critique of Temple policies) would have been shared by other Jews of his time.

3. Many of these negative "stock ideas," unfortunately, can become vividly alive in passion dramatizations. It is all too easy in dramatic presentations to resort to artificial oppositions in order

to heighten interest or provide sharp contrasts between the characters. Some of these erroneous oppositions, which are to be carefully avoided, are the following:

a) Jesus must not be depicted as opposed to the Law (Torah). In fact, as the *Notes* describe in greater detail, "there is no doubt that he wished to submit himself to the law (Gal 4:4)...extolled respect for it (Mt 5:17–20), and invited obedience to it (Mt 8:4) (cf. *Notes* III, 21, 22). Jesus should be portrayed clearly as a pious, observant Jew of his time *(Notes* III, 20 and 28).

b) The Old Testament and the Jewish tradition rounded on it must not be set against the New Testament in such a way that the former seems to constitute a religion of only justice, fear, and legalism with no appeal to the love of God and neighbor (Dt 6:5; Lv 19:18; Mt 22:34–40; cf. *Guidelines* III).

c) Jesus and the disciples must not be set dramatically in opposition to his people, the Jews. This is to misread, for example, the technical terminology employed by John's gospel *(Guidelines* II). It also ignores those parts of the gospel that show the Jewish populace well disposed toward Jesus. In his life and teaching, "Jesus was and always remained a Jew" *(Notes* III, 20), as, indeed, did the apostles *(Notes* III, 22).

d) Jews should not be portrayed as avaricious (e.g., in Temple money-changer scenes); blood thirsty (e.g., in certain depictions of Jesus' appearances before the Temple priesthood or before Pilate); or implacable enemies of Christ (e.g., by changing the small "crowd" at the governor's palace into a teeming mob). Such depictions, with their obvious "collective guilt" implications, eliminate those parts of the gospels that show that the secrecy surrounding Jesus' "trial" was motivated by the large following he had in Jerusalem and that the Jewish populace, far from wishing his death, would have opposed it had they known and, in fact, mourned his death by Roman execution (cf. Lk 23:27).

e) Any crowd or questioning scene, therefore, should reflect the fact that some in the crowd and among the Jewish leaders (e.g., Nicodemus, Joseph) supported Jesus and that the rest were manipulated by his opponents, as is made clear in the gospels (cf. *Nostra Aetate*, n. 4, "Jewish authorities"; *Notes* IV, 30).

f) Jesus and his teachings should not be portrayed as opposed to or by "the Pharisees" as a group *(Notes* III, 24). Jesus shared important Pharisaic doctrines *(Notes* III, 25) that set them apart from other Jewish groups of the time, such as the Sadducees. The Pharisees, in fact, are not mentioned in accounts of the passion except once in Luke, where Pharisees attempt to warn him of a plot against him by the followers of Herod (Lk 13:31). So, too, did a respected Pharisee, Gamaliel, speak out in a later time before the Sanhedrin to save the lives of the apostles (Acts 5). The Pharisees, therefore, should not be depicted as party to the proceedings against Jesus *(Notes* III, 24–27).

g) In sum, Judaism and Jewish society in the time of Christ and the apostles were complex realities, embracing many different trends, many spiritual, religious, social, and cultural values *(Guidelines* III). Presentations of the passion should strive to reflect this spiritual vitality, avoiding any implication that Jesus' death was a result of religious antagonism between a stereotyped "Judaism" and Christian doctrine. Many of the controversies (or "antitheses") between Jesus and his fellow Jews, as recorded in the gospels, we know today in fact reflect conflicts that took place long after the time of Christ between the early Christian communities and various Jewish communities *(Notes* IV, 29 A). To generalize from such specific and often later conflicts to an either/or opposition between Jesus and Judaism is to anachronize and, more basically, to vitiate the spirit and intent of the gospel texts *(Notes* III, 28; IV, 29 F).

h) In the light of the above criteria, it will also be useful to undertake a careful examination of the staging and costuming aspects of particular productions where this may apply. To give just one example, it is possible to project subtly yet powerfully any or all of the above "oppositions" by costuming: arraying Jesus' enemies in dark, sinister costuming and makeup, with Jesus and his friends in lighter tones. This can be effective on the stage. But it can also be disastrous if the effect is to isolate Jesus and the apostles from "the Jews," as if all were not part of the same people. It is important to portray Jesus and his followers clearly as Jews among Jews, both in dress and in actions such as prayer.

i) Similarly, the use of religious symbols requires careful evaluation. Displays of the menorah, tablets of the law, and other Jewish symbols should appear throughout the play and be connected with Jesus and his friends no less than with the Temple or with those opposed to Jesus. The presence of Roman soldiers should likewise be shown on the stage throughout the play, to represent the oppressive and pervasive nature of the Roman occupation.

## C. Difficulties and Sensitivities in Historical Reconstruction Based on the Four Gospel Accounts

The mixture of theological, historical, and artistic aspects mentioned above (B 1) gives rise to many difficulties in constructing an adequate presentation of the passion narratives (Mt 26–28; Mk 14–15; Lk 22-23; Jn 18–19). Below are some examples of the difficult choices facing those who would seek to do so with faithfulness to the gospels. In each, an attempt will be made to apply to the question principles adduced in sections A and B, above, in the hope that such discussion will be of help to those charged with evaluations of the wide range of possible depictions existing today.

### 1. The Question of Selectivity

a) Those constructing a single narrative from the versions of the events in the four gospels are immediately aware that the texts differ in many details. To take just two examples, the famous phrase, "His Blood be upon us and on our children," exists only in the Matthean text (Mt 27:24–25), while the question of whether or not there was a full Sanhedrin trial is given widely differing interpretations in each of the gospel narratives. John, for example, has no Sanhedrin trial scene as such, but only a questioning before the two chief priests at dawn (18:19). Also in John, it is a Roman cohort, merely accompanied by Temple guards, that arrests Jesus (Jn 18:3,12). How is one to choose between the differing versions?

b) First, it must be understood that the gospel authors did not intend to write "history" in our modern sense, but rather "sacred history" (i.e., offering "the honest truth about Jesus") *(Notes* IV, 29 A) in the light of revelation. To attempt to utilize the four passion narratives literally by picking one passage from one gospel and the next from another gospel, and so forth, is to risk violating the integrity of the texts themselves, just as, for example, it violates the sense of Genesis 1 to reduce the magnificence of its vision of the Creation to a scientific theorem.

c) A clear and precise hermeneutic and a guiding artistic vision sensitive to historical fact and to the best biblical scholarship are obviously necessary. Just as obviously, it is not sufficient for the producers of passion dramatizations to respond to responsible criticism simply by appealing to the notion that "it's in the Bible." One must account for one's selections.

In the above instances, for example, one could take from John's gospel the phrase "the Jews" and mix it with Matthew 27:24–25, clearly implying a "God guilt" on all Jews of all times in violation of *Nostra Aetate's* dictum that "what happened in his passion cannot be blamed on all the Jews then living without distinction nor upon the Jews of today." Hence, if the Matthean phrase is to be used (not here recommended), great care would have to be taken throughout the presentation to ensure that such an interpretation does not prevail. Likewise, the historical and biblical questions surrounding the notion that there was a formal Sanhedrin trial argue for extreme caution and, perhaps, even abandoning the device. As a dramatic tool, it can too often lead to misunderstanding.

d) The greatest caution is advised in all cases where "it is a question of passages that seem to show the Jewish people as such in an unfavorable light" (*Guidelines* II). A general principle might, therefore, be suggested that if one cannot show beyond reasonable doubt that the particular gospel element selected or paraphrased will not be offensive or have the potential for negative influence on the audience for whom the presentation is intended, that element cannot, in good conscience, be used. This, admittedly, will be a difficult principle to apply. Yet, given what has been said above, it would seem to be a necessary one.

## 2. *Historical Knowledge and Biblical Scholarship*

a) Often, what we have come to know from biblical scholarship or historical studies will place in doubt a more literalist reading of the biblical text. Here again, the hermeneutical principles of *Nostra Aetate*, the *Guidelines*, and the *Notes* should be of "overriding" concern. One such question suggests itself by way of example. This is the portrait of Pontius Pilate (cf. sec. A 3, above). It raises a very real problem of methodology in historical reconstruction of the events of Jesus' last days.

b) *The Role of Pilate.* Certain of the gospels, especially the two latest ones, Matthew and John, seem on the surface to portray Pilate as a vacillating administrator who himself found "no fault" with Jesus and sought, though in a weak way, to free him. Other data from the gospels and secular sources contemporary with the events portray Pilate as a ruthless tyrant. We know from these latter sources that Pilate ordered crucified hundreds of Jews without proper trial under Roman law, and that in the year 36 Pilate was recalled to Rome to give an account. Luke, similarly, mentions "the Galileans whose blood Pilate mingled with their sacrifices" in the Temple (Lk 13:1–4), thus corroborating the contemporary secular accounts of the unusual cruelty of Pilate's administration. John, as mentioned above, is at pains to show that Jesus' arrest and trial were essentially at Roman hands. Finally, the gospels agree that Jesus' "crime," in Roman eyes, was that of political sedition — crucifixion being the Roman form of punishment for such charges. The threat to Roman rule is implicit in the charge: "King of the Jews," nailed to the cross at Pilate's order (Mt 27:37; Mk 15:26; Lk 23:38; Jn 19:19). Matthew 27:38 and Mark 15:27 identify the "criminals" crucified with Jesus on that day as "insurgents."

There is, then, room for more than one dramatic style of portraying the character of Pilate while still being faithful to the biblical record. Again, it is suggested here that the hermeneutical insight of *Nostra Aetate* and the use of the best available biblical scholarship cannot be ignored in the creative process and provide the most prudent and secure criterion for contemporary dramatic reconstructions.

## Conclusion

*The Notes* emphasize that because the Church and the Jewish people are "linked together at the very level of their identity," an accurate, sensitive, and positive appreciation of Jews and Judaism "should not occupy an occasional or marginal place in Christian teaching, but be considered "essential" to Christian proclamation (I, 2; cf. I, 8).

This principle is nowhere more true than in depictions of the central events of the Paschal mystery. It is a principle that gives renewed urgency to the evaluation of all contemporary dramatizations of the passion and a renewed norm for undertaking that delicate and vital task.

# APPENDIX D

# Further Readings and Resources

## 1. WHERE TO GO FOR RESOURCES

Actual visits to synagogues remain one of the best methods for establishing positive attitudes about Judaism in both children and adults. These can be easily arranged simply by contacting a neighboring rabbi or the local Jewish community council. Any city with a sizable Jewish population is likely to have an office of both the American Jewish Committee and the Anti-Defamation League of B'nai B'rith. These can provide a variety of services to the school seeking to design a prejudice-free curriculum or to the parish community seeking to become active in the area of dialogue. The American Jewish Committee has many resources useful to teachers or parish groups, while the Anti-Defamation League maintains an excellent library of audiovisual materials that can be used in the classroom for introducing students to Jewish customs and traditions, the history of anti-Semitism, the analysis of prejudice, etc. Either would be glad to work with any interested group.

Finally, most Catholic dioceses in this country maintain an Office of Ecumenical and Interreligious Affairs. Such offices can usually provide speakers, resource lists, and guidelines for implementing the policies of the American bishops on the local level.

## 2. FURTHER READINGS
*(in paperback unless marked with an asterisk)*

### Chapter 1: A Bridge Across Time

*A. History of Jewish-Christian Relations*

Shmuel Almog, ed., *Anti-Semitism Through the Ages* (Oxford: Sassoon International Center, Hebrew University of Jerusalem, 1988).

Jeremy Cohen, *The Friars and the Jew: The Evolution of Medieval Anti-Judaism* (Ithaca and London: Cornell University Press, 1983).

John Edwards, *The Jews in Christian Europe 1400–1700* (London: Routledge, 1988).*

Eugene Fisher and Leon Klenicki, *Antisemitism is a Sin* (New York: Anti-Defamation League of B'nai B'rith.) Contains the text and discussion of the Holy See's 1988 document, "The Church and Racism," which confronts directly the history of anti-Semitism and the Church.

Eugene Fisher, *Homework for Christians Preparing for Christian-Jewish Dialogue* (New York: National Conference of Christians and Jews, 3rd revised edition, 1988).

Edward H. Flannery, *The Anguish of the Jews* (Mahwah, N.J.: Paulist Press, 1985). A Catholic priest describes the long history of Christian mistreatment of Jews and theological denigration of Judaism.

John G. Gager, *The Origins of Anti-Semitism* (New York: Oxford University Press, 1985). Attitudes toward Judaism in Pagan and Christian antiquity.

Jacob Neusner, *Torah Through the Ages: A Short History of Judaism* (London: SCM; and Philadelphia: Trinity Press International, 1990).

Heiko Oberman, *The Roots of Anti-Semitism in the Age of Renaissance and Reformation* (Philadelphia: Fortress, 1984). A Protestant scholar deals with such major figures, some more sympathetic than others, as Reuchlin, Pfefferkorn, Erasmus, Luther and others.*

Marc Saperstein, *Moments of Crisis in Jewish-Christian Relations* (London: SCM Press, and Philadelphia: Trinity Press, 1989). A Jewish scholar takes a new look at key points of ancient, medieval, Reformation and modern (i.e., Holocaust) history.

Michael Shermis and Arthur Zannoni, *Introduction to Jewish-Christian Relations* (Mahwah, N.J.: Paulist Press, 1991). Treats biblical issues, anti-Semitism and the Holocaust, the land of Israel, Jesus as a Pharisee, Feminism, and Education. Designed for classroom use.

J. Spiro and H. Hirsch, editors, *Persistent Prejudice* (Fairfax, Va.: George Mason University Press, 1988). Includes my own survey of the issues of anti-Semitism over the centuries in "Antisemitism and Christianity: Theories and Revisions of Theories" (pp. 11–30).*

Edward A. Synan, *The Popes and the Jews in the Middle Ages* (New York: Macmillan, 1965). Presents the actual legislation of the Popes over the centuries.*

Clemens Thoma and Michael Wyshogrod, editors, *Understanding Scripture: Explorations of Jewish and Christian Traditions of Interpretation* (Mahwah, N.J.: Paulist Press, 1987); and *Parable and Story in Judaism and Christianity* (Mahwah, N.J.: Paulist Press, 1989). These two *Stimulus* volumes both result from academic symposia and cover the interactions of Jewish and Christian modalities of spiritual thought over the centuries.

Clark Williamson, *When Jews and Christians Meet* (St. Louis: CBP Press, 1989). A guide for teachers and preachers covering biblical, historical, and contemporary issues.

R. L. Wilken, *John Chrysostom and the Jews: Rhetoric and Reality in the Late 4th Century* (University of California Press, 1983).*

Stephen Wylen, *Settings of Silver* (Mahwah, N.J.: Paulist Press, 1989). An introduction to Judaism covering basic beliefs and rituals as well as Jewish history.

## B. Documenting the Dialogue: The Second Vatican Council and Subsequent Official Church Teaching

Helga Croner, editor, *Stepping Stones to Further Jewish-Christian Relations* (New York: ADL/Stimulus Books, 1977); and *More Stepping Stones* (Mahwah, N.J.: Paulist Stimulus, 1985). Includes Protestant and Catholic, international and U.S. statements.

Eugene Fisher and Leon Klenicki, eds., *John Paul II on Jews and Judaism 1979–1986* (Washington, D.C.: U.S. Catholic Conference Publication No. 151–2, 1987).

Eugene Fisher and Leon Klenicki, eds., *In Our Time: The Flowering of Jewish-Catholic Dialogue* (Mahwah, N.J.: Paulist Stimulus, 1990). Contains key documents, commentaries on them, and an annotated bibliography (pp. 107–161).

Eugene Fisher and James Rudin, *Twenty Years of Jewish-Catholic Dialogue* (Mahwah, N.J.: Paulist Press, 1986). Discussions of the Council by pioneers in the field (G. Higgins and M. Tanenbaum); Israel (E. Flannery and R. Seltzer); Scripture (M. Cook and L. Boadt), Education (J. Banki); Liturgy (E. Fisher) and contemporary "trends" in Jewish and Christian theology of the other (I. Greenberg and J. Pawlikowski). Documents, appendix.

Eugene Fisher and Daniel Polish, *Formation of Social Policy in the Catholic and Jewish Traditions* (Notre Dame and London: University of Notre Dame Press, 1980) and *Foundations of Social Policy in the Catholic and Jewish Traditions* (Notre Dame and London: University of Notre Dame Press, 1983) provide the papers from a series of dialogues held annually between the Synagogue Council of America and the National Conference of Catholic Bishops. Similarly, James Rudin and Marvin Wilson have combined to produce three volumes of Evangelical Christian/Jewish dialogue for Baker Publishing (1978, 1984) and Eerdmans (1987).

International Catholic-Jewish Liaison Committee, *Fifteen Years of Catholic-Jewish Dialogue 1970–1985* (Rome: Lateran University, 1988). Selected papers from official dialogues, along with key Catholic documentation and interpretation. Similarly, Allan Brockway, et al., have put together the volume, *The Theology of the Churches and the Jewish People: Statements by the World Council of Churches and Its Churches* (Geneva: WCC Publications, 1988) and H. M. Ditmanson has edited *Stepping Stones to Further Jewish-Lutheran Relationships* (Minneapolis: Augsburg, 1990).

## C. The Holocaust

Rather than attempting a full bibliography, I will center on general popular-level books of particular pertinence to Jewish-Christian relations.

Michael R. Marrus, *The Holocaust in History* (Hanover, N.H., and London: University Press of New England for Brandeis University, 1987) The treatment of "The Catholic Church," (pp. 179–184) is well nuanced and helpful.

John Morley, *Vatican Diplomacy and the Jews During the Holocaust 1939–1943* (New York: KTAV, 1980). A Catholic priest analyzes records from the Vatican archives.*

Anthony Rhodes, *The Vatican in the Age of the Dictators 1922–1945* (New York: Holt, Rinehart, Winston, 1973). An historian gives the essential, wider context of the issues as they confronted the Holy See in the period itself.*

On the "righteous among the nations," there can be recommended: A. Ramati, *The Assisi Underground: Priests Who Rescued Jews* (New York: Stein and Day, 1978); P. Friedman, *Their Brother's Keepers* (New York: Holocaust Library, 1978); H. Rosenfeld, *Raul Wallenberg, Angel of Rescue* (New York: Prometheus, 1982); B. Wytwycky, *The Other Holocaust* (Washington, D.C.: The Novak Report, 1980); N. Tec, *When Light Pierced the Darkness* (Oxford and New York: Oxford University Press, 1986); C. Rittner and S. Myers, *The Courage to Care* (New York: New York University Press, 1986).

On what became one of the most difficult controversies between Jews and Catholics since World War II there are now two excellent books: W. Bartoszewski, *The Convent at Auschwitz* (New York: George Braziller, 1991); and C. Rittner and J. Roth, editors, *Memory Offended: The Auschwitz Convent Controversy* (New York: Praeger, 1991).

For a survey of Christian theological responses to the Holocaust, see John Pawlikowski, *The Challenge of the Holocaust for Christian Theology* (New York: Anti-Defamation League, 1980); and his and other articles in the October, 1984 Concilium volume: *The Holocaust as Interruption: A Question for Christian Theology*, co-edited by E. S.

Fiorenza and D. Tracy. See also A. Peck, ed., *Jews and Christians after the Holocaust* (Philadelphia: Fortress, 1982).

E. Fisher, ed., *John Paul II on the Holocaust* (Washington D.C.: Secretariat for Catholic-Jewish Relations, National Conference of Catholic Bishops, 1988).

E. Fisher and Leon Klenicki, *From Desolation to Hope* (Chicago: Archdiocese of Chicago, Liturgy Training Publications, 1990). An Interreligious Holocaust Memorial Service.

## D. The Modern State of Israel

Arthur Hertzberg, *The Zionist Idea* (New York: Harper Torchbooks, 1959). A collection of seminal essays.

Eugene Fisher, "The Holy See and the State of Israel: The Evolution of Attitudes and Policies," *Journal of Ecumenical Studies* (vol. 24, no. 2, Spring 1987, pp. 191–211).

Abraham Joshua Heschel, *Israel: An Echo of Eternity* (New York: Farrar, Straus and Giroux, 1969).

Lawrence Hoffman, ed., *The Land of Israel: Jewish Perspectives* (Notre Dame and London: University of Notre Dame Press, 1986). Biblical, rabbinic, medieval and modern Jewish understandings.

Anthony J. Kenny, *The Catholic-Jewish Dialogue and The State of Israel* (Victoria, Australia: The Council of Christians and Jews, 1991).

Andrej Kreutz, *Vatican Policy on the Palestinian-Israeli Conflict: The Struggle for the Holy Land* (New York: Greenwood Press, 1990).

A. James Rudin, *Israel for Christians: Understanding Modern Israel* (Philadelphia: Fortress, 1983).

David Burrell and Yehezkel Landau, *Voices from Jerusalem: Jews and Christians Reflect on the Holy Land* (Mahwah, N.J.: Paulist Press, 1992).

## Chapter II: Understanding Jesus, the Faithful Jew

Ben Zion and Baruch Bokser, ed. and transl., *The Talmud: Selected Writings* (Mahwah, N.J.: Paulist Classics of Western Spirituality, 1989).

Terrance Callan, *Forgetting the Root: The Emergence of Christianity from Judaism* (Mahwah, N.J.: Paulist Press, 1986). Categorizes New Testament books on the basis of their relative "liberal" or "conservative" reactions to the key issue of gentile inclusion in the Christian community.

James H. Charlesworth, *Jesus Within Judaism* (Garden City, N.Y.: Doubleday Anchor Bible, 1988). New Light from archaeology on the Pseudepigrapha, Dead Sea Scrolls, the Nag Hammadi Codices, etc.*

James H. Charlesworth, editor, *Jews and Christians: Exploring the Past, Present, and Future* (New York: Crossroad, 1990); and *Jesus' Jewishness: Exploring the Place of Jesus in Early Judaism* (New York: Crossroad, 1991). Bring together major essays of leading Protestant, Catholic and Jewish theologians, historians and biblical scholars.*

Philip Cunningham, *Jewish Apostle to the Gentiles: Paul as He Saw Himself* (Mystic, Conn.: Twenty-Third Publications, 1986). A popular summary of recent Pauline scholarship.

W. D. Davies, *The Setting of the Sermon on the Mount* (Cambridge: Cambridge University Press, 1966) and *Jewish and Pauline Studies* (Philadelphia: Fortress, 1984).*

Eugene Fisher and Leon Klenicki, *Root and Branches* (Winona, Minn.: St. Mary's Press, 1987). Popular treatment of relationships between biblical Judaism, rabbinic Judaism and early Christianity.

Lloyd Gaston, *Paul and the Torah* (Vancouver: University of British Columbia Press, 1987). A survey and analysis of recent Pauline studies.*

Andrew M. Greeley and Jacob Neusner, *The Bible and Us* (New York: Warner Books, 1990). A Priest and a Rabbi read the scriptures together.

Harvey Falk, *Jesus the Pharisee* (Mahwah, N.J.: Paulist Press, 1985). Places Jesus in the Hillelite as opposed to the Shammaite "school" of Pharisaism.

Asher Finkel, *The Pharisees and the Teacher of Nazareth* (Leiden: Brill, 1964). Compares and contrasts Jesus and Pharisaic teachings.*

Michael Hilton and Gordon Marshall, *The Gospels and Rabbinic Judaism: A Study Guide* (New York: KTAV and ADL, 1988). Compares texts on similar topics.

Daniel J. Harrington, S.J., *God's People in Christ* (Philadelphia: Fortress, 1980). New Testament Perspectives on the Church and Judaism.

John Koenig, *Jews and Christians in Dialogue: New Testament Foundations* (Philadelphia: Westminster, 1979). A Lutheran perspective.

Pinchas Lapide, *The Sermon on the Mount* (Maryknoll, N.Y.: Orbis Books, 1986). Talmudic parallels to gospel sayings.

Tobias Lach, *A Rabbinic Commentary on the New Testament* (New York: ADL, 1987).

Franz Mussner, *Tractate on the Jews* (Philadelphia: Fortress, 1984). Biblical based systematic approach.

Jacob Neusner, *Understanding Rabbinic Judaism* (New York: KTAV and ADL, 1974); *Christian Faith and the Bible of Judaism* (Grand Rapids: Eerdmans, 1987). Renowned Jewish scholar comments on key issues in the current dialogue.

John Pawlikowski and James Wilde, *When Catholics Speak about Jews* (Chicago: Archdiocese of Chicago, Liturgy Training Publications, 1987). For preachers and teachers. Pawlikowski's *Christ in the Light of the Christian-Jewish Dialogue* (Mahwah, N.J.: Paulist Stimulus, 1982) surveys much of the work on Jesus and the Pharisees to that point.

H. G. Perelmuter, *Siblings: Rabbinic Judaism and Early Christianity at their Beginnings* (Mahwah, N.J.: Paulist Press, 1989). Rabbinic texts organized around key figures: Simeon b. Shetah, Hillel, Johanan b. Zakkai, Eliezer and Joshua, Akiba, Meir and Elisha b. Abuya. Popular level.

Ellis Rivkin, *The Hidden Revolution: The Pharisees Search for the Kingdom* (Nashville: Abingdon, 1978).

E. P. Sanders, *Paul, the Law and the Jewish People* (Philadelphia: Fortress, 1977); *Jewish and Christian Self-Definition* (edited 2 volumes, Philadelphia: Fortress, 1980, 1982); *Paul, the Law, and the Jewish People* (Philadelphia: Fortress, 1983); *Jesus and Judaism* (Philadelphia: Fortress, 1985); *Jewish Law from Jesus to Mishnah* (London: SCM; and Philadelphia: Trinity Press, 1990).

Samuel Sandmel, *Judaism and Christian Beginnings* (Oxford and New York: Oxford University Press, 1978). Surveys the sources, institutions and ideas of the richly complex world of first century Judaism that relate to the emergence of Christianity.

Alan F. Segal, *Rebecca's Children: Judaism and Christianity in the Roman World* (Cambridge, Mass.: Harvard University Press, 1986) and *Paul the Convert* (New Haven and London: Yale University Press, 1990).

H. L. Strack and G. Stermberger, *Introduction to the Talmud and Midrash* (Edinburgh, Scotland: T & T Clark, 1991). Update of a classic text.

Brad H. Young, *Jesus and His Jewish Parables: Rediscovering the Roots of Jesus' Teaching* (Mahwah, N.J.: Paulist Press, 1989).


## Chapter III: Are the Gospels Anti-Semitic?

Norman A. Beck, *Mature Christianity: The Recognition and Repudiation of the Anti-Jewish Polemic of the New Testament* (Selinsgrove, Pa.: Susquehanna University Press, Associated University Presses, 1985).

Alan T. Davies, *Anti-Semitism and the Foundations of Christianity* (Mahwah, N.J.: Paulist Press, 1979). Twelve Christian scholars explore the development and dynamics of anti-Semitism within the New Testament and Patristic tradition.

Samuel Sandmel, *Antisemitism in the New Testament?* (Philadelphia: Fortress, 1978). A book-by-book analysis.

Gerard Sloyan, *Is Christ the End of the Law?* (Philadelphia: Westminster, 1978). Re-reading a classical polemic text in its larger Pauline context.

Clark M. Williamson, *Has God Rejected His People? Anti-Judaism in the Christian Church* (Nashville: Abingdon, 1982); and *Interpreting Difficult Texts: Anti-Judaism and Christian Preaching* (London and Philadelphia: SCM and Trinity Press, 1989).


## Chapter IV: Who Killed Jesus?

Haim Cohen, *The Trial and Death of Jesus* (New York: KTAV, 1977). Argues that there was no "Jewish trial" of Jesus at all, but only a Roman one under Pontius Pilate.

Joseph Fitzmyer, S.J., "Jesus the Lord," in *Chicago Studies* 17 (1978, pp. 87–90) and *A Christological Catechism* (Mahwah, N.J.: Paulist Press, 1982).

Philip S. Kaufman, O.S.B., *The Beloved Disciple: Witness against Anti-Semitism* (Collegeville, Minn.: Liturgical Press, 1991). Popular level treatment of St. John's Passion Narrative for adult education courses.

Gerard Sloyan, *Jesus on Trial* (Philadelphia: Fortress, 1973). Surveys the issues and literature to that point. Updated in "Recent Literature on the Trial Narratives" in T. J. Ryan, ed., *Critical History and Biblical Faith* (Villanova, Pa.: Villanova University, College Theology Society, 1979).

John T. Townsend, *A Liturgical Interpretation of Our Lord's Passion in Narrative Form* (New York: National Conference of Christians and Jews, 1985).

National Conference of Catholic Bishops' Committee for Ecumenical and Interreligious Affairs, *Criteria for the Evaluation of Dramatizations of the Passion* (Washington, D.C.: U.S. Catholic Conference Publications, 1988). For parish and school use. In English and Spanish.

See also on this and the above New Testament topics the relevant entries in D. Senior, et al., editors, *The Catholic Study Bible* (Oxford and New York: Oxford University Press, 1990); and R. Brown, et al., editors, *The New Jerome Biblical Commentary* (Englewood Cliffs, N.J.: Prentice-Hall, 1990).

## Chapter V: Dialogue for the Future: The Relationship Between the Covenants

Roger Brooks, editor, *Unanswered Questions: Theological Views of Jewish-Catholic Relations* (Notre Dame and London: University of Notre Dame Press, 1988). A significant collection of essays.*

Helga Croner and Leon Klenicki, editors, *Issues in the Jewish-Christian Dialogue: Jewish Perspectives on Covenant, Mission and Witness* (Mahwah, N.J.: Paulist Stimulus, 1979).

Eugene J. Fisher, "Covenant Theology and Jewish-Christian Dialogue" *American Journal of Theology and Philosophy* (Vol. 9, No. 2, January–May, 1988) pp. 5–39.

Leon Klenicki, ed., *Toward a Theological Encounter: Jewish Understandings of Christianity* (Mahwah, N.J.: Paulist Press, 1991). Selected and provocative essays.

Norbert Lohfink, *The Covenant Never Revoked: Biblical Reflections on Christian-Jewish Dialogue* (Mahwah, N.J.: Paulist Press, 1991). New Testament insights from a major German Christian scholar.

John T. Pawlikowski, *Jesus and the Theology of Israel* (Wilmington, Del.: Michael Glazier, 1989). Survey of Protestant, Catholic and Jewish scholarship in the field.

Clemens Thoma, *A Christian Theology of Judaism* Mahwah, N.J.: Paulist Stimulus, 1980).

Norma Thompson and Bruce Cole, editors, *The Future of Jewish-Christian Relations* (Schenectady, N.Y.: Character Research Press, 1982).

Paul M. Van Buren, *A Christian Theology of the People Israel* (3 volumes, New York: Seabury, and Harper and Row, 1980–1988). A major excursus in Christian systematic theology.

Clark Williamson, ed., *A Mutual Witness* (St. Louis: Chalice Press, 1992). Essays on "critical solidarity" between Jews and Christians.

M. Zeik and M. Siegel, *Root and Branch: The Jewish/Christian Dialogue* (New York: Roth Publishing, 1984). Popular level introductory essays.

## Chapter VI: Celebrations and Activities

Anti-Defamation League Pamphlets and Videos: *Your Neighbor Celebrates; Your Neighbor Worships; American Jews, Their Story*, etc. Catalogues available from Anti-Defamation League offices regionally and nationally (823 United Nations Plaza, New York, NY 10017). Materials are also available from the American Jewish Committee (165 E. 56th Street, New York, NY 10022) and local Jewish Community Relations Centers.

Bishops' Committee on the Liturgy, National Conference of Catholic Bishops, *God's Mercy Endures Forever: Guidelines on the Presentation of Jews and Judaism in Catholic Preaching* (Washington, D.C.: USCC Publication No: 247–0; Phone: 800–235–USCC).

Martin Cohen and Helga Croner, editors, *Christian Mission — Jewish Mission* (Mahwah, N.J.: Paulist Stimulus, 1982).

Annette Daum and Eugene Fisher, *The Challenge of Shalom for Catholics and Jews* (New York: Union of American Hebrew Congregations, 1985). A dialogical discussion guide to the Catholic Bishops Pastoral on Peace and War.

Darrell Fasching, *The Jewish People in Christian Preaching* (Lewiston, N.Y.: Mellen Press, 1984). Insights for homilies.*

Asher Finkel and Lawrence Frizzell, editors, *Standing Before God: Studies on Prayer in Scripture and Tradition* (New York: KTAV, 1981). Essays in honor of Msgr. John Oesterreicher.*

Eugene J. Fisher, editor, *The Jewish Roots of Christian Liturgy* (Mahwah, N.J.: Paulist Press, 1990). Essays on the origins of Christian liturgy in Judaism, on life cycle liturgies (marriage and death); on Sabbath and Sunday; and liturgical renewal today.

Irving Greenberg, *The Jewish Way: Living the Holidays* (New York: Summit Books, 1988). A distinctive approach to understanding Judaism as revealed through its holy days.

Leon Klenicki and Eugene Fisher, *From Desolation to Hope: An Interreligious Holocaust Memorial Service* (Chicago: Archdiocese of Chicago, Liturgy Training Publications, 1983, revised edition 1990; Phone: 800–933–1800).

Leon Klenicki, *The Passover Celebration: A Haggadah for the Seder* (New York: The Anti-Defamation League of B'nai B'rith, and Chicago:

Archdiocese of Chicago, Liturgy Training Publications, 1980 reprinted, 1985). Phone: 800–933–1800.

Leon Klenicki and Gabe Huck, editors *Spirituality and Prayer: Jewish and Christian Understandings* (Mahwah, N.J.: Paulist Stimulus, 1983).

Leon Klenicki and Geoffrey Wigoder, editors, *A Dictionary of the Jewish-Christian Dialogue* (Mahwah, N.J.: Paulist Stimulus, 1984). Fifty key terms, each defined by a Jew and a Christian.

Anthony J. Saldarini, *Jesus and Passover* (Mahwah, N.J.: Paulist Press, 1984).

Elie Wiesel and Albert Friedlander, *The Six Days of Destruction: Meditation Toward Hope* (Mahwah, N.J.: Paulist Press, 1988).

Eric Werner, *The Sacred Bridge* (vol. 1: New York: Schocken, 1970; vol. 2: New York: KTAV, 1984). Liturgy and music in the synagogue and church in the first millennium.

Alfred Wolf and Royale Vadakin, editors, *A Journey of Discovery: A Resource Manual for Jewish-Catholic Dialogue* (Valencia, Calif.: Tabor Publishing, 1989). Joint statements, resources and "how-tos" developed by the Los Angeles Catholic-Jewish Respect Life, Priest-Rabbi, and Women's Dialogues over the course of two decades.

## Chapter VII: Christian Teaching and Judaism Today

### A. Analyses of Christian Teaching Materials

Claire Huchet Bishop, *How Catholics Look at Jews* (Mahwah, N.J.: Paulist Press, 1974). Surveys European textbook studies of treatment of Jews and Judaism.

Philip A. Cunningham, *A Content Analysis of the Presentation of Jews and Judaism in Current Roman Catholic Textbooks* (Ph.D. Dissertation, Boston College, 1992). Updates Fisher, 1976. (Ann Arbor: University of Michigan Microfilms International.)

Eugene J. Fisher, *A Content Analysis of the Treatment of Jews and Judaism in Current Roman Catholic Textbooks and Manuals on the Primary and Secondary Levels* (Ph.D. Dissertation, New York University, 1976; Ann Arbor, Mich.: University Microfilms International).

Bernhard Olson, *Faith and Prejudice* (New Haven and London: Yale University Press, 1963). The classic study of Protestant texts for their treatment of Jews and Judaism.*

John Pawlikowski, *Catechetics and Prejudice* (Mahwah, N.J.: Paulist Press, 1973). Surveys the pioneering Catholic textbook studies of Sisters Rose Thering, Rita Mudd, and Mary Gleason.

Stuart Polly, *the Portrayal of Jews and Judaism in Currewnt Protestant Teaching Materials: A Context Analysis* (Ann Arbor, Mich.: University Microfilms International, 1992). Update of Olson and Strohes studies of Protestant texts.

Gerald S. Strober, *Portrait of the Elder Brother: Jews and Judaism in Protestant Teaching Materials* (New York: American Jewish Committee, 1972). Updated Olson, 1963.

## B. General Educational Studies and Resources

ADL and American Jewish Committee, cited above, again, have a wealth of information and resources available for Christian teachers interested in the themes and issues raised in this book).

Eugene J. Fisher, *Seminary Education and Christian-Jewish Relations* (Washington, D.C.: National Catholic Education Association, 1983, revised, 1988). How to integrate the new insights of the dialogue into the existing Christian seminary curriculum.

Eugene Fisher, editor, *Within Context: Guidelines for the Catechetical Presentation of Jews and Judaism in the New Testament* (Morristown, N.J.: Silver, Burdett and Ginn, 1987). In preparation: David Efroymson and Eugene Fisher, editors, *Within Context: Essays on Jews and Judaism in the New Testament*, a companion volume to the above short pamphlet guidelines (Collegeville, Minn.: The Liturgical Conference, 1993).

Eugene Fisher and Leon Klenicki, editors, *Understanding the Jewish Experience* (Washington, D.C.: U.S. Catholic Conference Department of Education/Anti-Defamation League, 1982; reprinted in expanded form with a series of articles on religious education published over the years by the authors in the journal *PACE* (Professional Approaches for Christian Educators), now published by *Our Sunday Visitor* press. Published in Spanish by CELAM, the Latin American Bishops' Conference (Bogota, Colombia).

Rose Thering, O.P., *Jews, Judaism and Catholic Education* (Anti-Defamation League of B'nai B'rith, American Jewish Committee, Seton Hall University, 1986). A documentary survey report of Catholic educational institutions' programs, courses, workshop offerings, etc., in the area of Catholic-Jewish understanding and Judaica.

Archdiocese of Philadelphia, Superintendent of Schools Office, *Abraham Our Father in Faith A Religion Teacher's Curriculum Guide* (1979, updated 1990). Excellent and highly practical resource tool for Catholic religious teachers. Also translated into Spanish by CELAM.

With regard to Holocaust education, the recently founded "National Catholic Institute for Holocaust Education" has programs of study for high school teachers that include a seminar at YAD VASHEM in Israel. Write: Sr. Mary Noel Kernan, S.C., Seton Hill College, Greensburg, PA 15601.

The U.S. Holocaust Memorial Museum, now nearing completion on the Mall in Washington D.C., will also have a strong educational component.

# APPENDIX E

# A Future Curriculum
# for Catholic Education

At a workshop at St. Louis University sponsored by the American Jewish Committee in 1975, Fr. Alfred McBride, president of the National Forum of Religious Educators, presented a series of ideas for "a future curriculum of Catholic education." After declaring that Catholic education must become "prejudice-free" by avoiding deicidal references, pejorative use of the term "Pharisees," and other "inaccurate and narrow-minded concepts," he proposed some "guidelines for Catholic education" that will help recover a sense of transcendence on all levels of instruction, from primary grades through adult education. (Suggestions in brackets have added to Fr. McBride's presentation by the author.)

*PRIMARY GRADES* (1st, 2nd, and 3rd year classes) — Based on the teachings of the late Rabbi Abraham Joshua Heschel that "religion begins in wonder, and from wonder we turn to the infinite," discuss concepts of *wonder, love,* and *praise* of God. (Deut. 6:4; Deut. 19:18 — the summary of Torah).

*INTERMEDIATE* (4th, 5th and 6th year classes) — Teach the facts, the meaning of the facts, and the values associated with these meanings that emerge out of the eight acts that constitute "the great religious lifecycle" of the Jewish people in the "Old Testament" (Hebrew Scriptures) stories: *Patriarch; Exodus; Pilgrims; Sinai; Conquest; Kingdom; Exile; Return.*

[New Testament events and facts should be approached in such a way that Jesus' Jewishness is clearly seen. The Pharisees can be pictured in a positive light and their lives used as models of faithfulness. The Roman role in Jesus' passion and death can be brought out so that a balanced view of New Testament events is presented. The Jewish character of Jesus' teaching should be taught. Judaism and Christianity should both be seen as "religions of love," not fear.]

Rather than teach "salvation history" which emphasizes abstract concepts of "covenant" and "prophecy" that are difficult for children to grasp, or "fulfillment language" (the New Testament is contained in the Old, and the Old Testament is fulfilled in the New), teach about Elijah, Joshua — actual lives that are overflowing with reality and that raise concrete value questions.

Help children experience liturgically the Passover feast of unleavened bread and the feast of the lamb, which are the basis of the Eucharist. In that way, "Catholic children will learn that we owe so much to Judaism and to the Jews, and let us say it."

*JUNIOR HIGH SCHOOL* (7th, 8th and 9th year classes) — This is a period when children have "a *rendezvous* with beauty and reverence." As part of larger courses on religion, special courses should be developed to introduce Catholic children to the feasts and festivals of *Judaism* — *Rosh Hashonah* (the Jewish New Year), *Yom Kippur* (the Day of Atonement), *Sukkoth* (Tabernacles), *Hanukah* (Lights), *Shavuoth* (Pentecost), and especially *Shabbat* (the Sabbath — read Heschel on the Sabbath for learning reverence for the holy day). Catholics have a sense for the whole year, and this will strengthen Catholic appreciation of the calendar of feast days.

Catholic children should also learn about the temple and the synagogue, the rabbi and the cantor, the ark of the Torah, and the Torah scrolls. Such concepts as the following should be introduced: *Shechinah* (the divine presence), *yeshiva* (community of faith), *minyan* (a gathering of ten people to pray, "shared prayer").

Jewish family customs are important — circumcision, *bar-mitzvah*, *bas-mitzvah*, marriage customs, funerals, blessings. These experiences will do much to create a sense of reverence.

*HIGH SCHOOL* (10th, 11th, and 12th year classes) — This is a period for developing transcendence in our teaching, and exposing children to the spirituality and mystical prayer that was preserved in the *shtetls* (villages) and ghettos of East European Jewish communities. Rabbi Heschel makes a critical distinction between *kevah* (literally, "set time"), or fixed ritual, and *kavanah*, the mystical outpouring of the human heart. (Read Heschel's, *Mans Quest for God*). We need both.

Ideas should be taught on prophecy and kings. Children at this age level should learn to agonize with Jeremiah and Daniel, and develop social concern by reading the confessions of Jeremiah in Chapter 20. The confrontation between "charismatic" judges and "institutional" kings, as in Samuel, discloses how modern the Bible can be.

There is need for learning the emphasis on *mitzvah* (religious deed) and Law as a "light unto my people."

This is the grade level to teach the history of the Jewish people *after* the Bible period. Children should be exposed to a knowledge of the history of the pogroms against Jews carried out by Christian-affiliated people — the Crusades, the Inquisition, culminating in the death camps in our own century [as well as to the contribution of Jews to Western religious history: the Talmud, Scholasticism, etc.]

The Nazi Holocaust must be taught. But First Isaiah's references to holy martyred men and the suffering servant must not be used for masochistic purposes. The notion that seeking martyrdom is a blessing is utter nonsense: it is an act of pride and that is sin. Martyrdom is grace thrust upon you, and you are lucky to come into it if it comes your way. [An appreciation for the modern state of Israel and the current Arab/Israeli conflict would also be appropriate at this age level.]

I approve discussions of the Holocaust and recommend the controversial book *After Auschwitz* by Rabbi Richard Rubenstein, and the extraordinary book, *Israel — Echo of Eternity* by Rabbi Heschel who regards Auschwitz and the rebirth of Israel as the death and resurrection of the Jewish people.

*ADULTS* — We need to apprise Catholic adults of Vatican Council II's declarations, particularly that which deals with Catholic-Jewish relations. We also must concentrate on "Family Education," and try to eradicate prejudice which often comes with mother's milk. Discussion of prejudice should take place at Cana conferences, marriage conferences, and tribunals. Parents should be asked to examine their prejudices, and should be helped not to pass them on. A check-list of consciousness-raising themes and issues should be shared with them.

Catholic parents should know synagogue practices. They should know the plurality of Orthodox, Conservative and Reform branches of Judaism. Our families profit by exposure to strong family life in some Jewish communities.